Cardboard

anytime, anywhei

Panel 1: You read Magic articles, listen to Magic podcasts, watch Magic videos, and are always discussing Magic with your friends.

Panel 2: You have special Magic deck boxes, fancy dice and counters, sleeves, playmats, and even Magic apparel.

Panel 3: What's wrong with just playing the game?!

Magic isn't a game, it's a lifestyle.

A collection of comics about the world's most addictive game.

Cardboard Crack anytime, anywhere

Check out these other Cardboard Crack books:
Cardboard Crack
I will never quit Cardboard Crack

No dolphins or Magic cards were hurt during the making of the cover.

This book collects comics that originally appeared online between January 30, 2014 and June 8, 2014, and can also be viewed at:
cardboard-crack.com
facebook.com/CardboardCrack

For information write:
cardboardcrack.mtg@gmail.com

Printed in the U.S.A.

For my readers, whose encouragement
and support never ceases to amaze me.

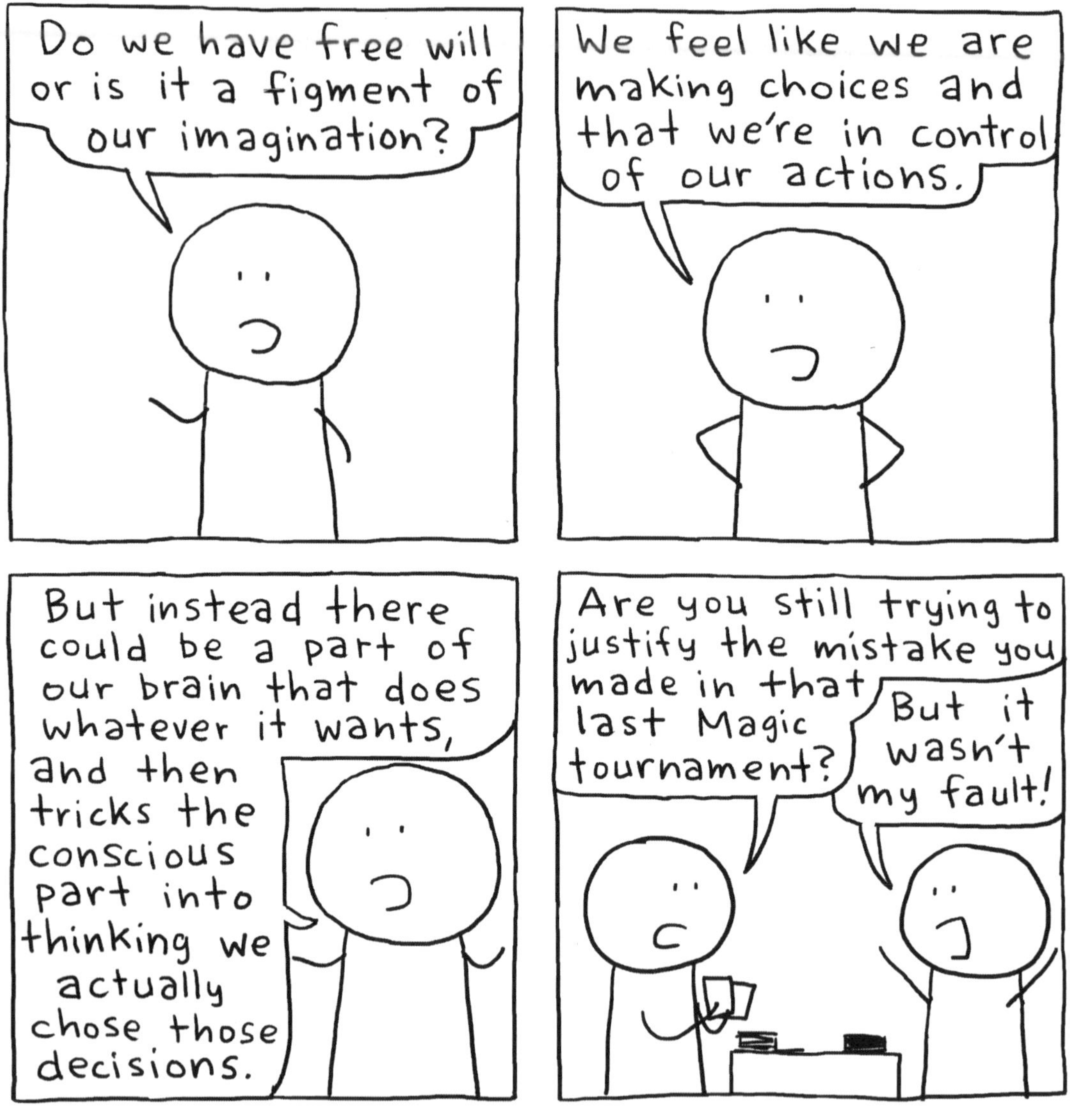
Do we have free will or is it a figment of our imagination?
We feel like we are making choices and that we're in control of our actions.
But instead there could be a part of our brain that does whatever it wants,
and then tricks the conscious part into thinking we actually chose those decisions.
Are you still trying to justify the mistake you made in that last Magic tournament?
But it wasn't my fault!

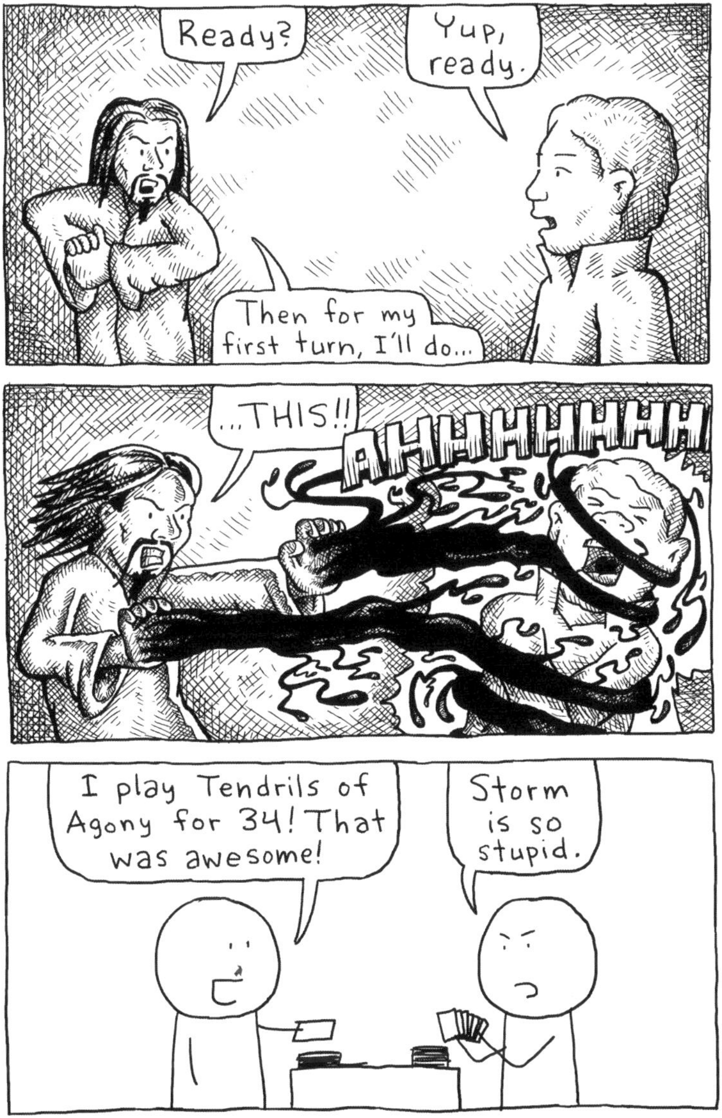
Ready?
Yup, ready.
Then for my first turn, I'll do...
...THIS!!
AHHHHHHHH
I play Tendrils of Agony for 34! That was awesome!
Storm is so stupid.

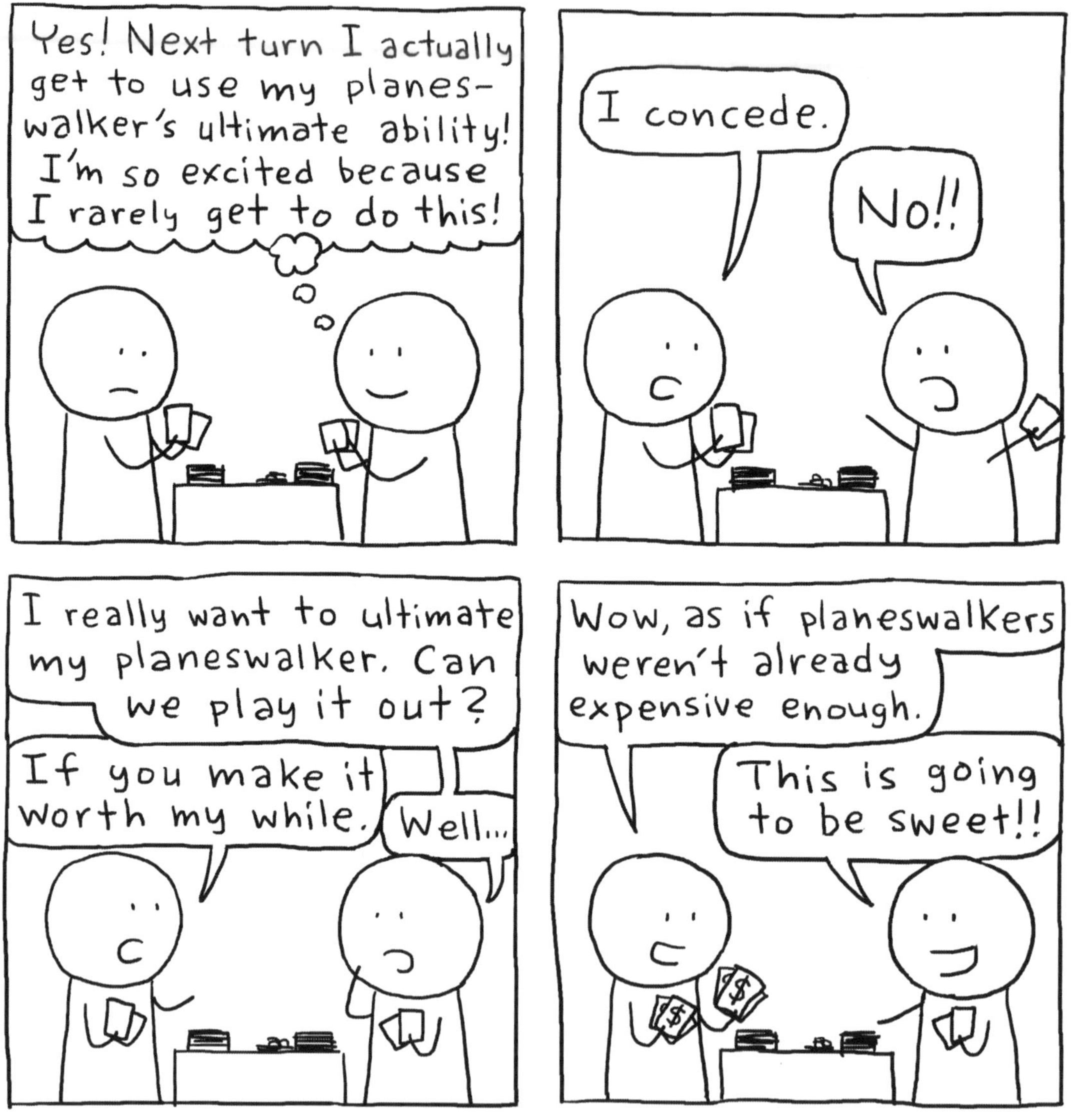
Yes! Next turn I actually get to use my planes-walker's ultimate ability! I'm so excited because I rarely get to do this!
I concede.
No!!
I really want to ultimate my planeswalker. Can we play it out?
If you make it worth my while.
Well...
Wow, as if planeswalkers weren't already expensive enough.
This is going to be sweet!!

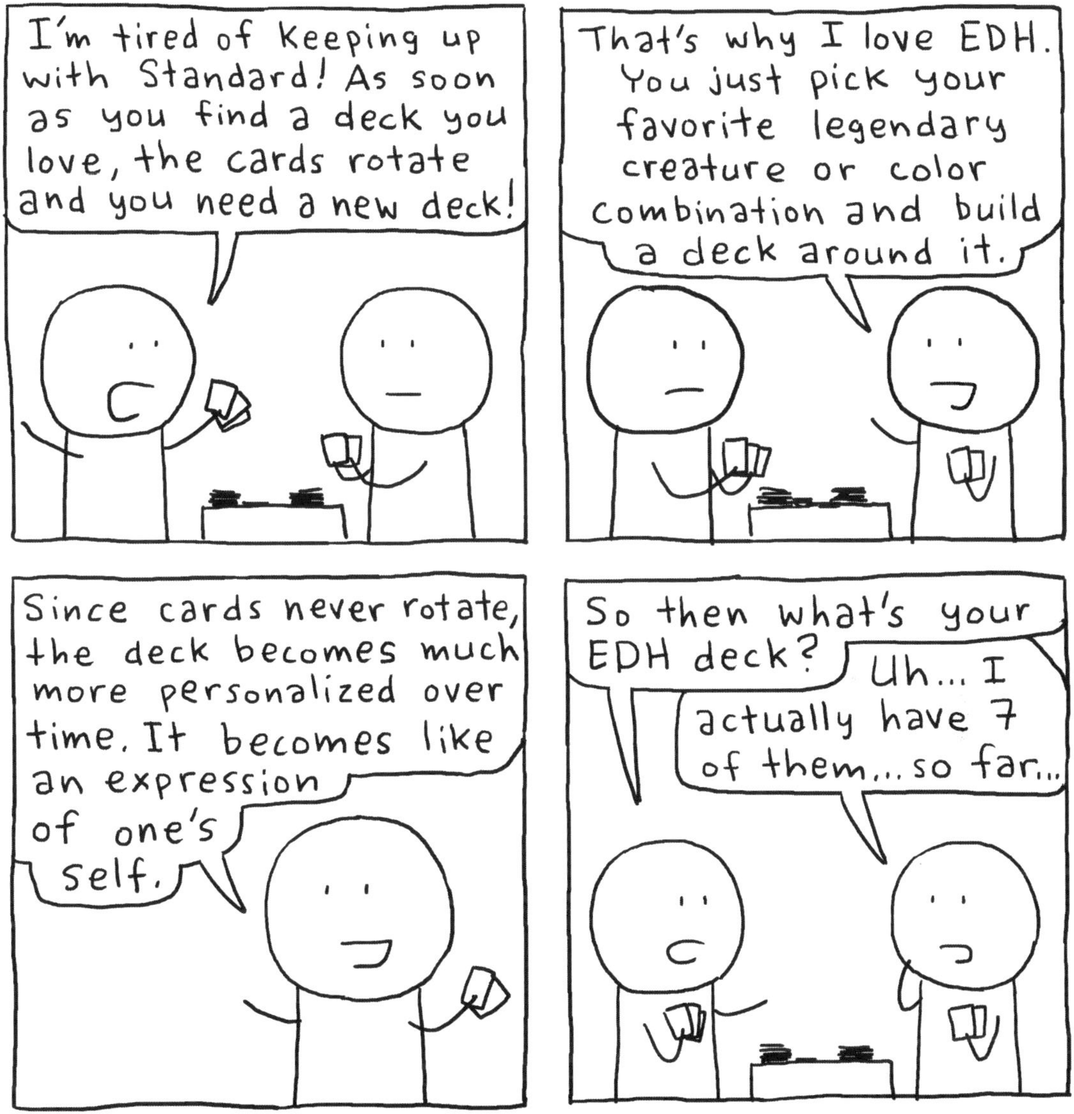
I'm tired of keeping up with Standard! As soon as you find a deck you love, the cards rotate and you need a new deck!
That's why I love EDH. You just pick your favorite legendary creature or color combination and build a deck around it.
Since cards never rotate, the deck becomes much more personalized over time. It becomes like an expression of one's self.
So then what's your EDH deck?
Uh... I actually have 7 of them... so far...

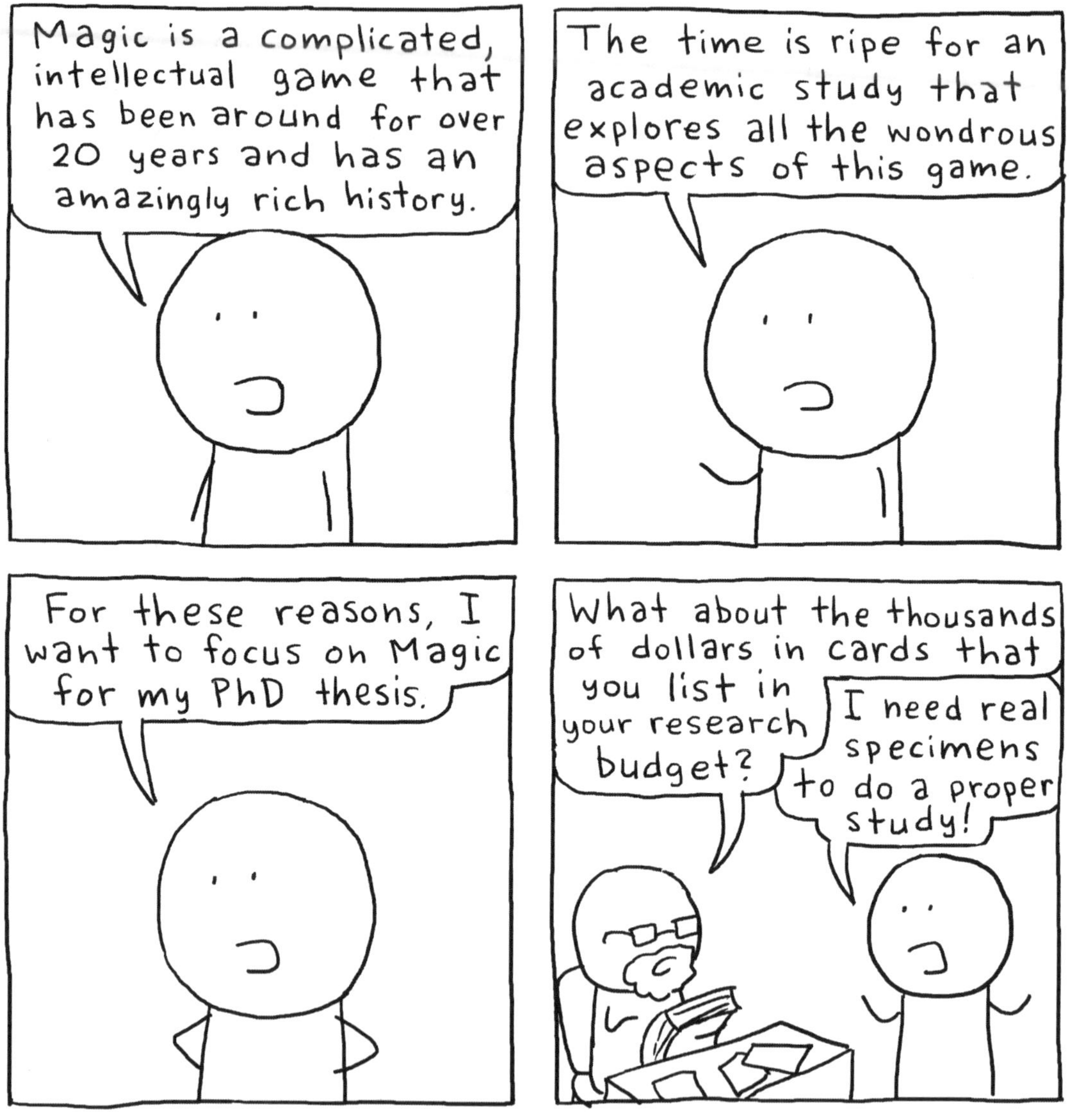
Magic is a complicated, intellectual game that has been around for over 20 years and has an amazingly rich history.
The time is ripe for an academic study that explores all the wondrous aspects of this game.
For these reasons, I want to focus on Magic for my PhD thesis.
What about the thousands of dollars in cards that you list in your research budget?
I need real specimens to do a proper study!

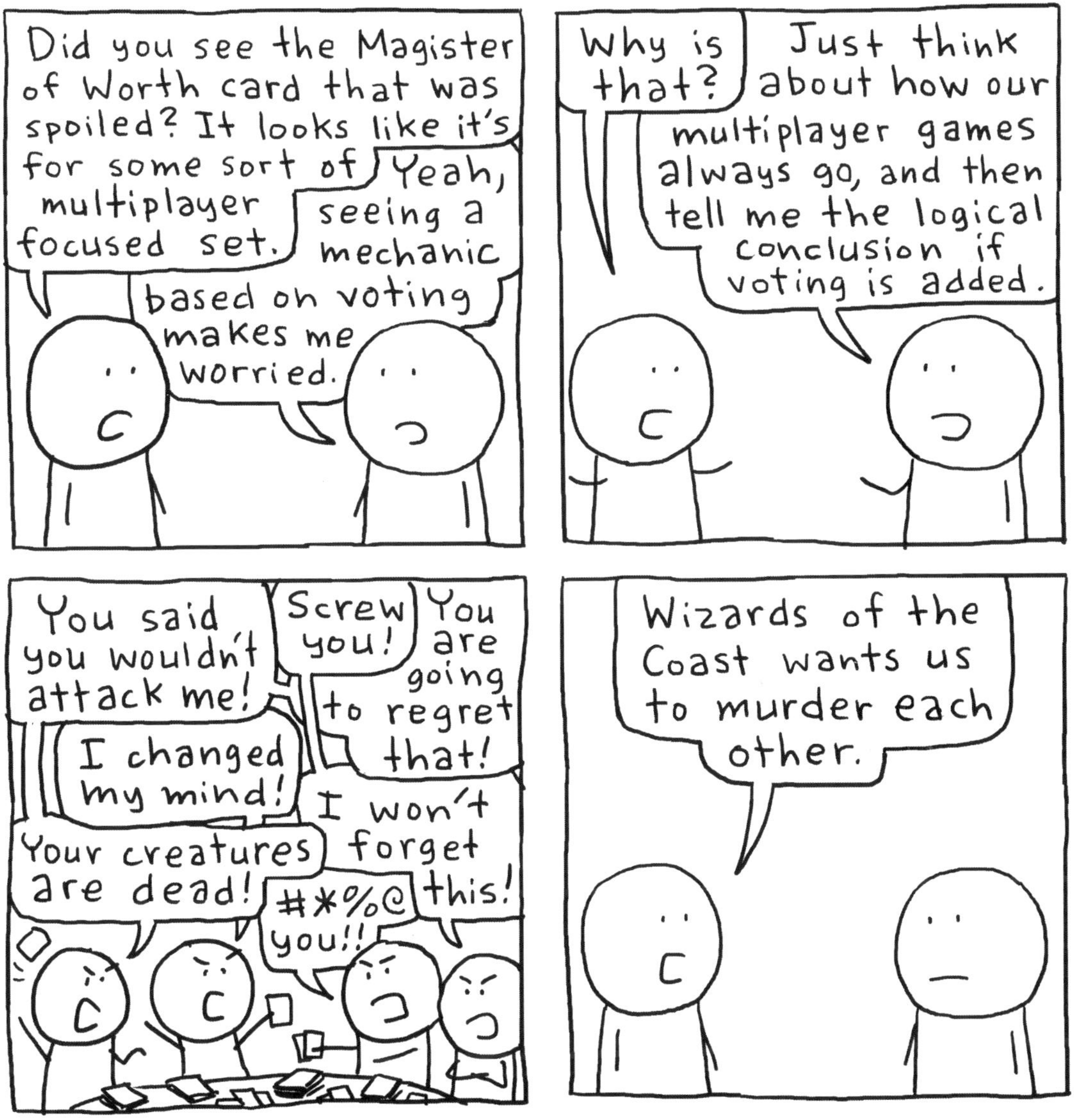
Did you see the Magister of Worth card that was spoiled? It looks like it's for some sort of multiplayer focused set.
Yeah, seeing a mechanic based on voting makes me worried.
Why is that?
Just think about how our multiplayer games always go, and then tell me the logical conclusion if voting is added.
You said you wouldn't attack me!
Screw you!
You are going to regret that!
I changed my mind!
I won't forget this!
Your creatures are dead!
#*%@ you!!
Wizards of the Coast wants us to murder each other.

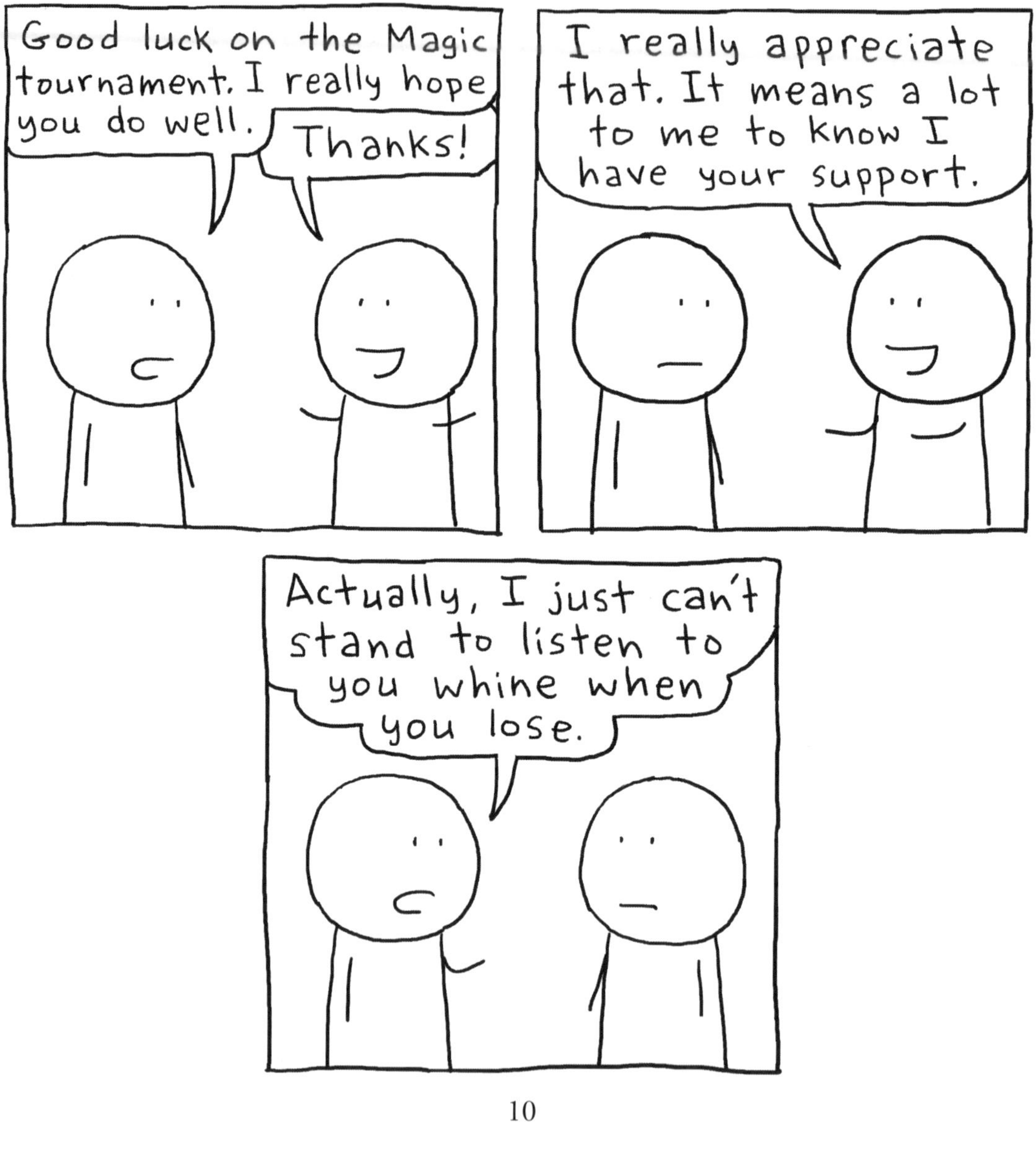
Good luck on the Magic tournament. I really hope you do well.
Thanks!
I really appreciate that. It means a lot to me to know I have your support.
Actually, I just can't stand to listen to you whine when you lose.

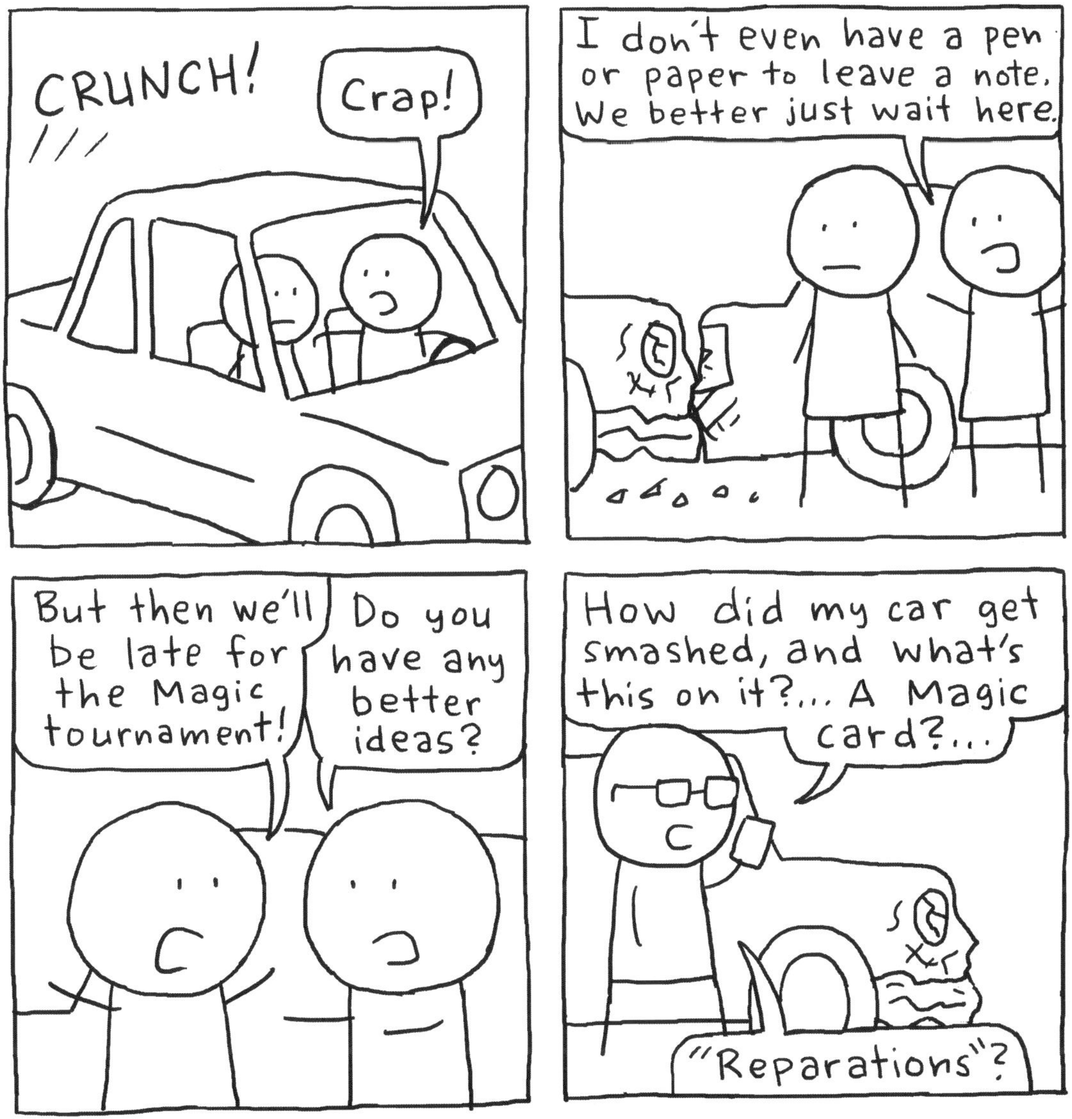
CRUNCH!
Crap!
I don't even have a pen or paper to leave a note. We better just wait here.
But then we'll be late for the Magic tournament!
Do you have any better ideas?
How did my car get smashed, and what's this on it?... A Magic card?...
"Reparations"?

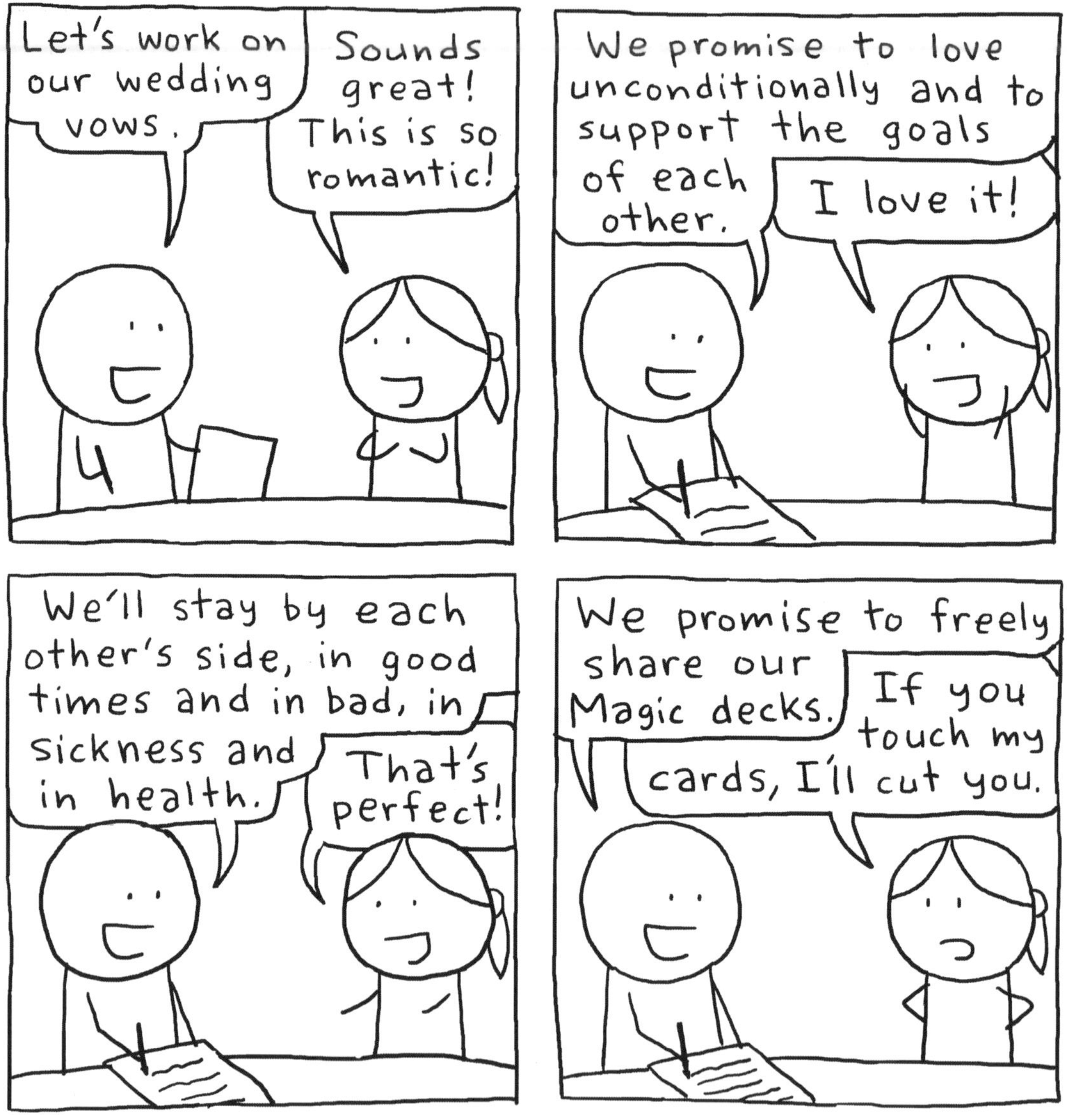
Let's work on our wedding vows.
Sounds great! This is so romantic!
We promise to love unconditionally and to support the goals of each other.
I love it!
We'll stay by each other's side, in good times and in bad, in sickness and in health.
That's perfect!
We promise to freely share our Magic decks.
If you touch my cards, I'll cut you.

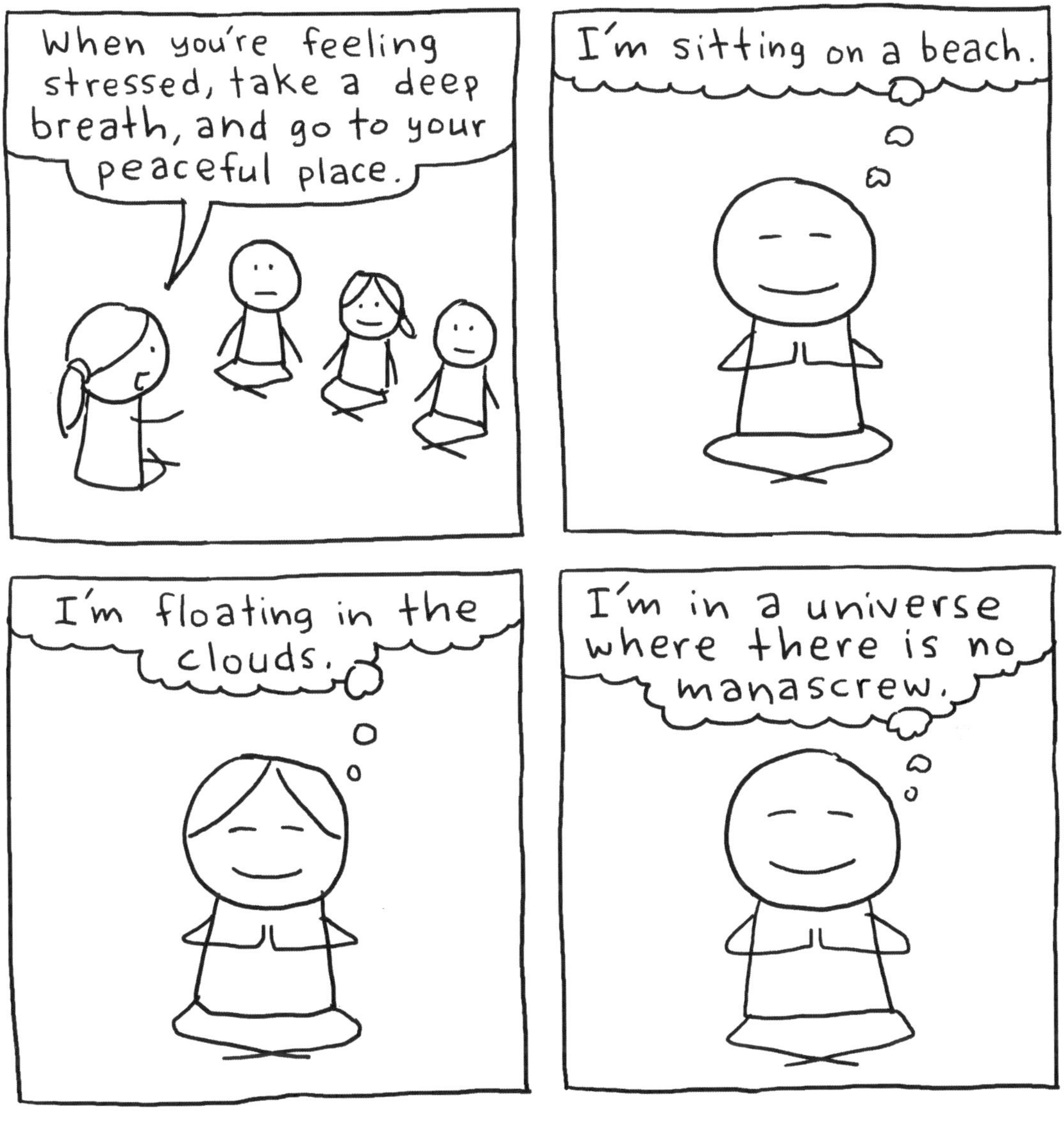
When you're feeling stressed, take a deep breath, and go to your peaceful place.
I'm sitting on a beach.
I'm floating in the clouds.
I'm in a universe where there is no manascrew.

Number of mistakes I notice...
...when I'm playing Magic.
...when I'm watching others play Magic.
This must mean that I almost always play perfectly, right?!

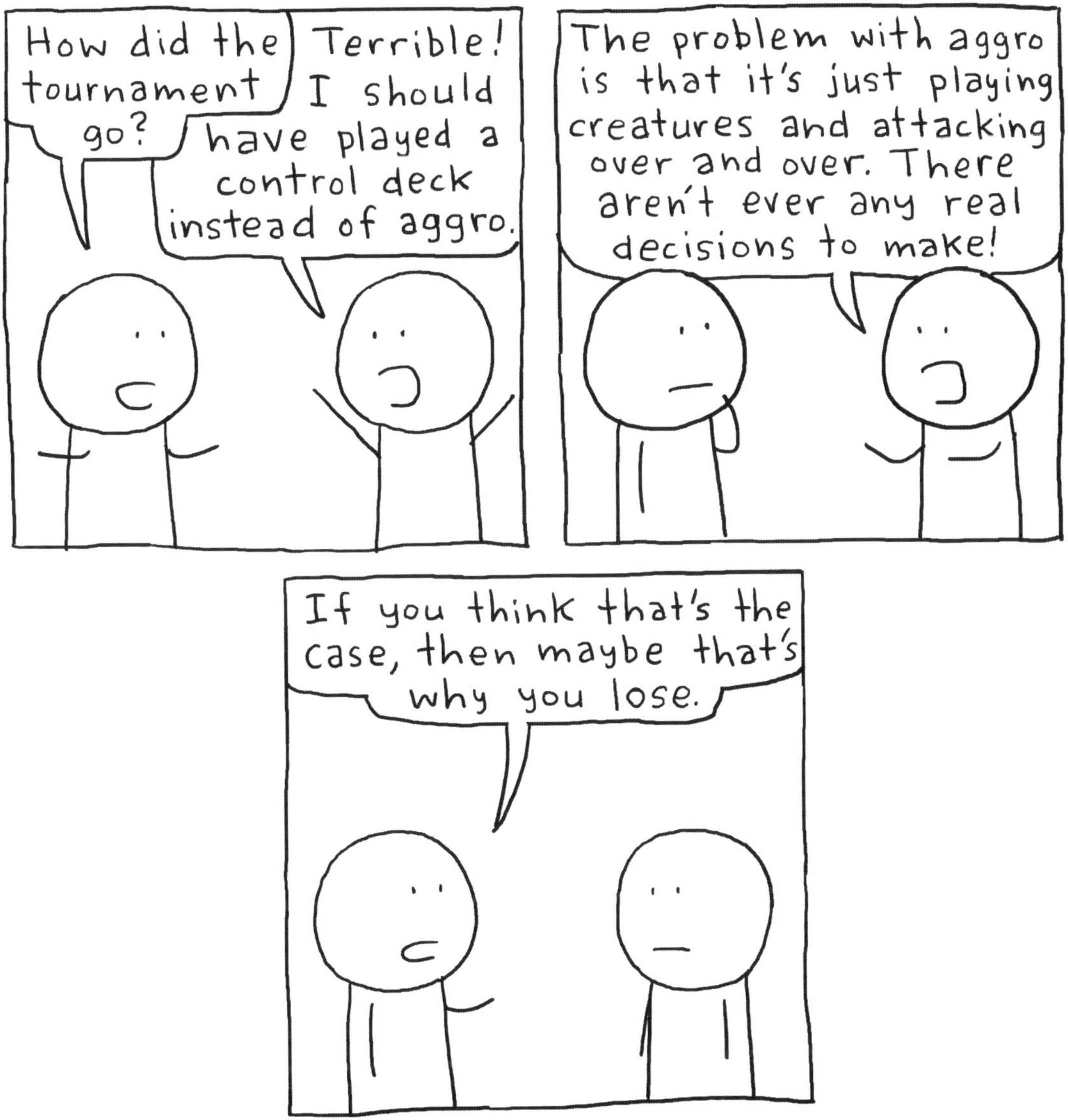
How did the tournament go?
Terrible! I should have played a control deck instead of aggro.
The problem with aggro is that it's just playing creatures and attacking over and over. There aren't ever any real decisions to make!
If you think that's the case, then maybe that's why you lose.

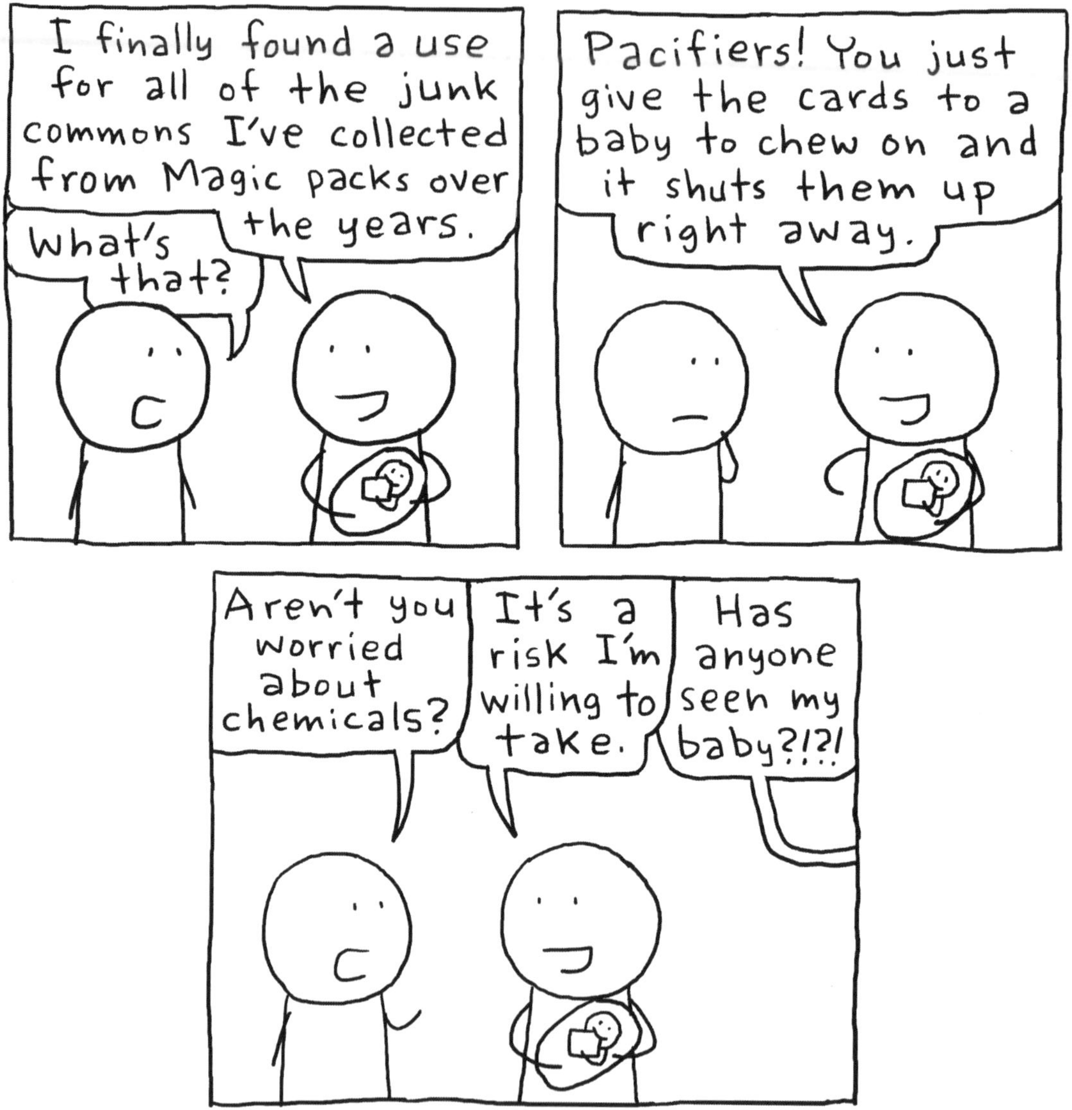
I finally found a use for all of the junk commons I've collected from Magic packs over the years.
What's that?
Pacifiers! You just give the cards to a baby to chew on and it shuts them up right away.
Aren't you worried about chemicals?
It's a risk I'm willing to take.
Has anyone seen my baby?!?!

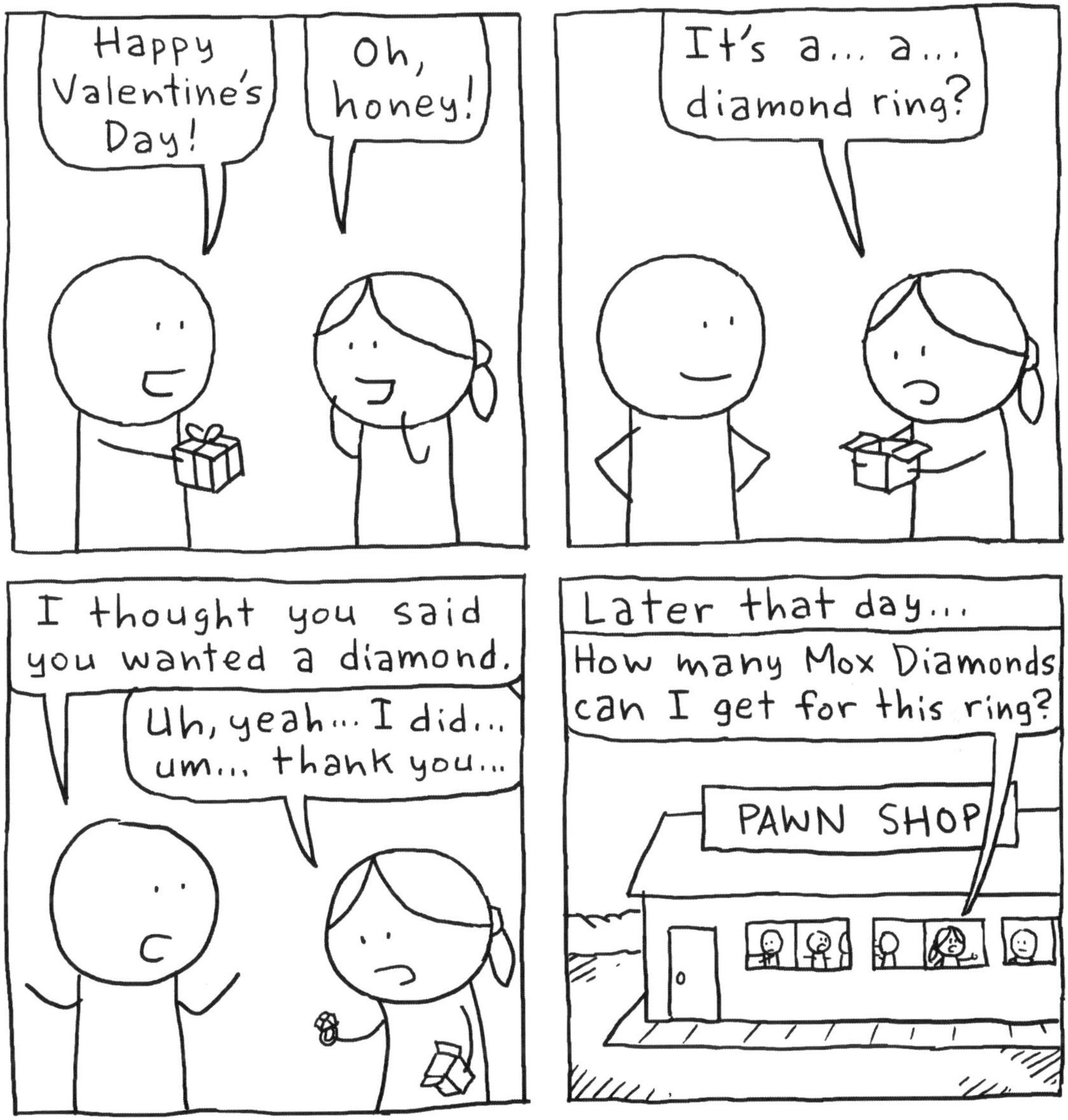
Happy Valentine's Day!
Oh, honey!
It's a... a... diamond ring?
I thought you said you wanted a diamond.
Uh, yeah... I did... um... thank you...
Later that day...
How many Mox Diamonds can I get for this ring?
PAWN SHOP

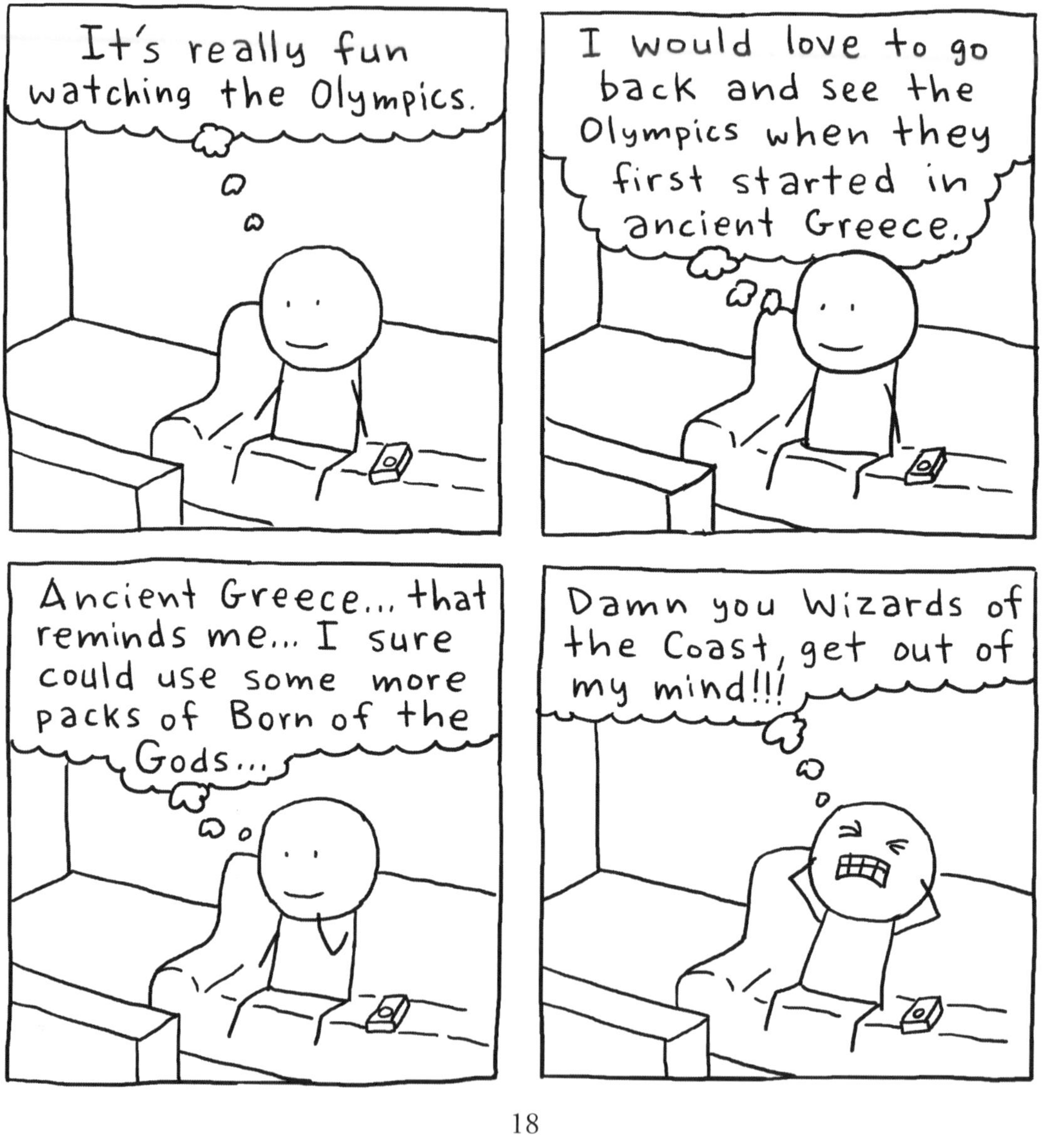
It's really fun watching the Olympics.
I would love to go back and see the Olympics when they first started in ancient Greece.
Ancient Greece... that reminds me... I sure could use some more packs of Born of the Gods...
Damn you Wizards of the Coast, get out of my mind!!!

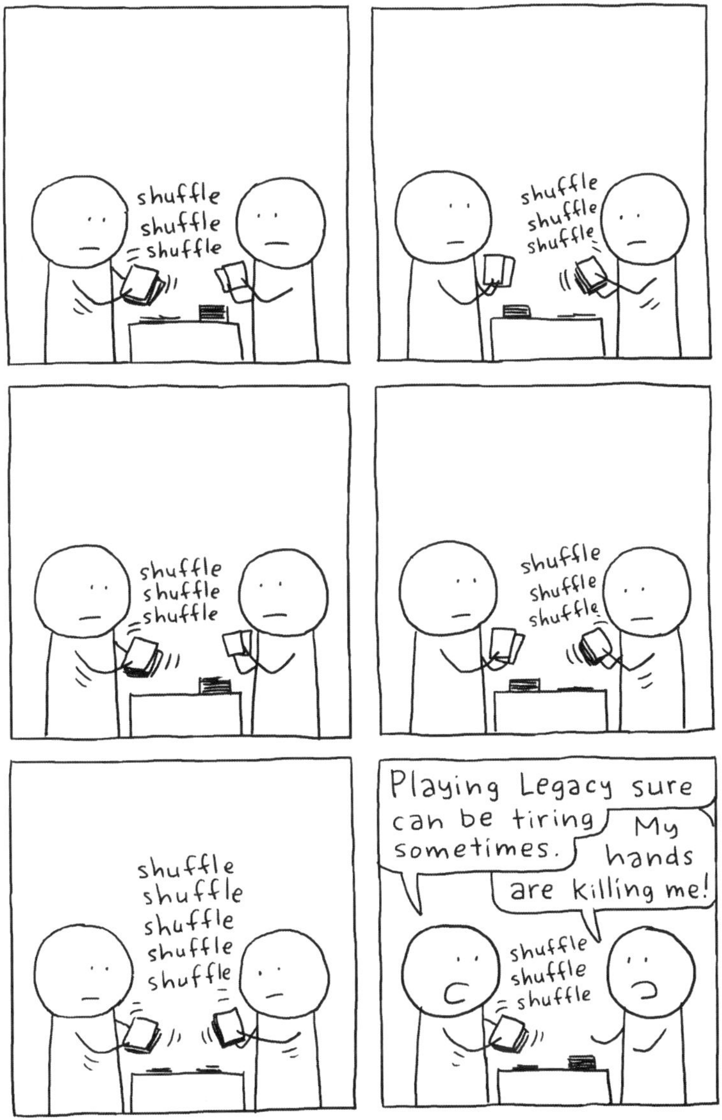
shuffle
shuffle
shuffle
shuffle
shuffle
shuffle
shuffle
shuffle
shuffle
shuffle
shuffle
shuffle
shuffle
shuffle
shuffle
shuffle
shuffle
Playing Legacy sure can be tiring sometimes.
My hands are killing me!
shuffle
shuffle
shuffle

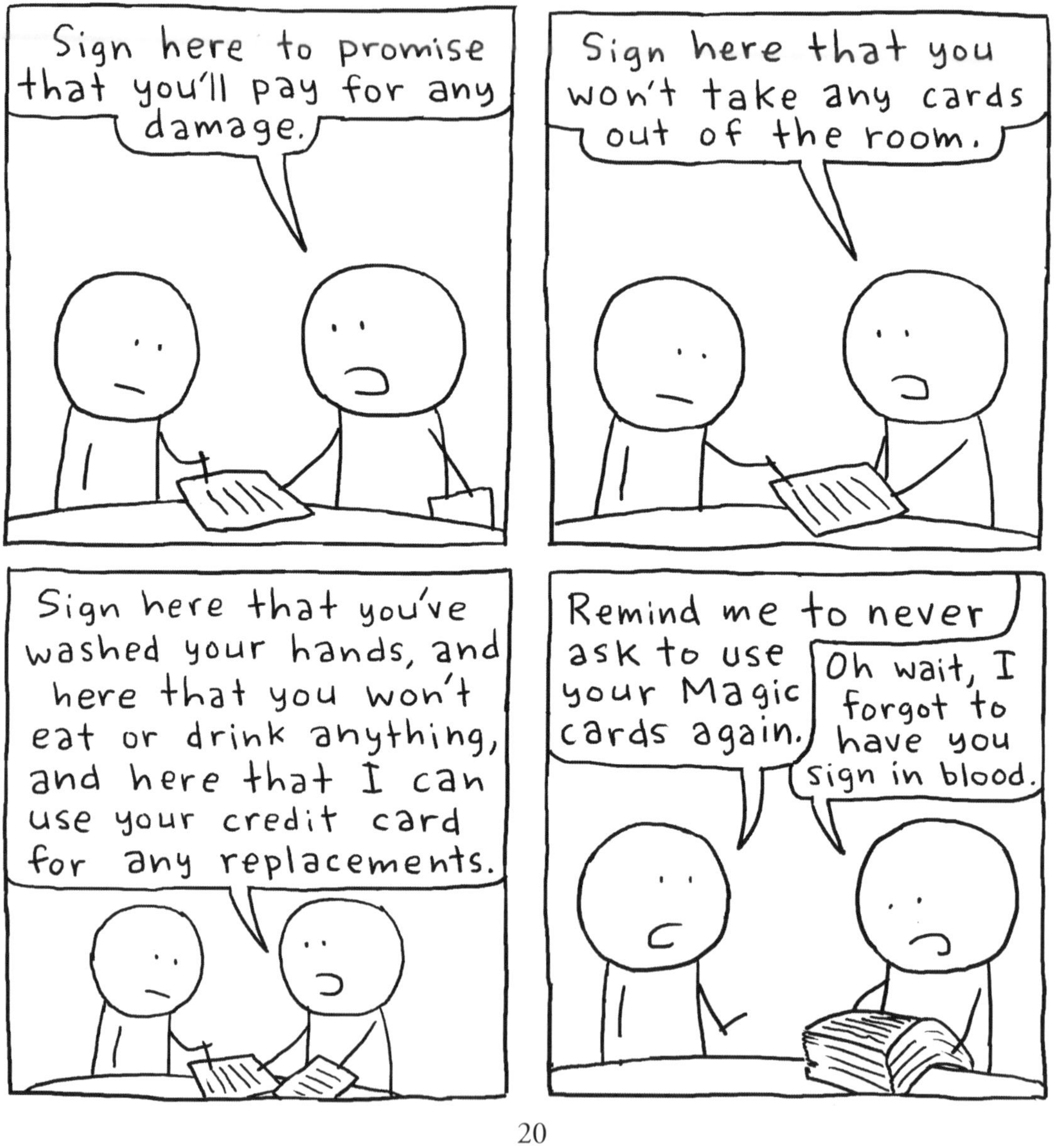
Sign here to promise that you'll pay for any damage.
Sign here that you won't take any cards out of the room.
Sign here that you've washed your hands, and here that you won't eat or drink anything, and here that I can use your credit card for any replacements.
Remind me to never ask to use your Magic cards again.
Oh wait, I forgot to have you sign in blood.

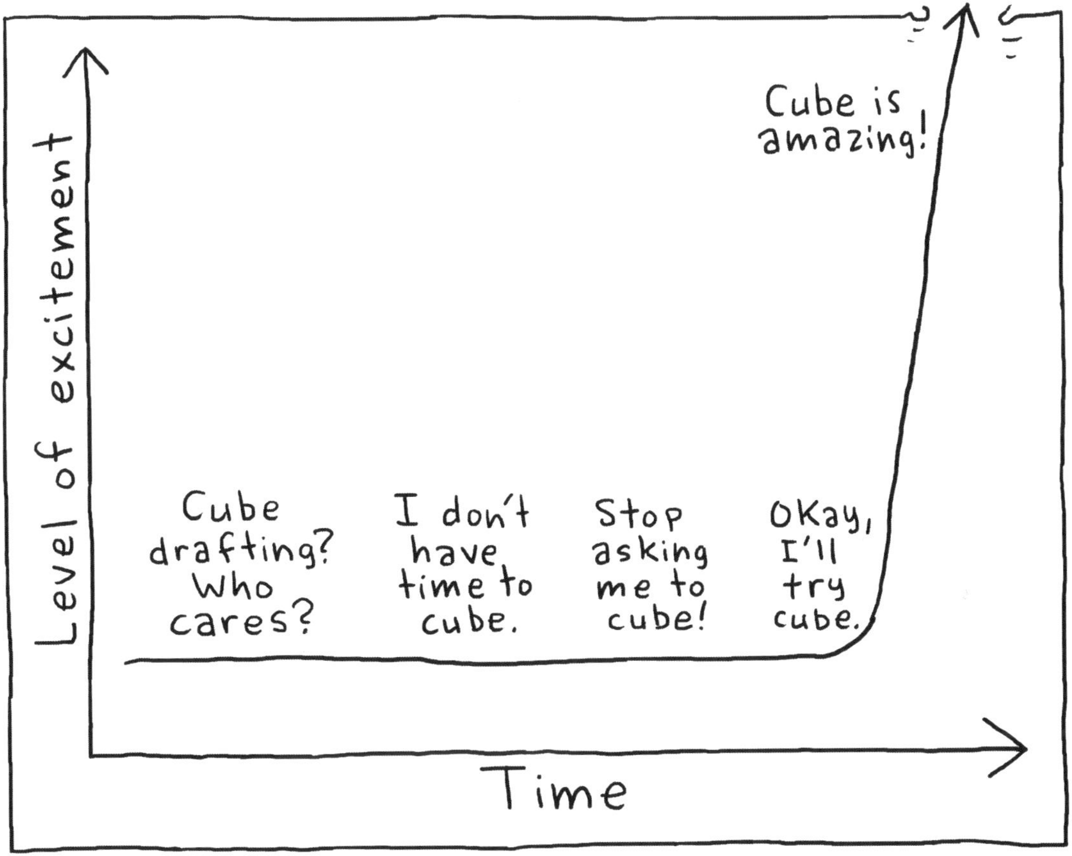
Level of excitement
Time
Cube drafting? Who cares?
I don't have time to cube.
Stop asking me to cube!
Okay, I'll try cube.
Cube is amazing!

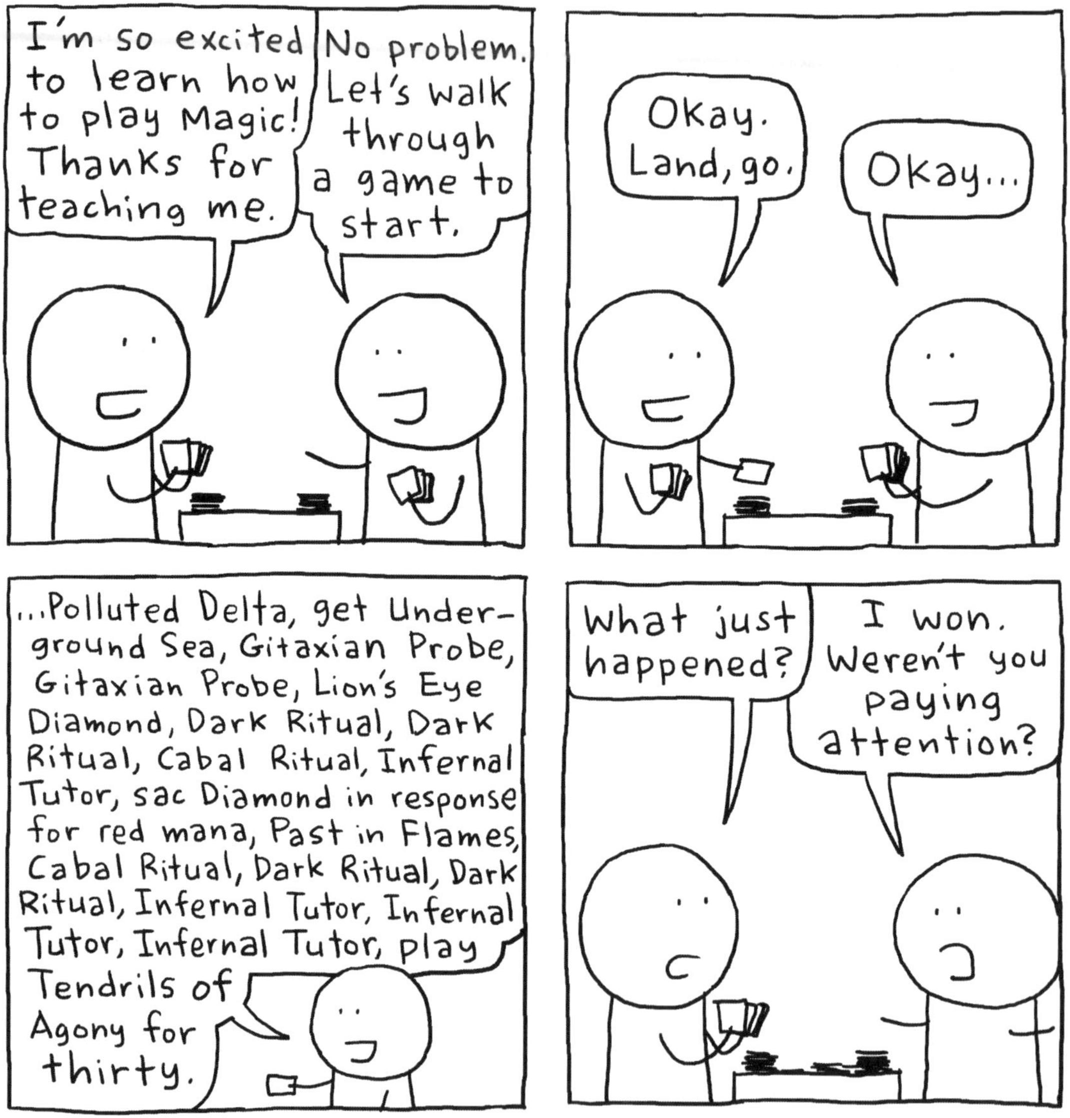
I'm so excited to learn how to play Magic! Thanks for teaching me.
No problem. Let's walk through a game to start.
Okay. Land, go.
Okay...
...Polluted Delta, get Underground Sea, Gitaxian Probe, Gitaxian Probe, Lion's Eye Diamond, Dark Ritual, Dark Ritual, Cabal Ritual, Infernal Tutor, sac Diamond in response for red mana, Past in Flames, Cabal Ritual, Dark Ritual, Dark Ritual, Infernal Tutor, Infernal Tutor, Infernal Tutor, play Tendrils of Agony for thirty.
What just happened?
I won. Weren't you paying attention?

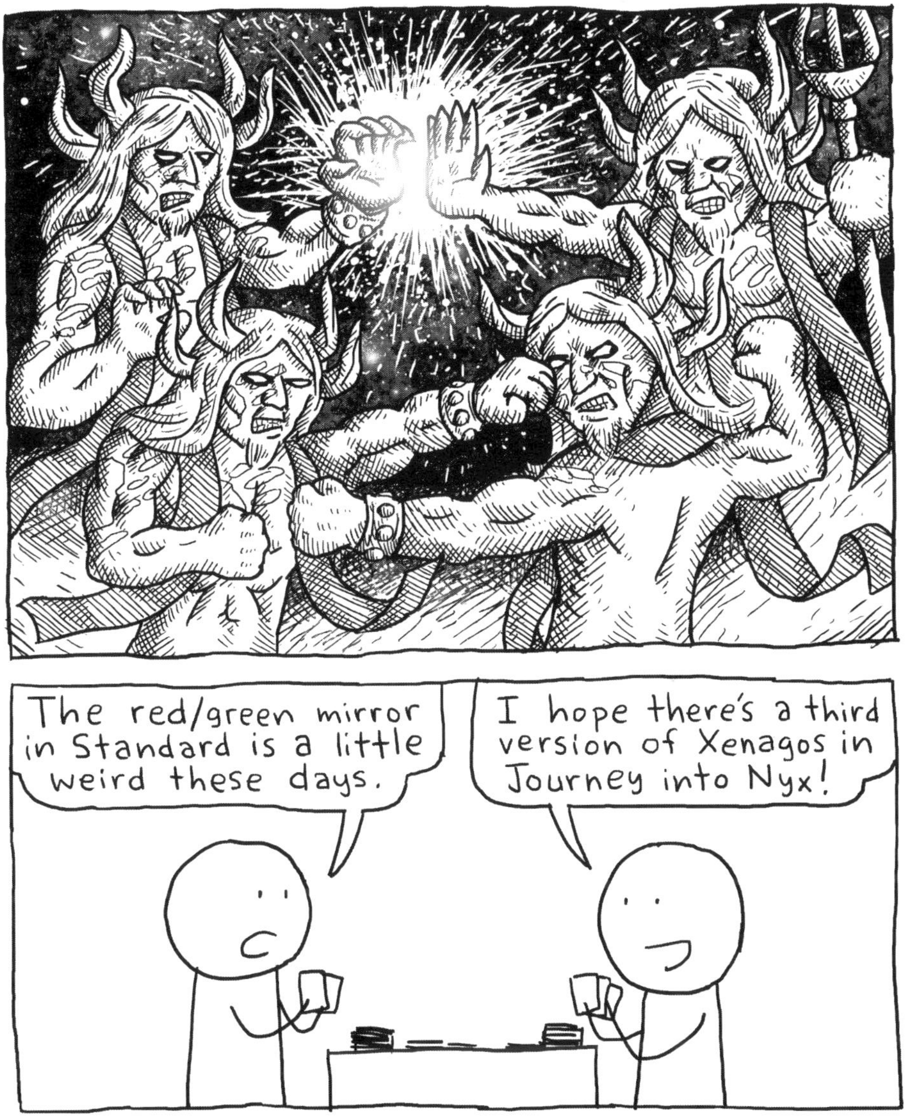
The red/green mirror in Standard is a little weird these days.
I hope there's a third version of Xenagos in Journey into Nyx!

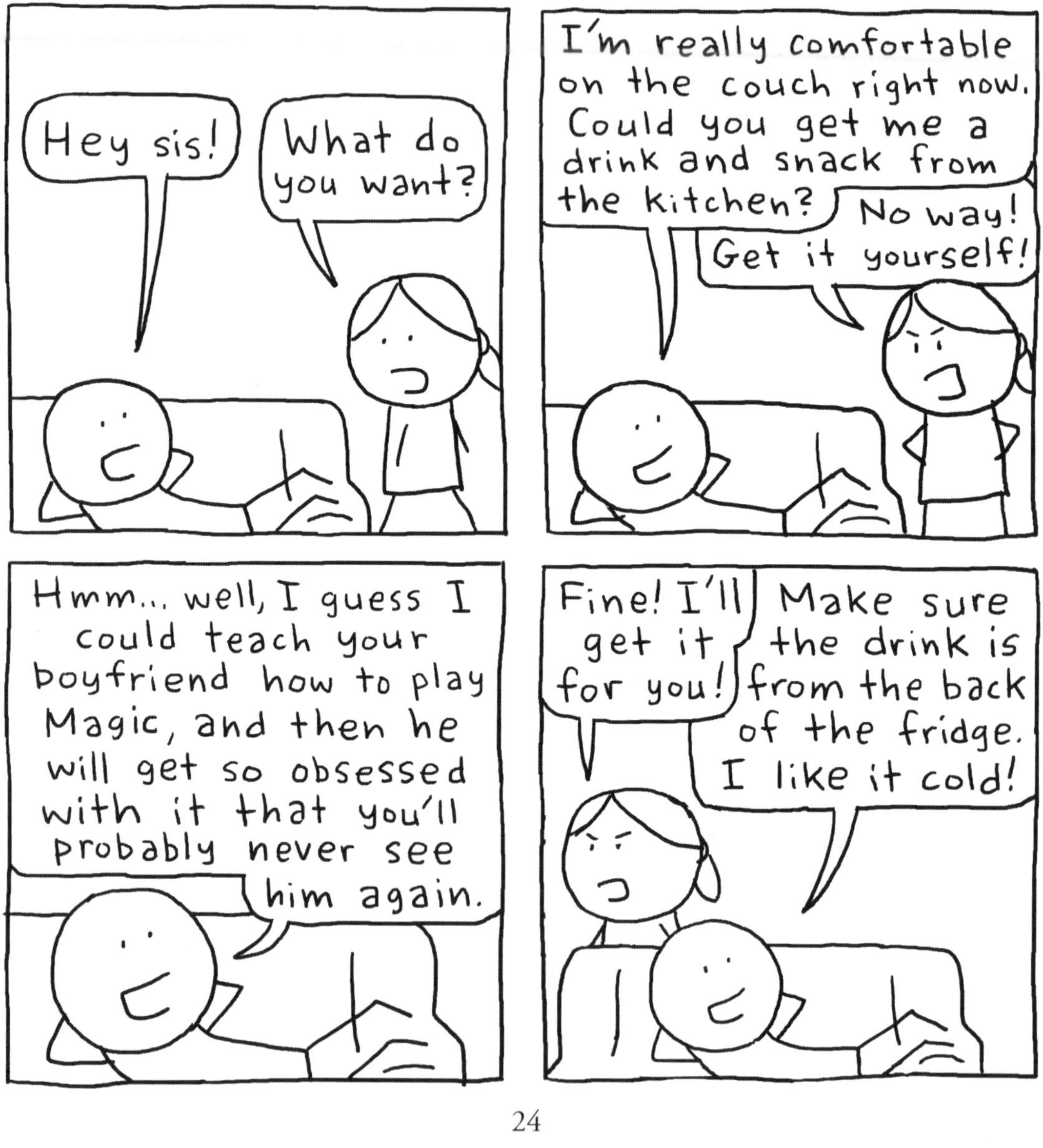

Hey sis!
What do you want?
I'm really comfortable on the couch right now. Could you get me a drink and snack from the kitchen?
No way! Get it yourself!
Hmm... well, I guess I could teach your boyfriend how to play Magic, and then he will get so obsessed with it that you'll probably never see him again.
Fine! I'll get it for you!
Make sure the drink is from the back of the fridge. I like it cold!

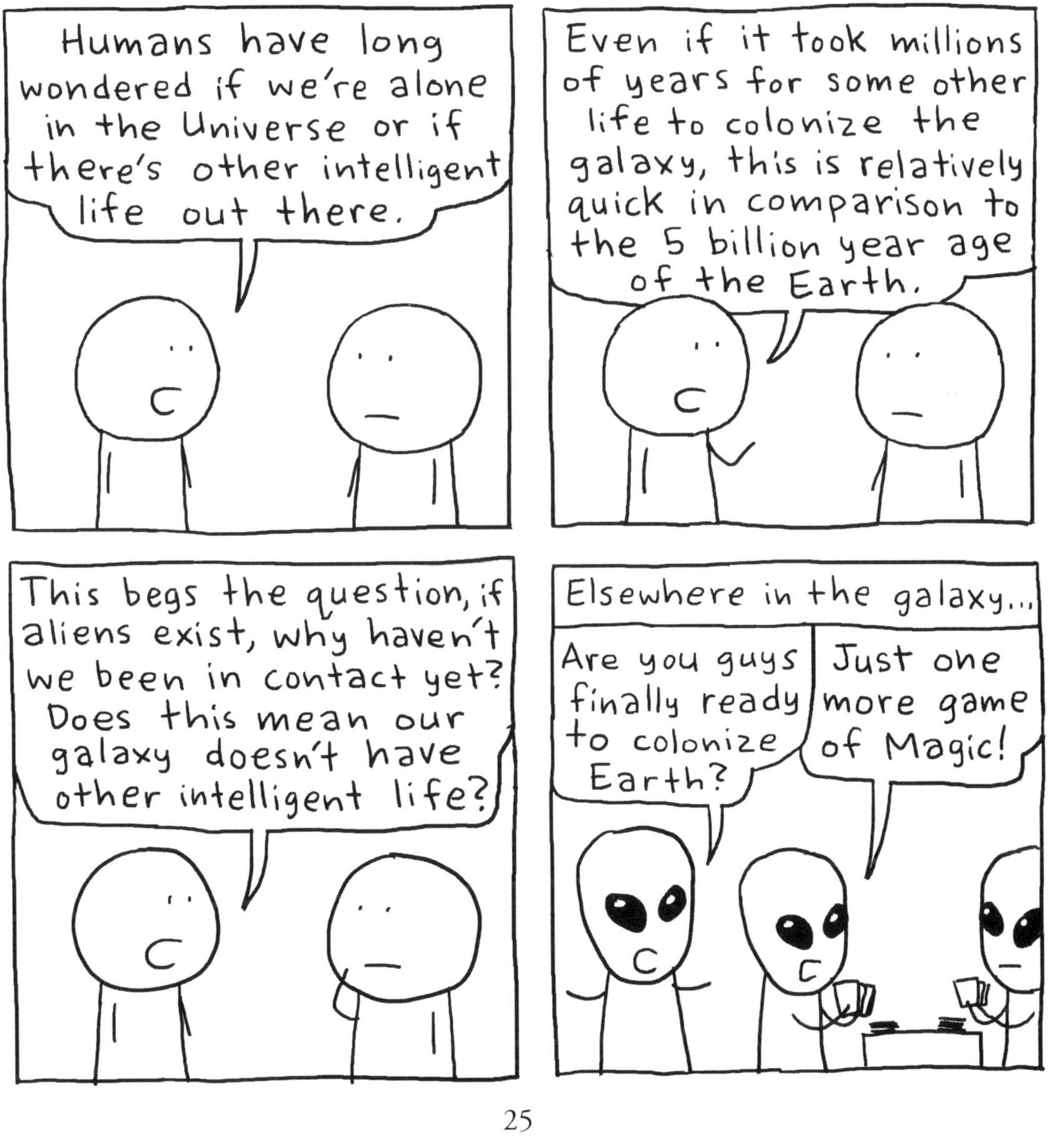
Humans have long wondered if we're alone in the Universe or if there's other intelligent life out there.
Even if it took millions of years for some other life to colonize the galaxy, this is relatively quick in comparison to the 5 billion year age of the Earth.
This begs the question, if aliens exist, why haven't we been in contact yet? Does this mean our galaxy doesn't have other intelligent life?
Elsewhere in the galaxy...
Are you guys finally ready to colonize Earth?
Just one more game of Magic!

Tip for playing Magic: Only use altered, foreign cards, and then every game you can play "Mental Magic".
I cast Hero's Downfall to kill your planeswalker.
Wait, is that an Underworld Connections?
Uh... um... no! Of course not!

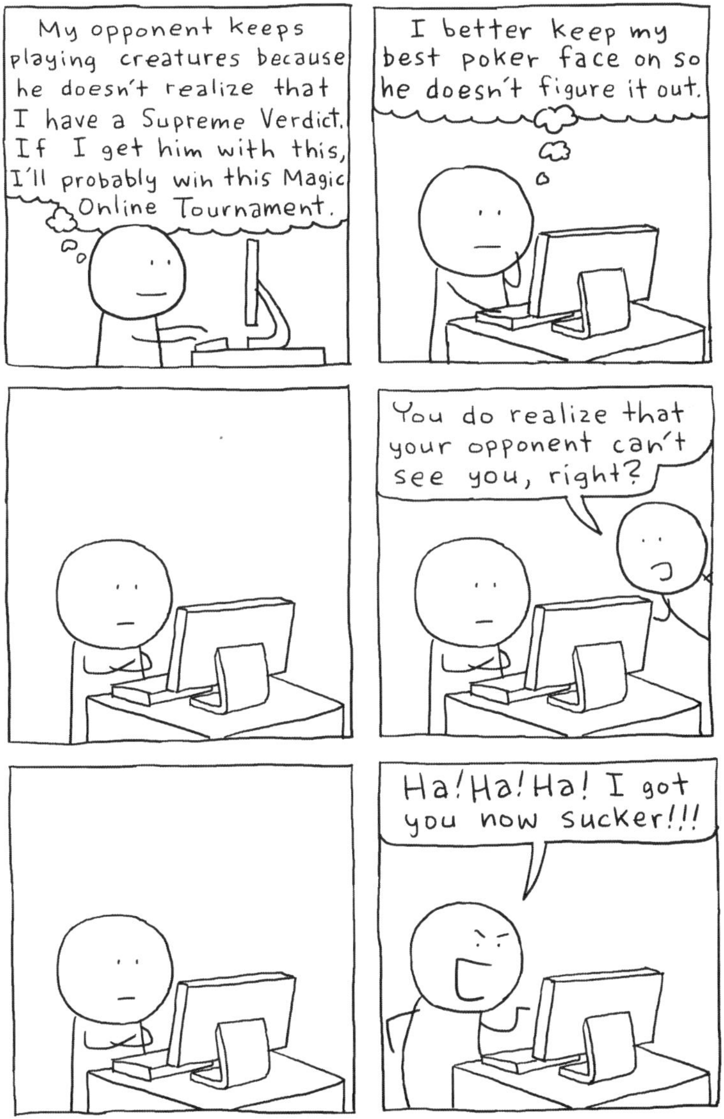
My opponent keeps playing creatures because he doesn't realize that I have a Supreme Verdict. If I get him with this, I'll probably win this Magic Online Tournament.
I better keep my best poker face on so he doesn't figure it out.
You do realize that your opponent can't see you, right?
Ha! Ha! Ha! I got you now sucker!!!

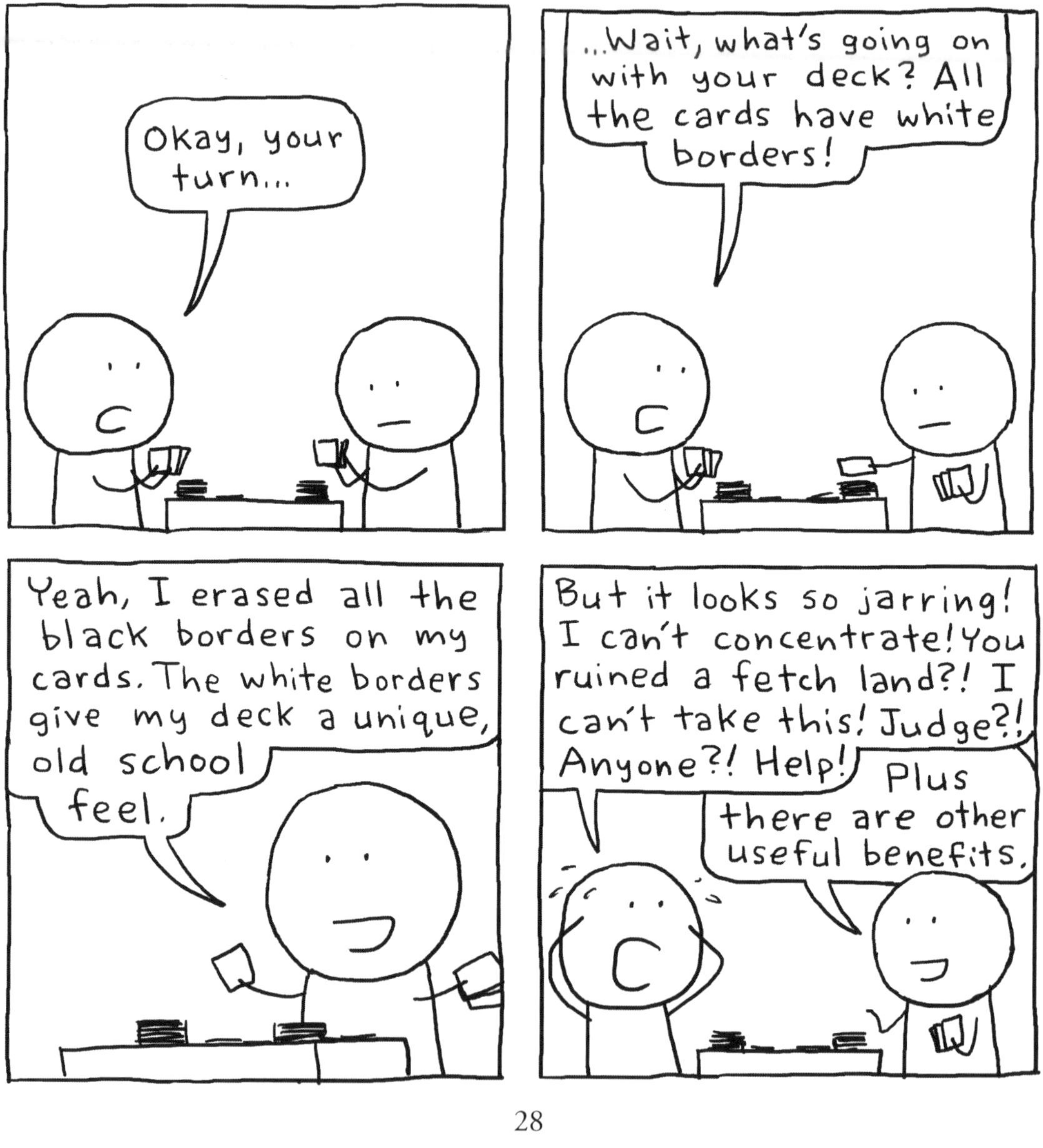
Okay, your turn...
...Wait, what's going on with your deck? All the cards have white borders!
Yeah, I erased all the black borders on my cards. The white borders give my deck a unique, old school feel.
But it looks so jarring! I can't concentrate! You ruined a fetch land?! I can't take this! Judge?! Anyone?! Help!
Plus there are other useful benefits.

Modern human beings have been around for about 200,000 years, which is relatively short in comparison to the time-scale for significant evolution to take place.

This means that humans were basically optimized by evolution for things like foraging for food, reproducing, and not getting eaten by predators.

And now these same humans are expected to work 40 hours per week, sitting in front of a computer all day long!

Wow, it's inhumane!

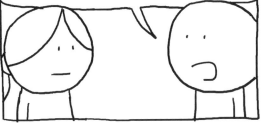

By the way, how long have we been sitting here playing Magic?

Probably like 34 hours straight. Why?

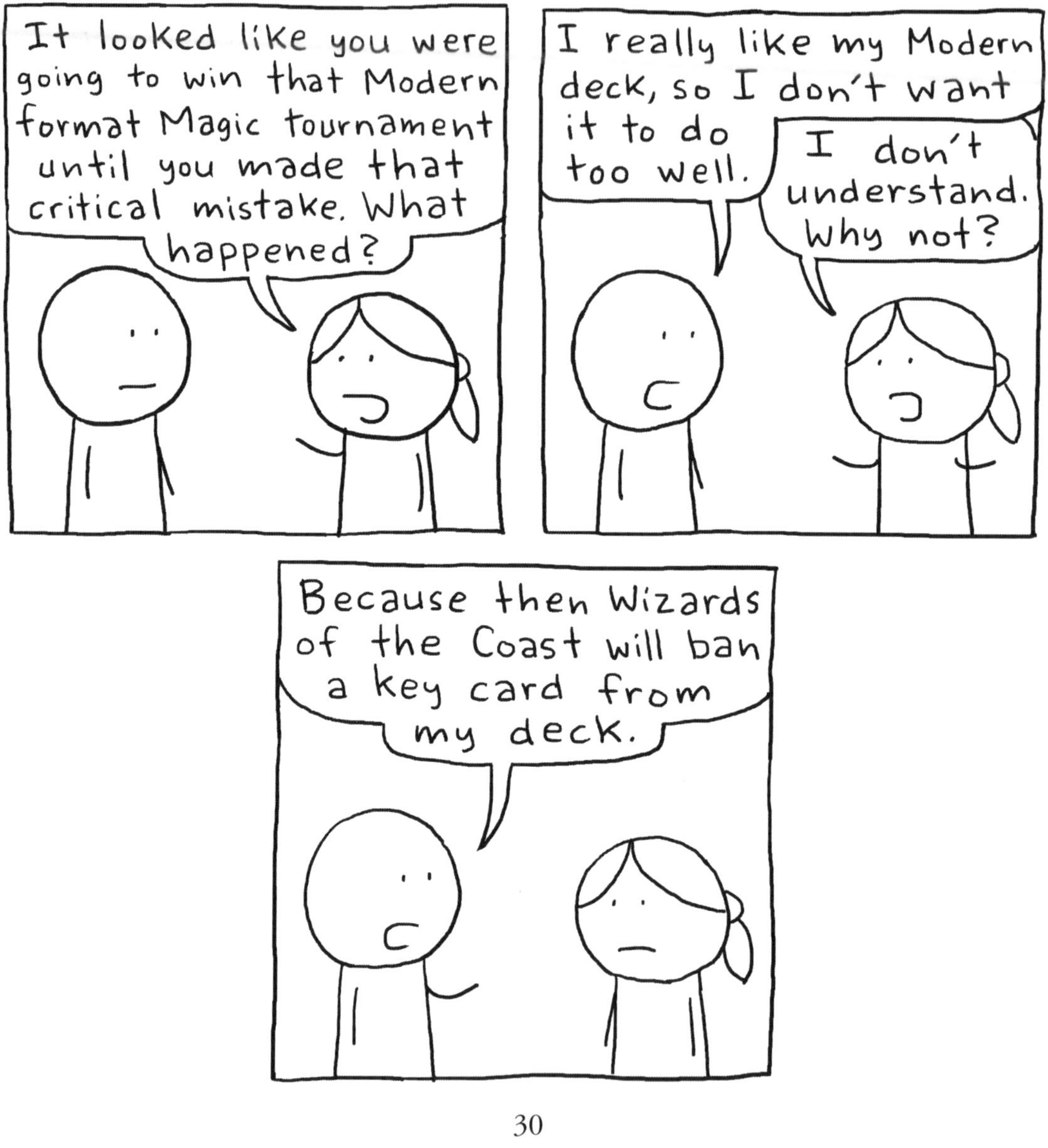
It looked like you were going to win that Modern format Magic tournament until you made that critical mistake. What happened?
I really like my Modern deck, so I don't want it to do too well.
I don't understand. Why not?
Because then Wizards of the Coast will ban a key card from my deck.

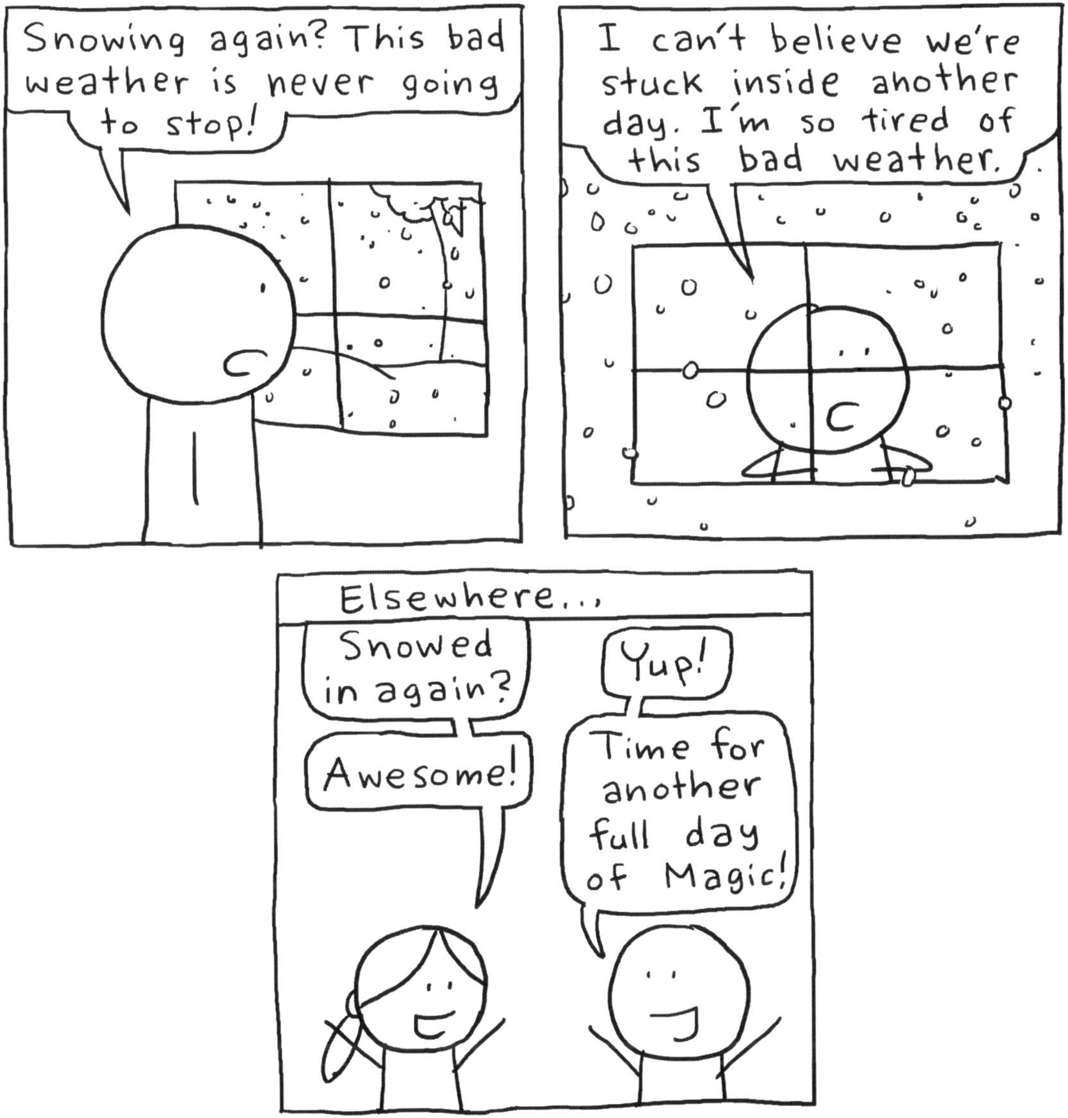
Snowing again? This bad weather is never going to stop!
I can't believe we're stuck inside another day. I'm so tired of this bad weather.
Elsewhere...
Snowed in again?
Awesome!
Yup!
Time for another full day of Magic!

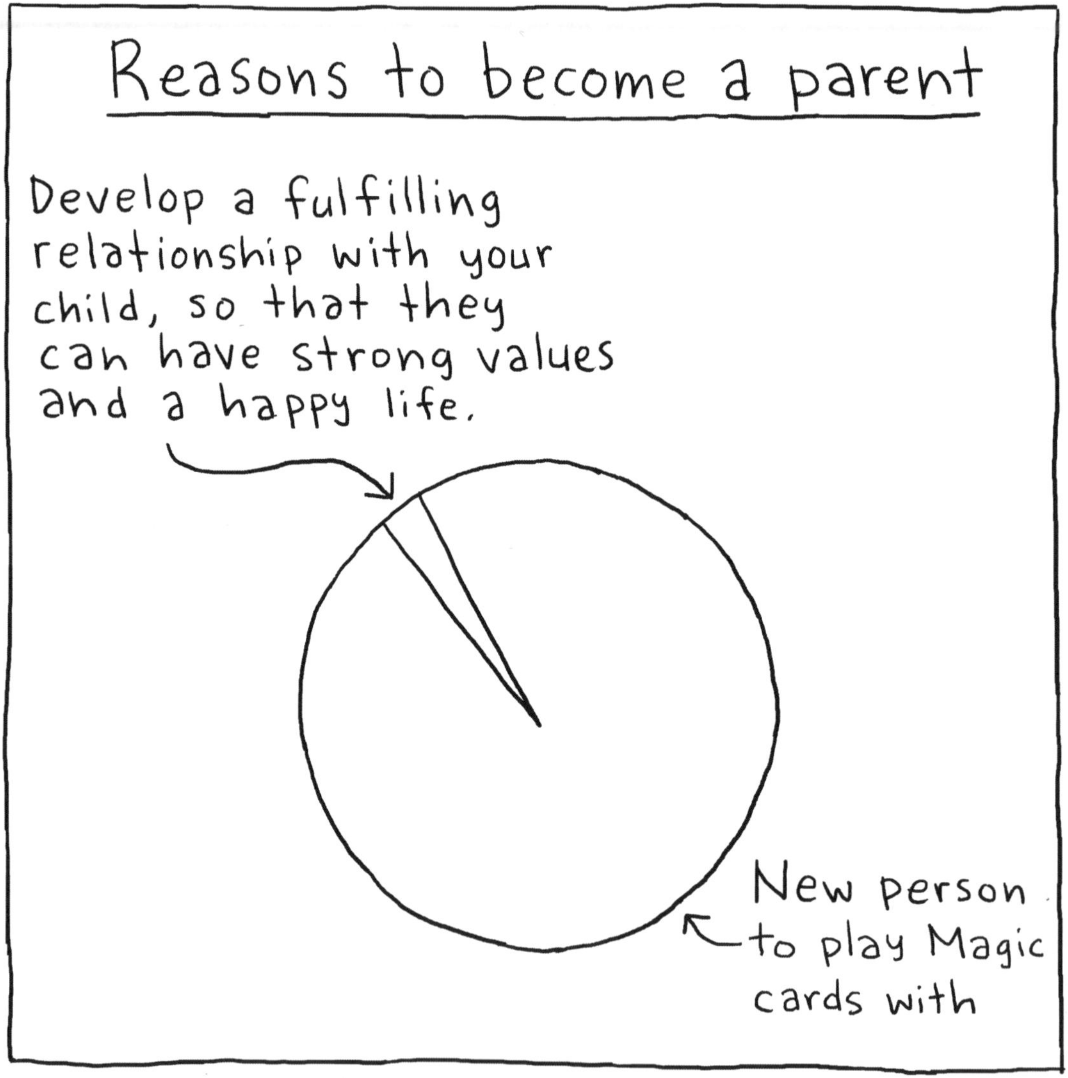

Reasons to become a parent

Develop a fulfilling
relationship with your
child, so that they
can have strong values
and a happy life.

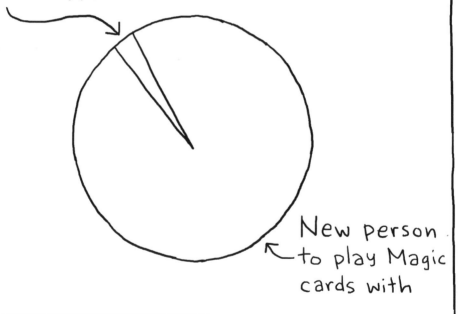

New person
to play Magic
cards with

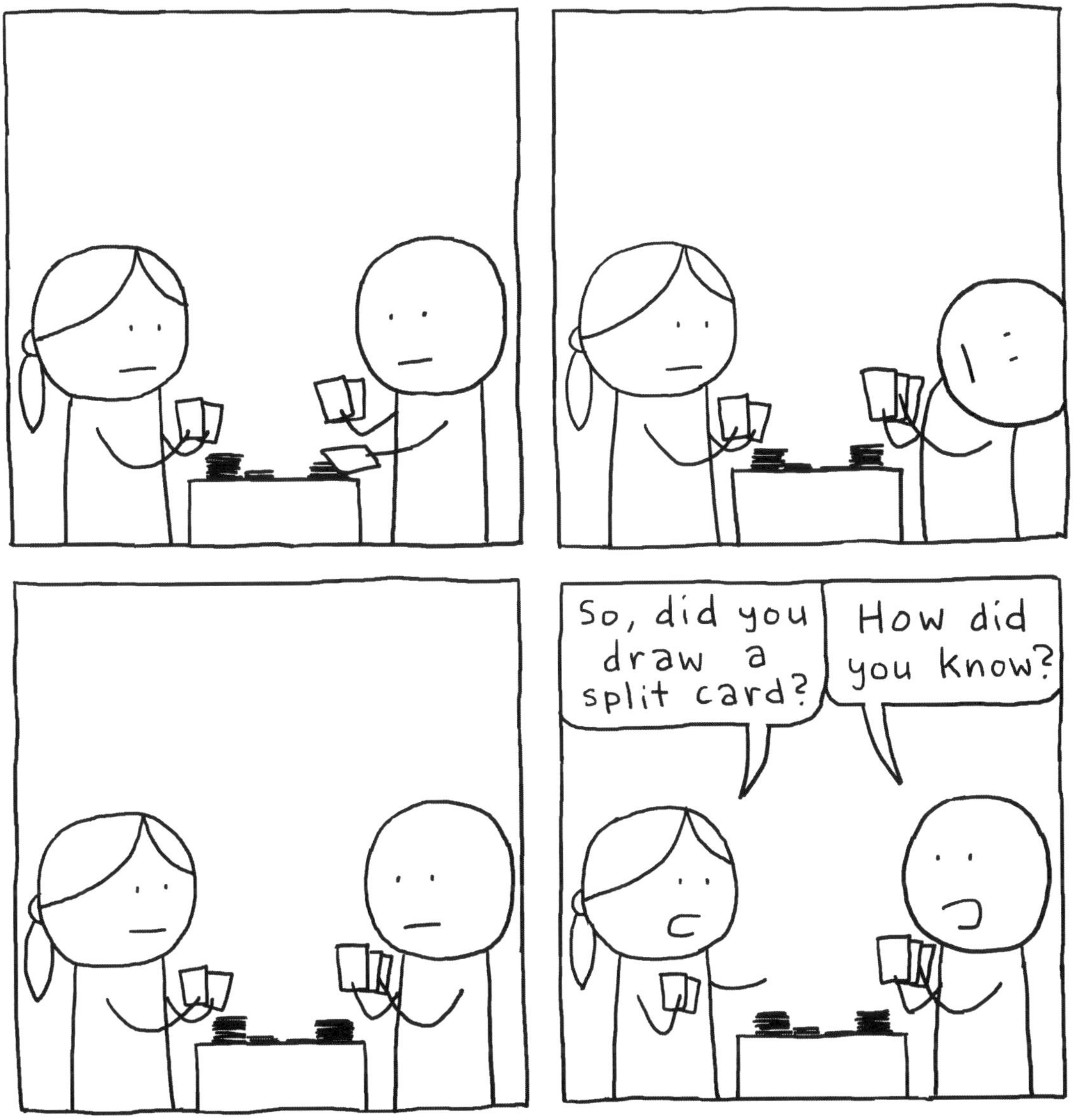
So, did you draw a split card?
How did you know?

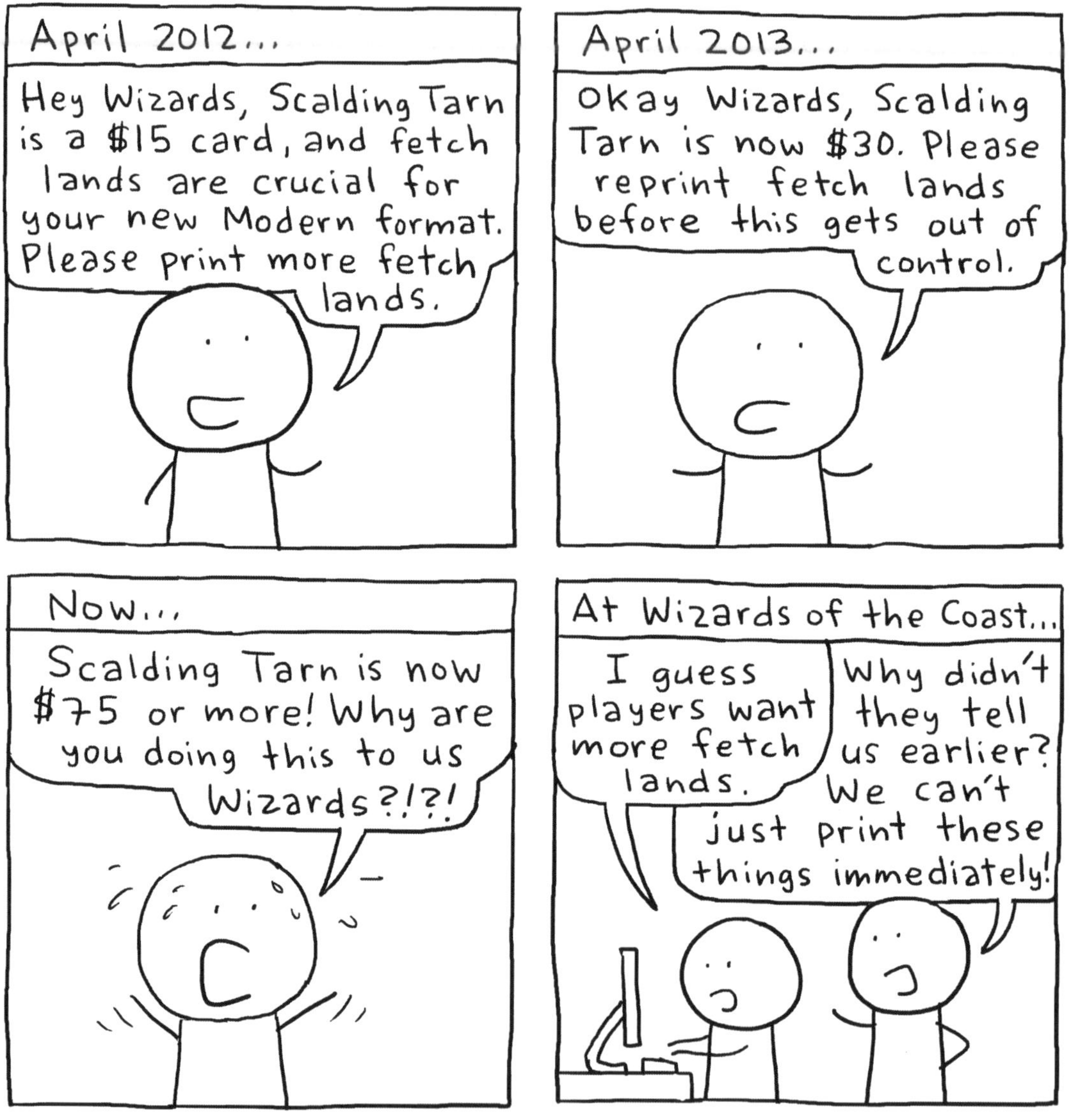
April 2012...
Hey Wizards, Scalding Tarn is a $15 card, and fetch lands are crucial for your new Modern format. Please print more fetch lands.
April 2013...
Okay Wizards, Scalding Tarn is now $30. Please reprint fetch lands before this gets out of control.
Now...
Scalding Tarn is now $75 or more! Why are you doing this to us Wizards?!?!
At Wizards of the Coast...
I guess players want more fetch lands.
Why didn't they tell us earlier? We can't just print these things immediately!

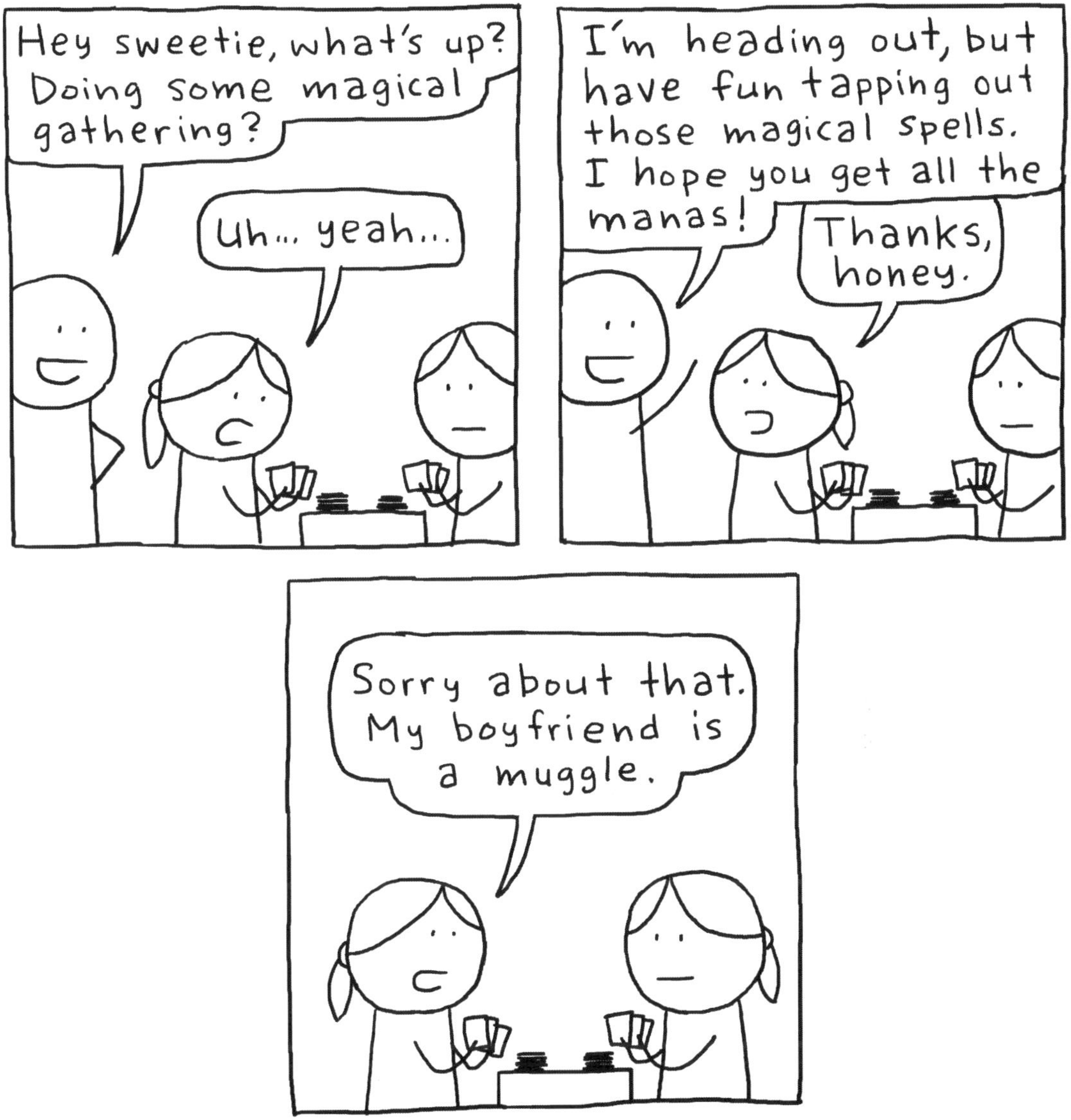
Hey sweetie, what's up? Doing some magical gathering?
Uh... yeah...
I'm heading out, but have fun tapping out those magical spells. I hope you get all the manas!
Thanks, honey.
Sorry about that. My boyfriend is a muggle.

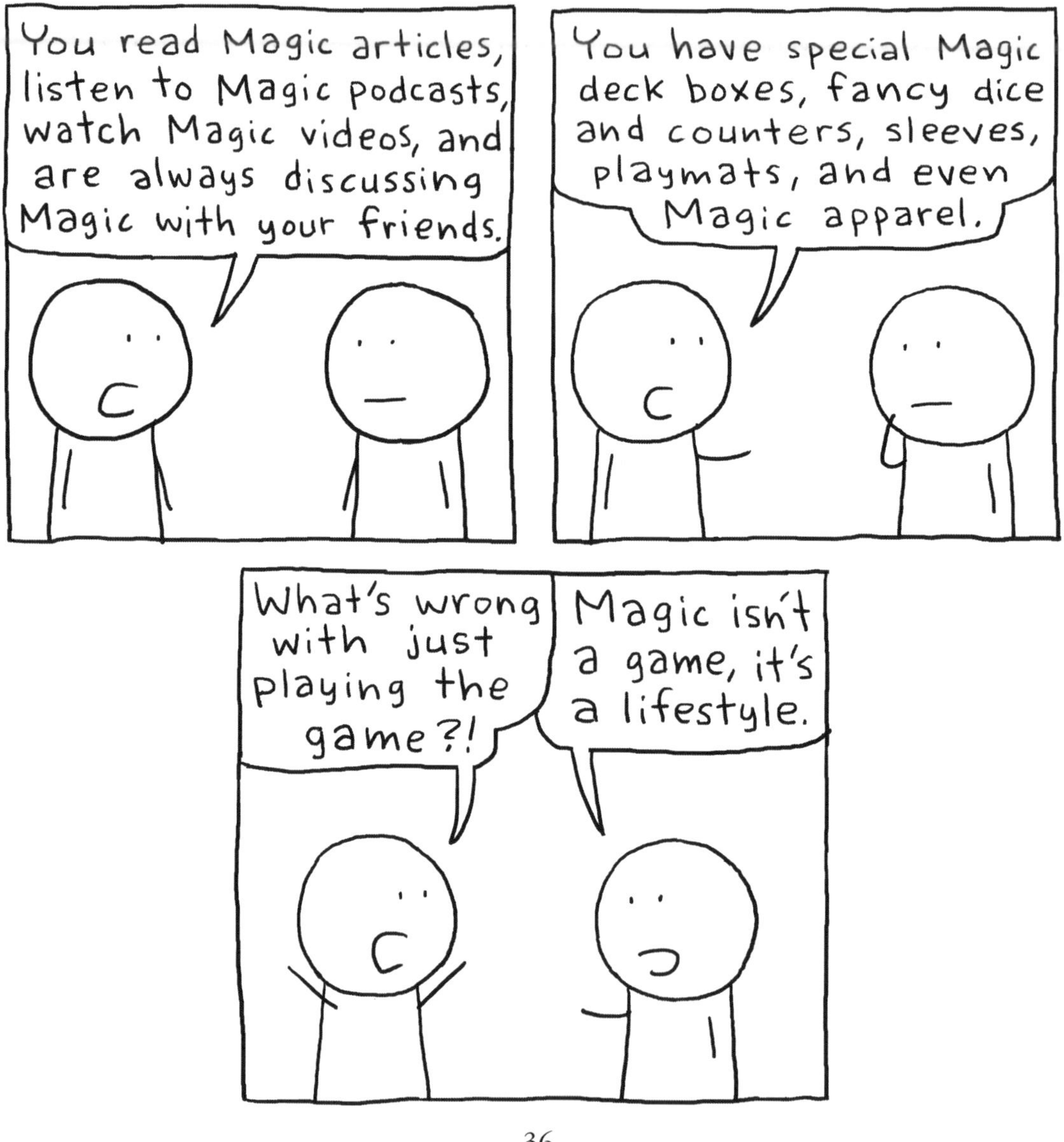
You read Magic articles, listen to Magic podcasts, watch Magic videos, and are always discussing Magic with your friends.
You have special Magic deck boxes, fancy dice and counters, sleeves, playmats, and even Magic apparel.
What's wrong with just playing the game?!
Magic isn't a game, it's a lifestyle.

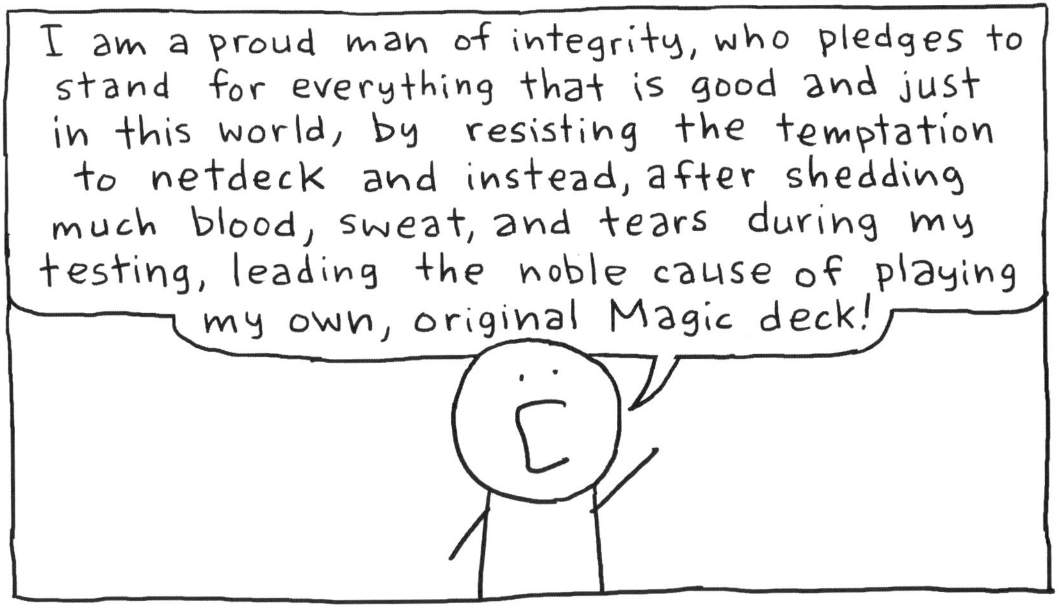
I am a proud man of integrity, who pledges to stand for everything that is good and just in this world, by resisting the temptation to netdeck and instead, after shedding much blood, sweat, and tears during my testing, leading the noble cause of playing my own, original Magic deck!

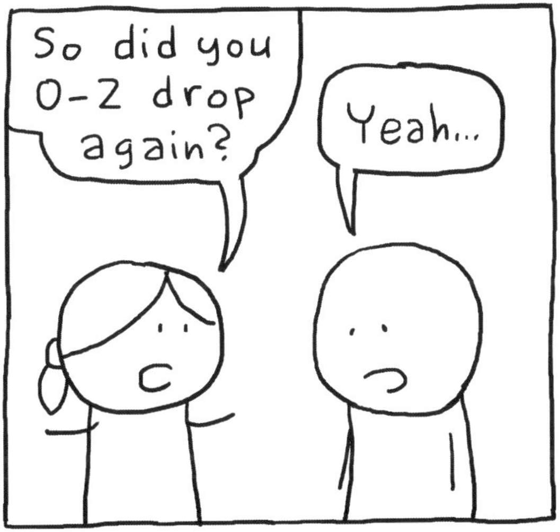
So did you 0-2 drop again?
Yeah...

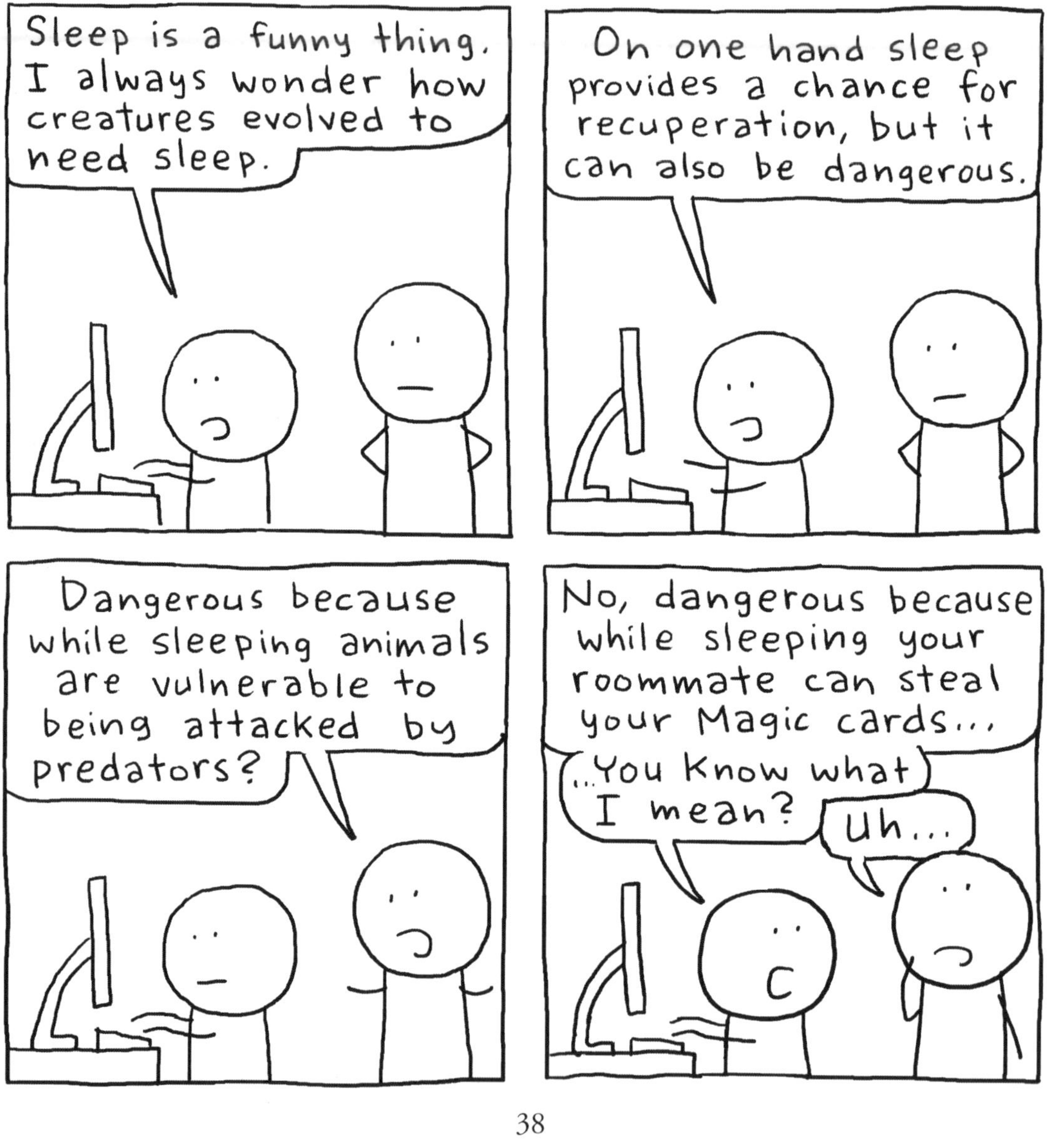
Sleep is a funny thing. I always wonder how creatures evolved to need sleep.
On one hand sleep provides a chance for recuperation, but it can also be dangerous.
Dangerous because while sleeping animals are vulnerable to being attacked by predators?
No, dangerous because while sleeping your roommate can steal your Magic cards...
...You know what I mean?
Uh...

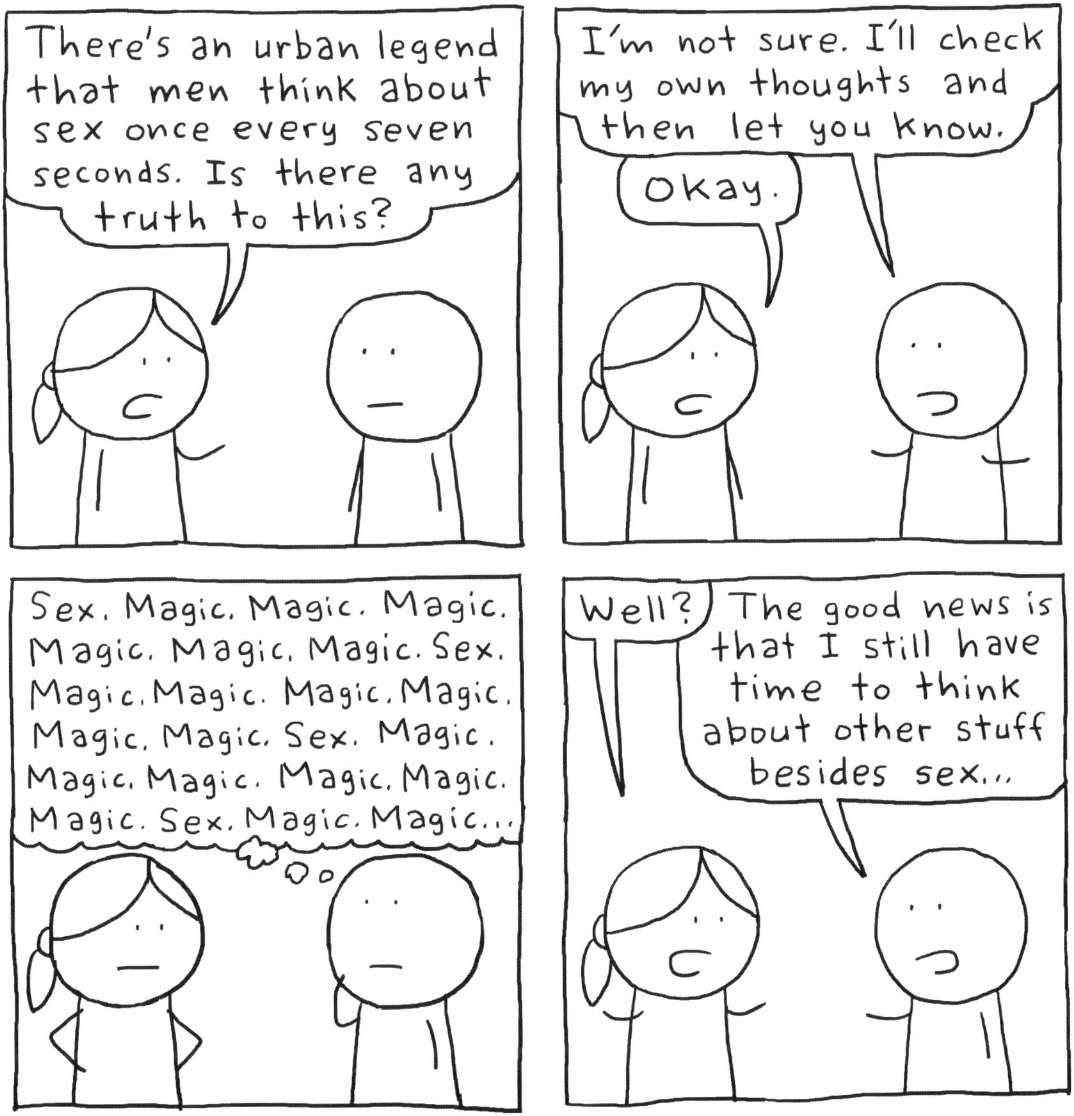
There's an urban legend that men think about sex once every seven seconds. Is there any truth to this?
I'm not sure. I'll check my own thoughts and then let you know.
Okay.
Sex. Magic. Magic. Magic. Magic. Magic. Magic. Sex. Magic. Magic. Magic. Magic. Magic. Magic. Sex. Magic. Magic. Magic. Magic. Magic. Magic. Sex. Magic. Magic...
Well?
The good news is that I still have time to think about other stuff besides sex...

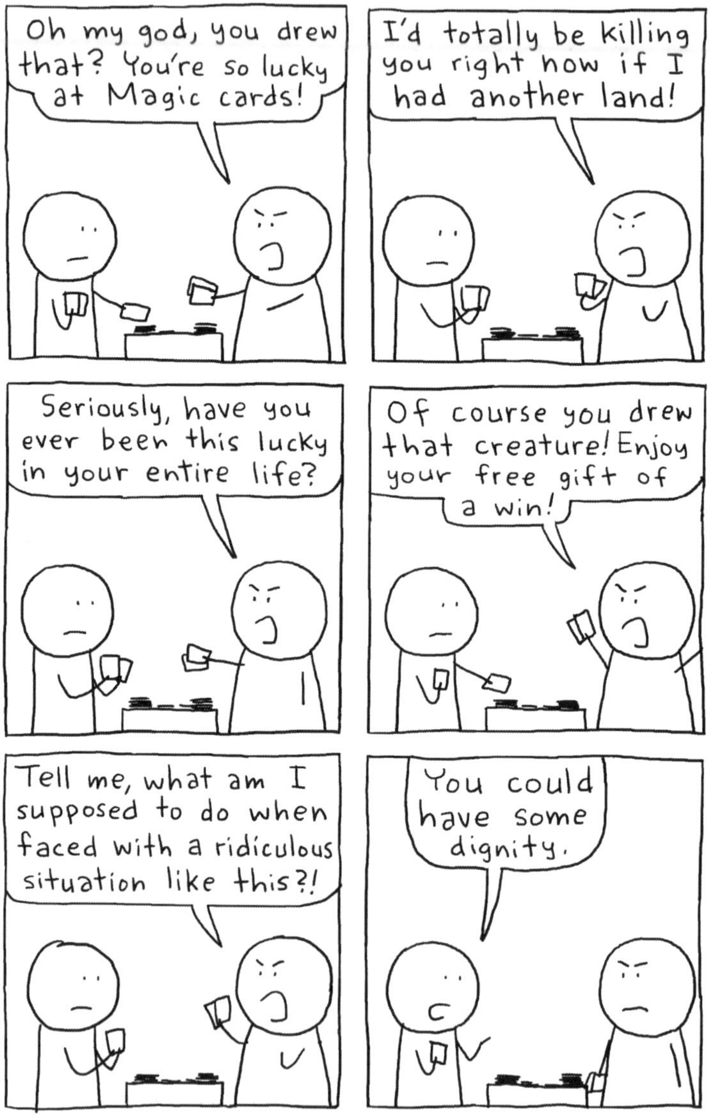
Oh my god, you drew that? You're so lucky at Magic cards!
I'd totally be killing you right now if I had another land!
Seriously, have you ever been this lucky in your entire life?
Of course you drew that creature! Enjoy your free gift of a win!
Tell me, what am I supposed to do when faced with a ridiculous situation like this?!
You could have some dignity.

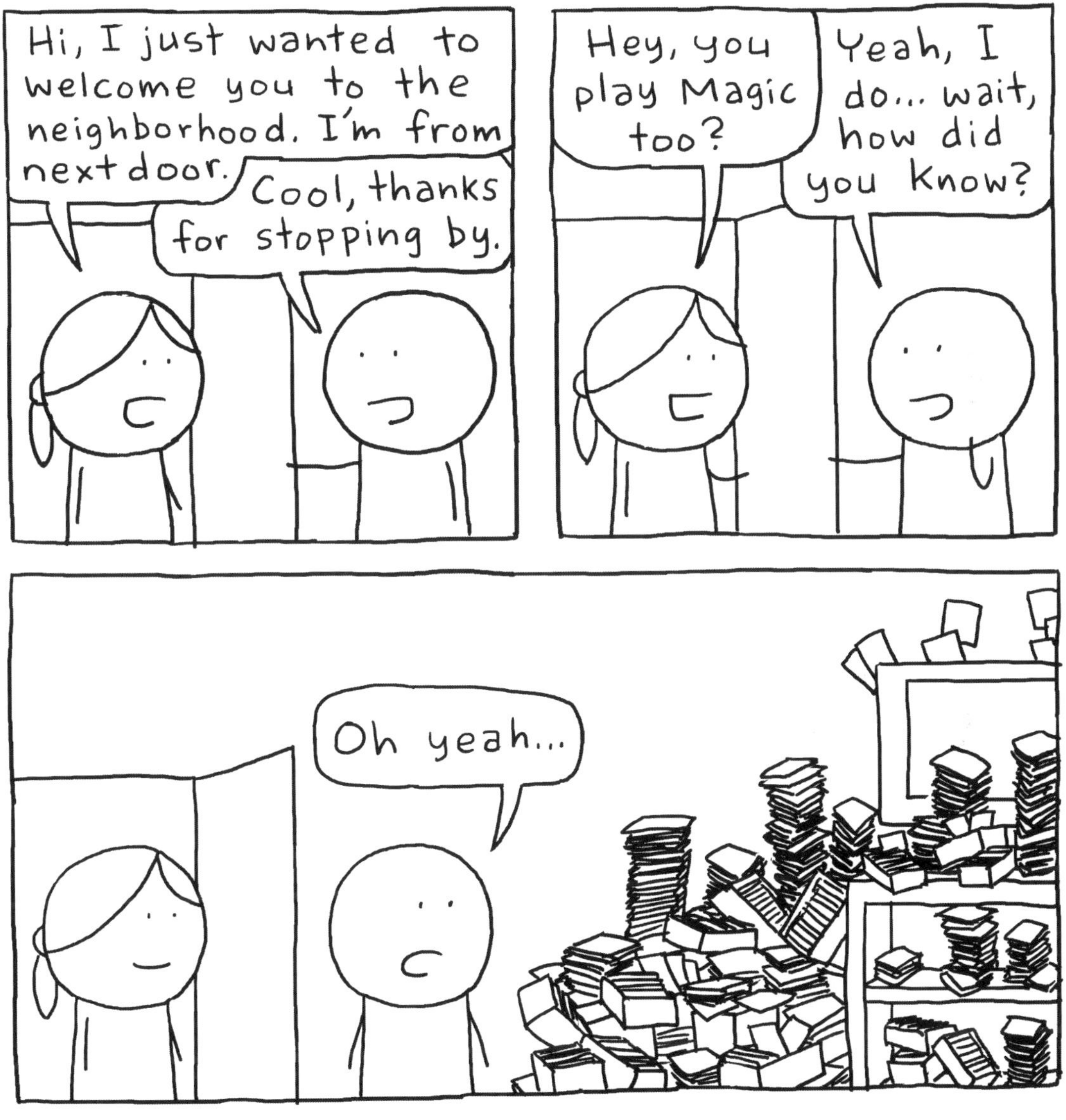
Hi, I just wanted to welcome you to the neighborhood. I'm from next door.
Cool, thanks for stopping by.
Hey, you play Magic too?
Yeah, I do... wait, how did you know?
Oh yeah...

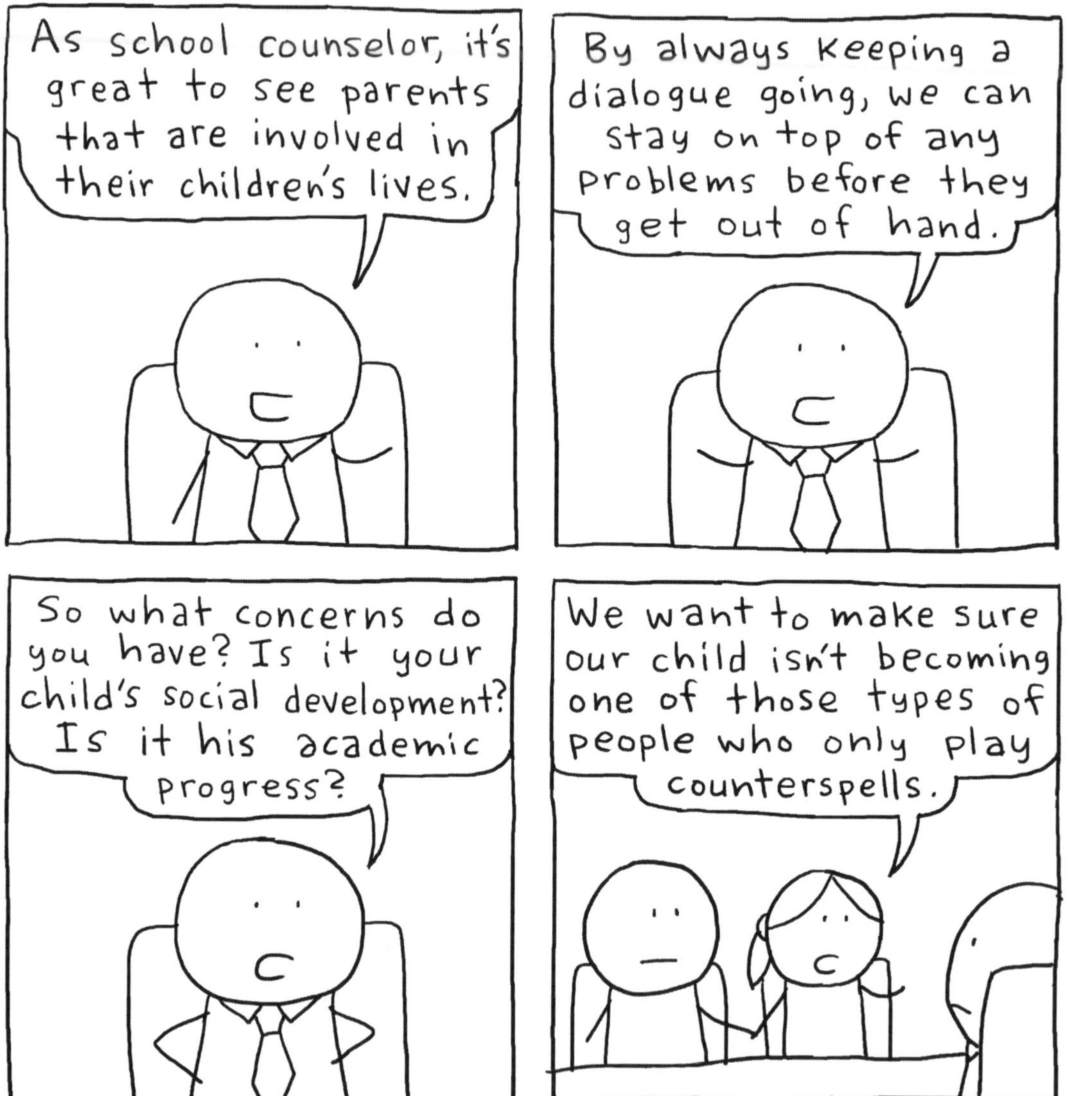

As school counselor, it's great to see parents that are involved in their children's lives.
By always keeping a dialogue going, we can stay on top of any problems before they get out of hand.
So what concerns do you have? Is it your child's social development? Is it his academic progress?
We want to make sure our child isn't becoming one of those types of people who only play counterspells.

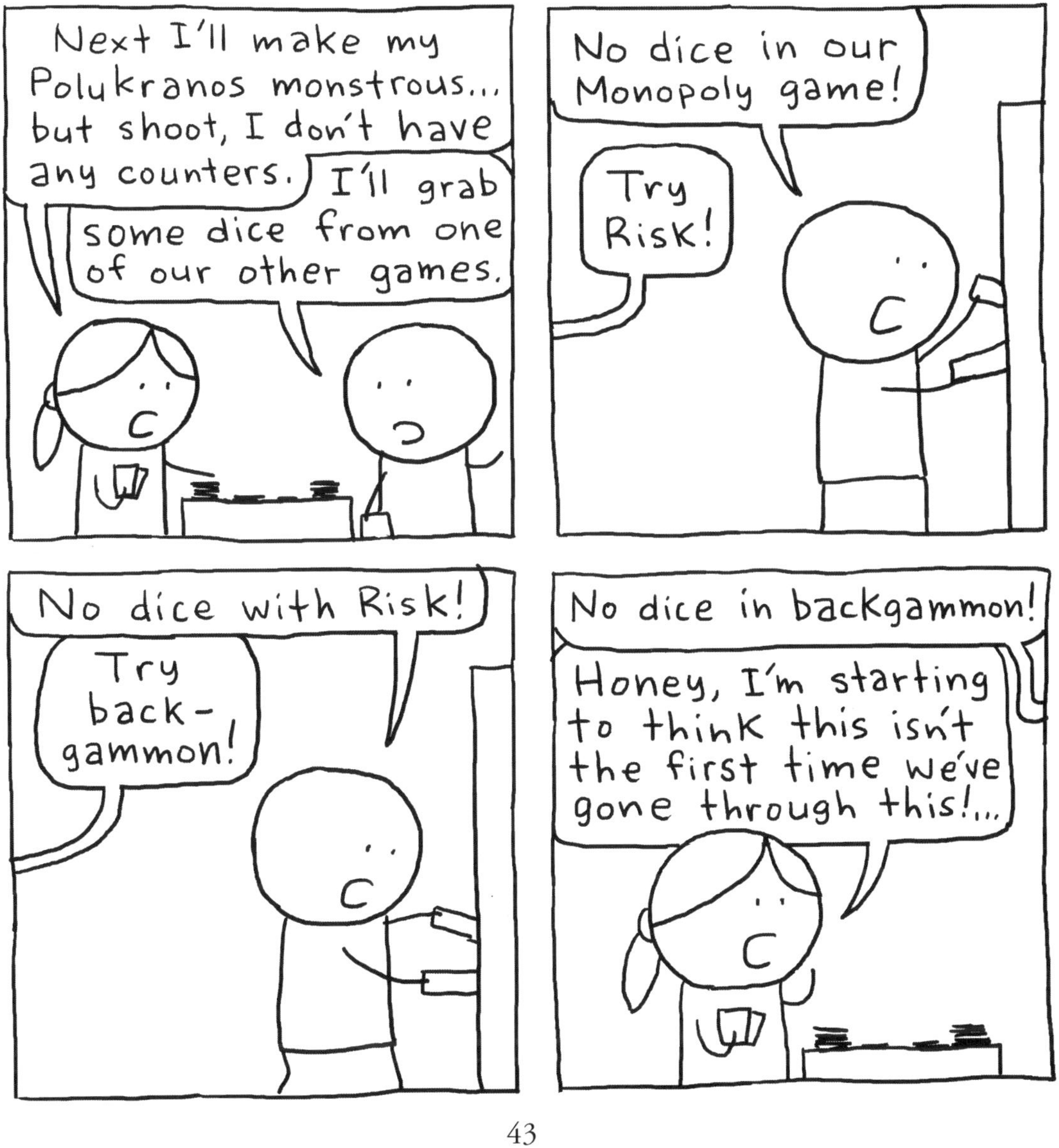
Next I'll make my Polukranos monstrous... but shoot, I don't have any counters.
I'll grab some dice from one of our other games.
No dice in our Monopoly game!
Try Risk!
No dice with Risk!
Try back-gammon!
No dice in backgammon!
Honey, I'm starting to think this isn't the first time we've gone through this!...

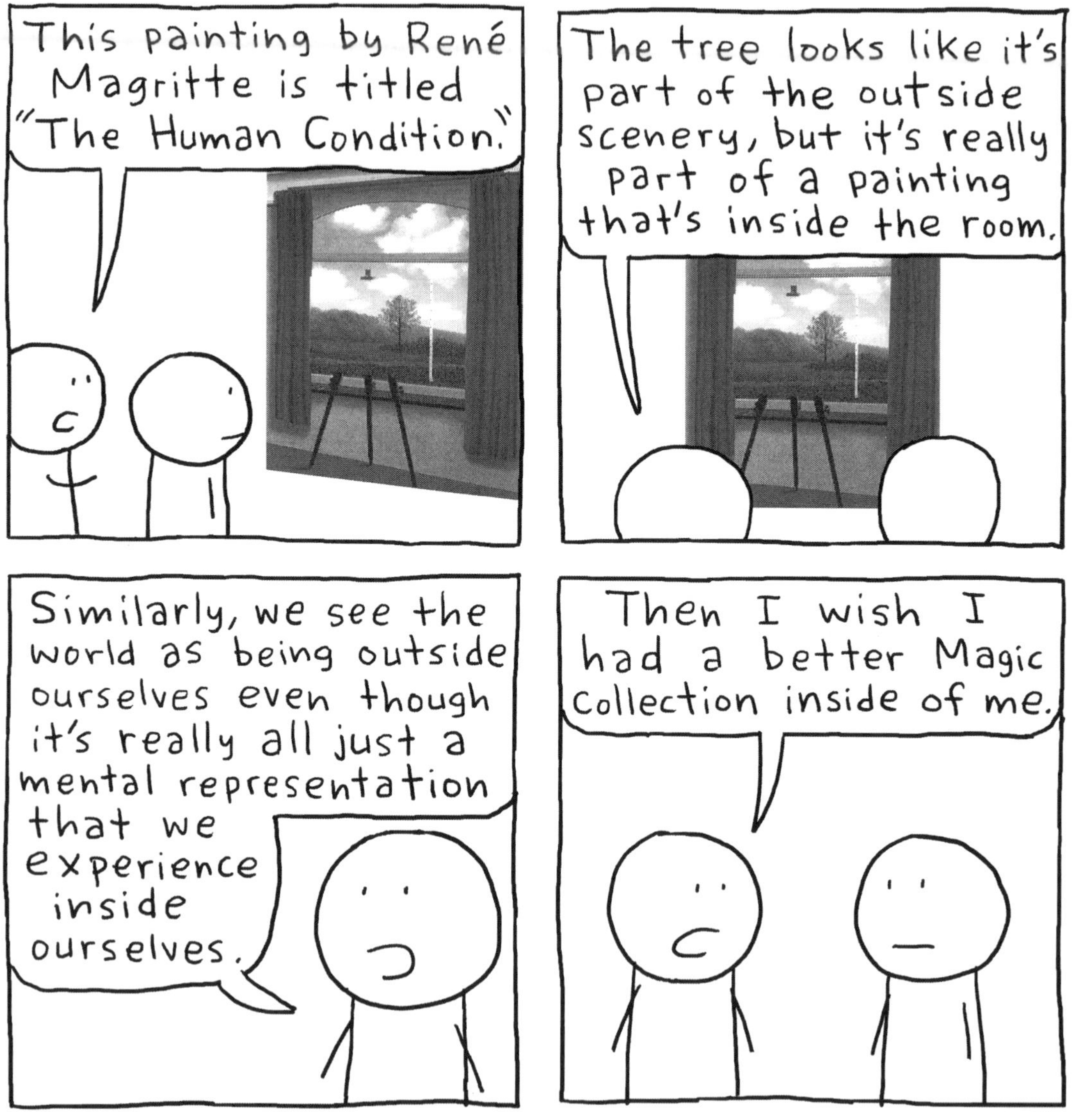
This painting by René Magritte is titled "The Human Condition."
The tree looks like it's part of the outside scenery, but it's really part of a painting that's inside the room.
Similarly, we see the world as being outside ourselves even though it's really all just a mental representation that we experience inside ourselves.
Then I wish I had a better Magic Collection inside of me.

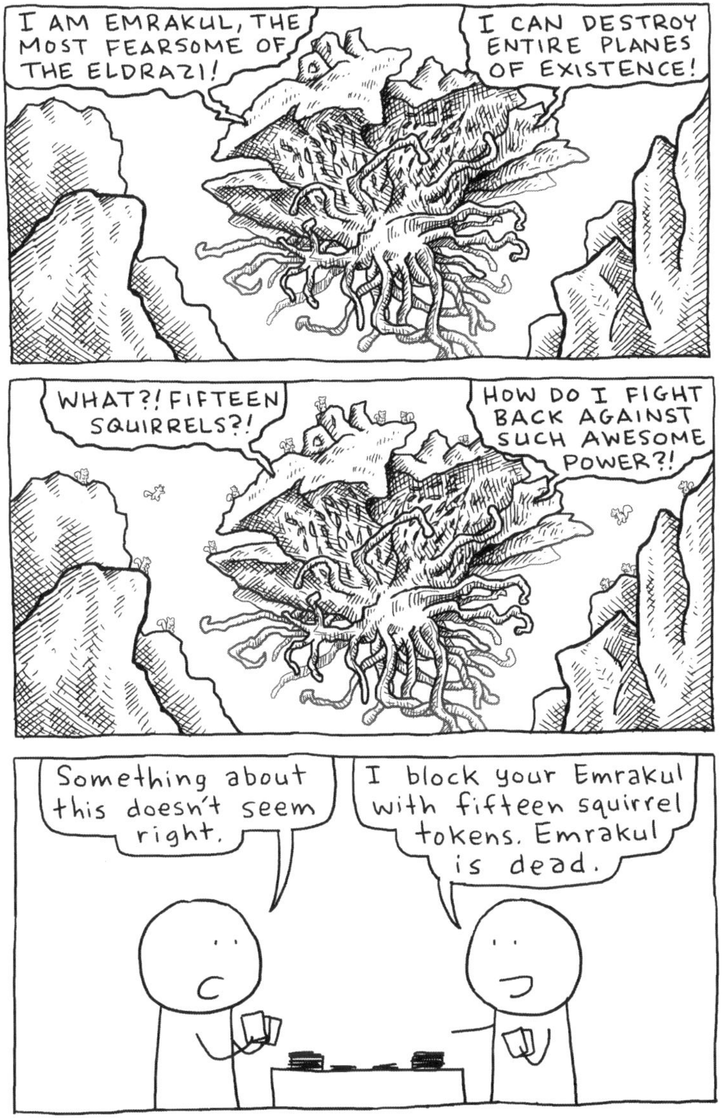
I AM EMRAKUL, THE MOST FEARSOME OF THE ELDRAZI!
I CAN DESTROY ENTIRE PLANES OF EXISTENCE!
WHAT?! FIFTEEN SQUIRRELS?!
HOW DO I FIGHT BACK AGAINST SUCH AWESOME POWER?!
Something about this doesn't seem right.
I block your Emrakul with fifteen squirrel tokens. Emrakul is dead.

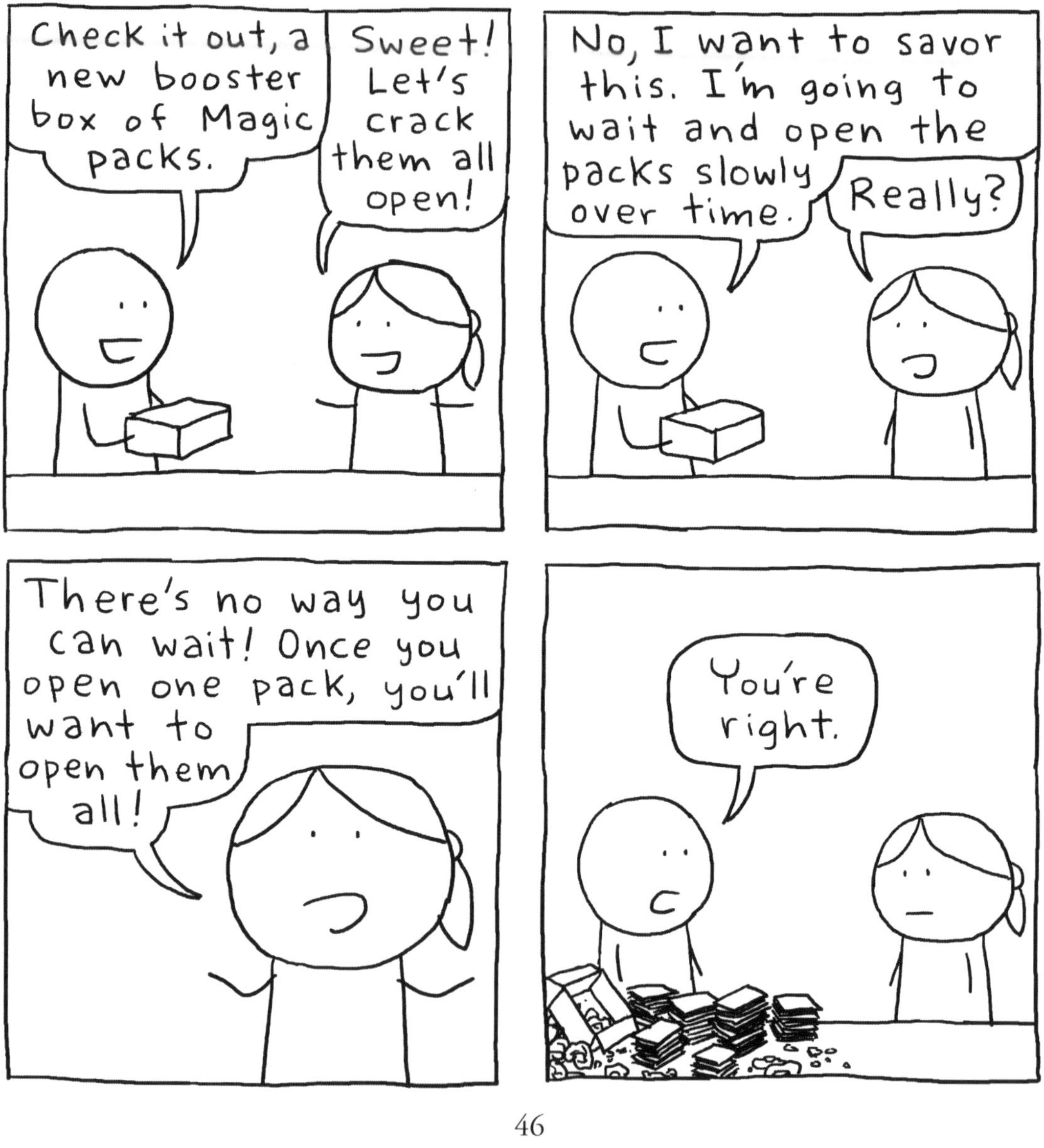
Check it out, a new booster box of Magic packs.
Sweet! Let's crack them all open!
No, I want to savor this. I'm going to wait and open the packs slowly over time.
Really?
There's no way you can wait! Once you open one pack, you'll want to open them all!
You're right.

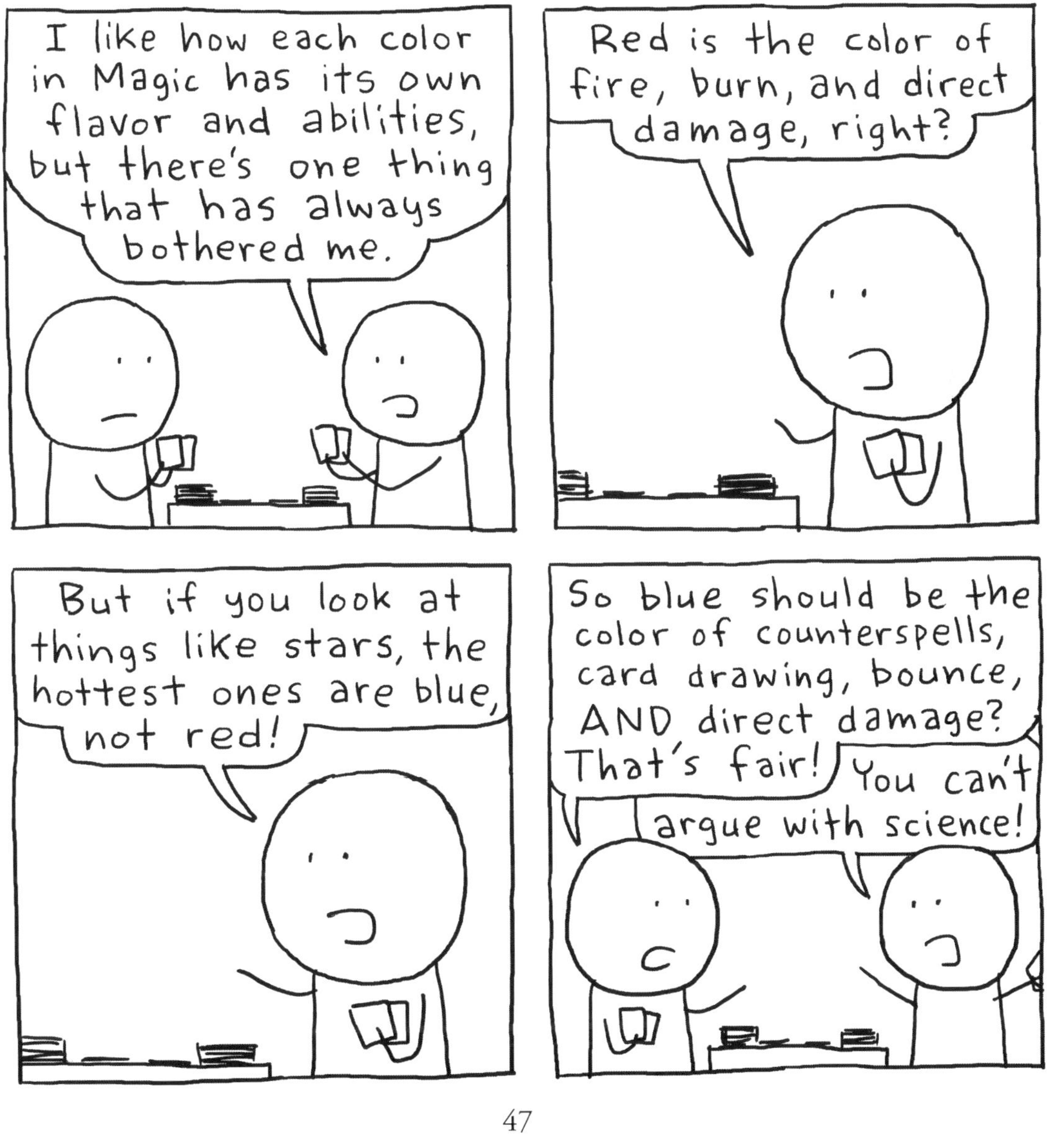
I like how each color in Magic has its own flavor and abilities, but there's one thing that has always bothered me.
Red is the color of fire, burn, and direct damage, right?
But if you look at things like stars, the hottest ones are blue, not red!
So blue should be the color of counterspells, card drawing, bounce, AND direct damage?
That's fair!
You can't argue with science!

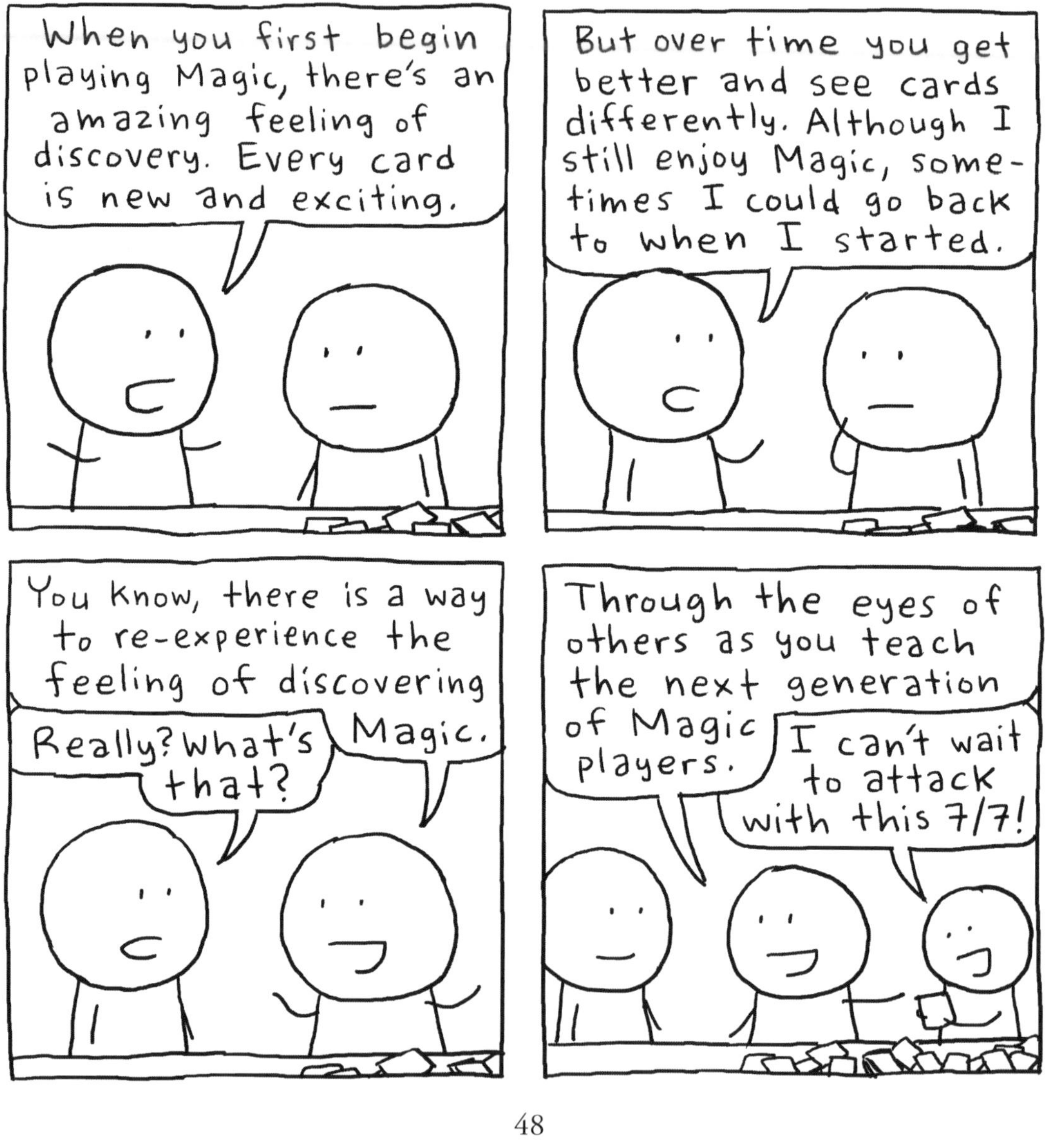
When you first begin playing Magic, there's an amazing feeling of discovery. Every card is new and exciting.
But over time you get better and see cards differently. Although I still enjoy Magic, some-times I could go back to when I started.
You know, there is a way to re-experience the feeling of discovering Magic.
Really? What's that?
Through the eyes of others as you teach the next generation of Magic players.
I can't wait to attack with this 7/7!

Looking at Magic cards again? Seriously, how many hours per day do you spend thinking about Magic?
That depends. Does dreaming about Magic when I'm sleeping count?

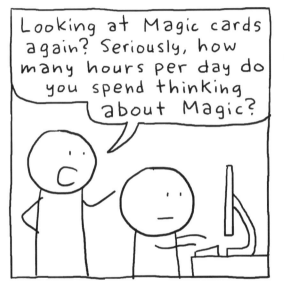

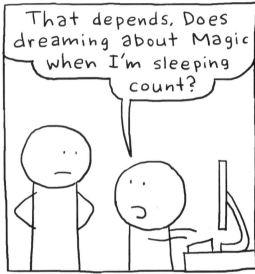

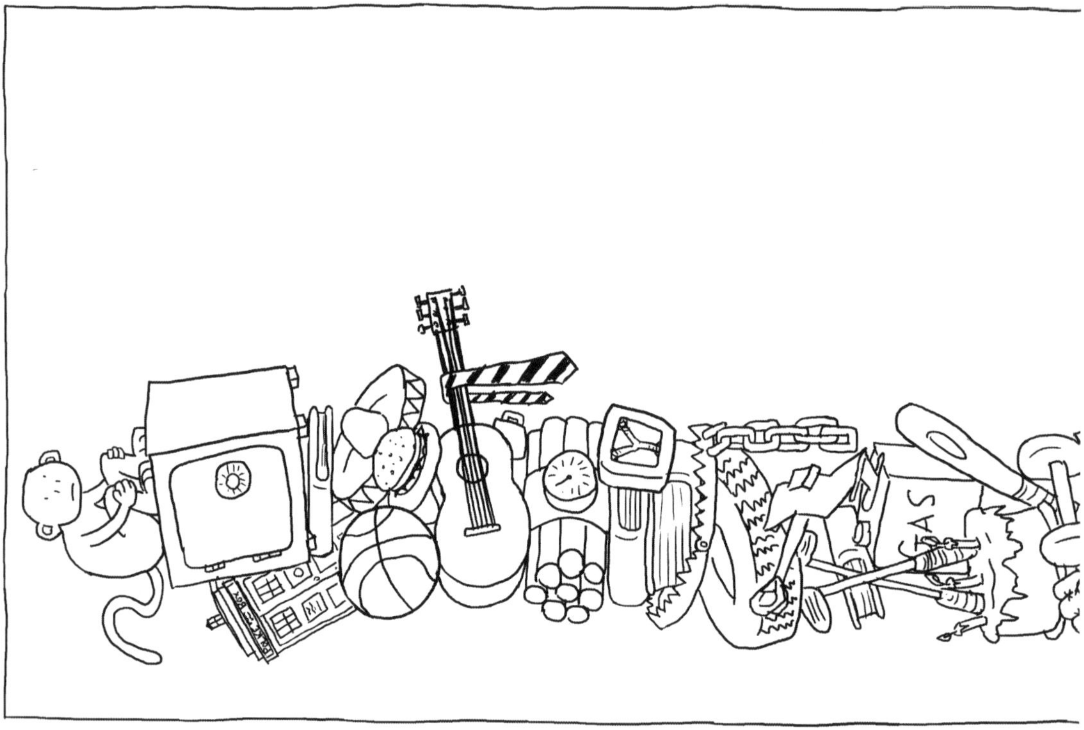
GAS

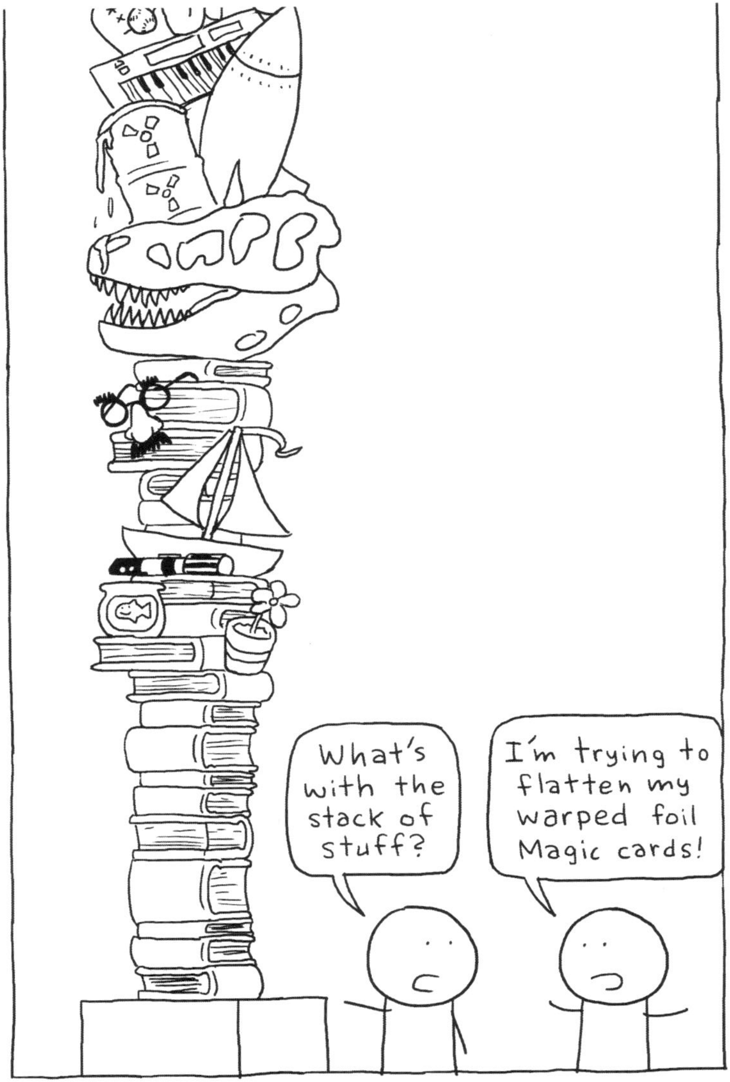
What's with the stack of stuff?
I'm trying to flatten my warped foil Magic cards!

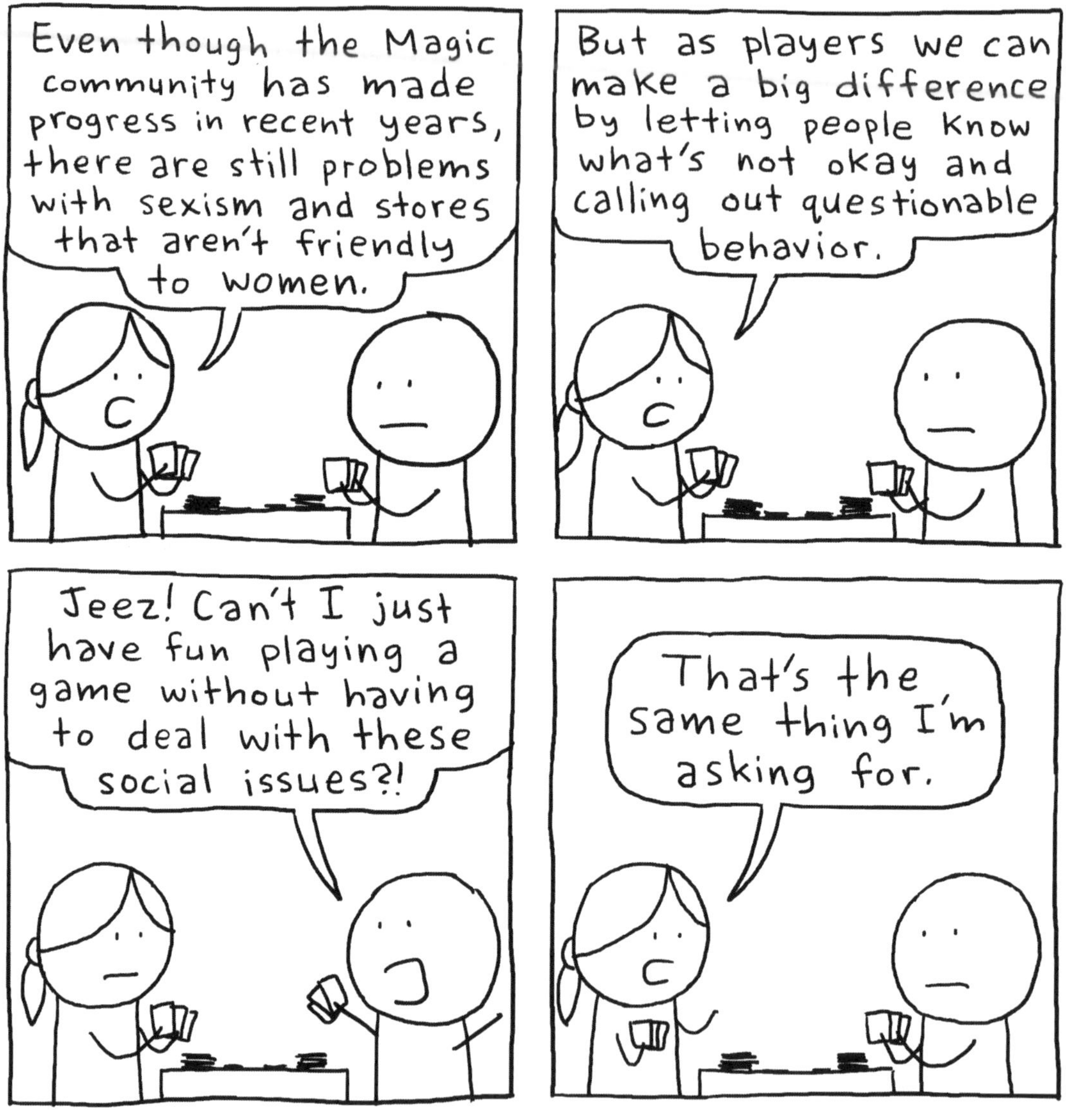

Even though the Magic community has made progress in recent years, there are still problems with sexism and stores that aren't friendly to women.
But as players we can make a big difference by letting people know what's not okay and calling out questionable behavior.
Jeez! Can't I just have fun playing a game without having to deal with these social issues?!
That's the same thing I'm asking for.

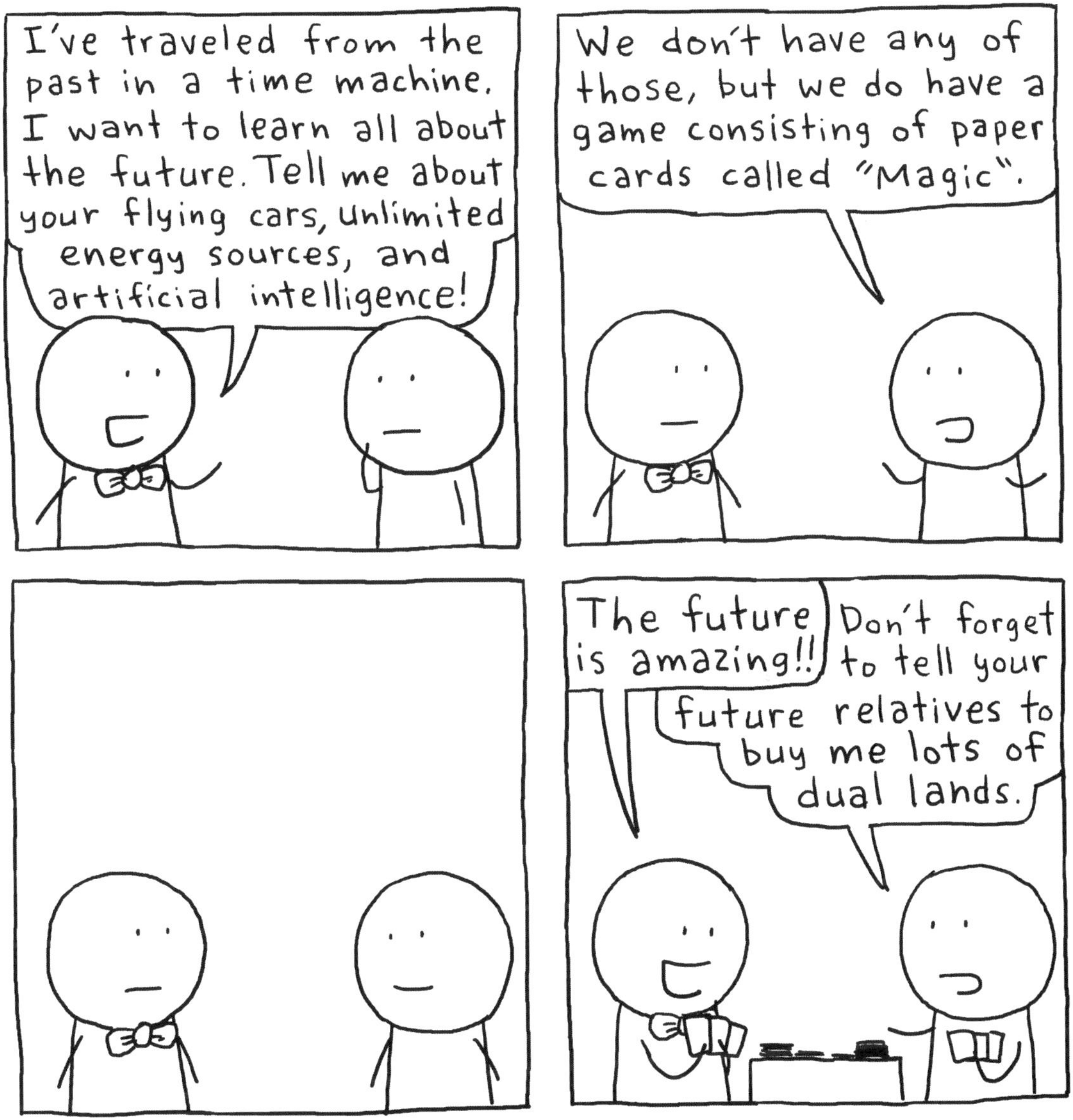
I've traveled from the past in a time machine. I want to learn all about the future. Tell me about your flying cars, unlimited energy sources, and artificial intelligence!
We don't have any of those, but we do have a game consisting of paper cards called "Magic".
The future is amazing!!
Don't forget to tell your future relatives to buy me lots of dual lands.

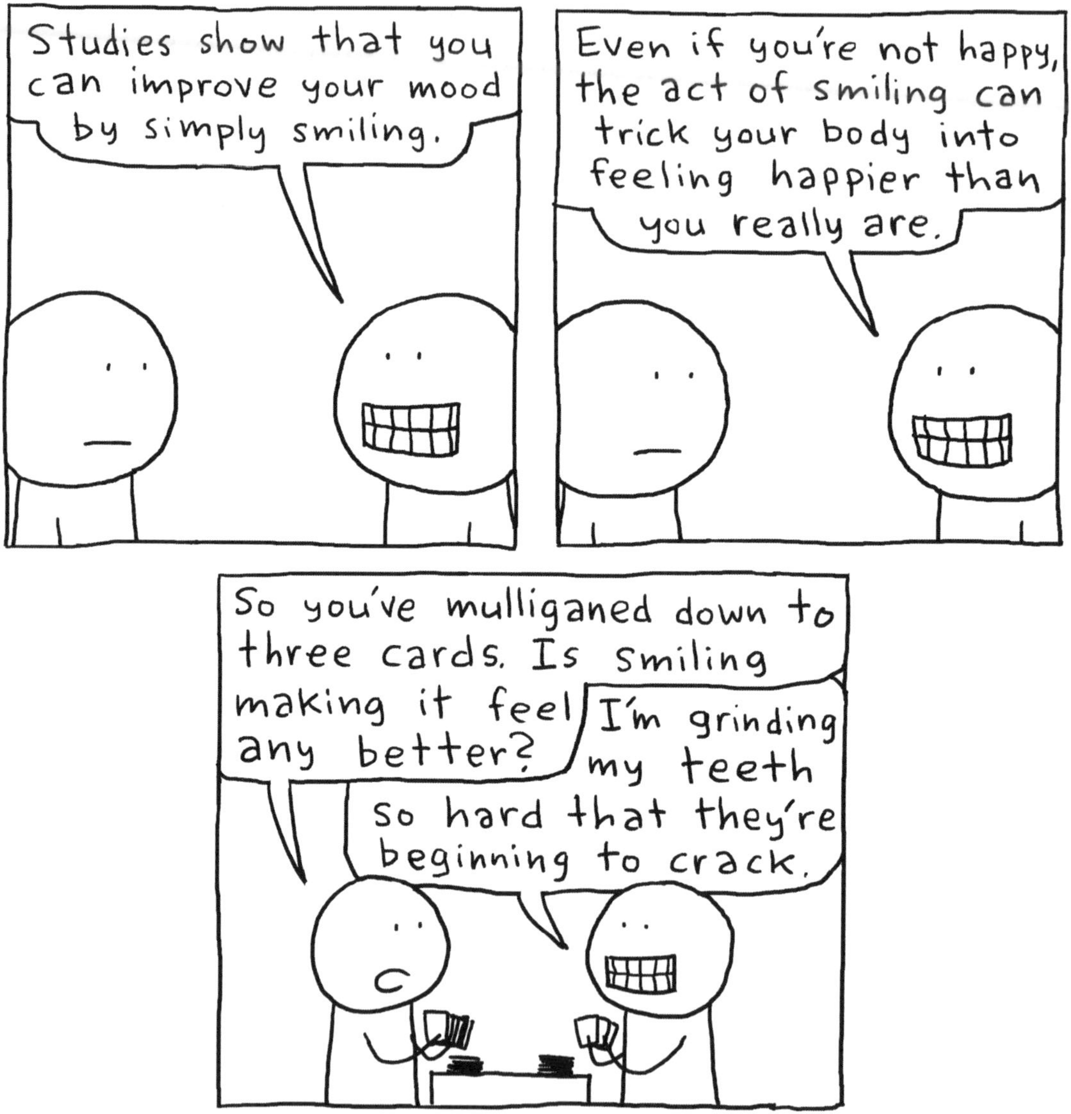
Studies show that you can improve your mood by simply smiling.
Even if you're not happy, the act of smiling can trick your body into feeling happier than you really are.
So you've mulliganed down to three cards. Is smiling making it feel any better?
I'm grinding my teeth so hard that they're beginning to crack.

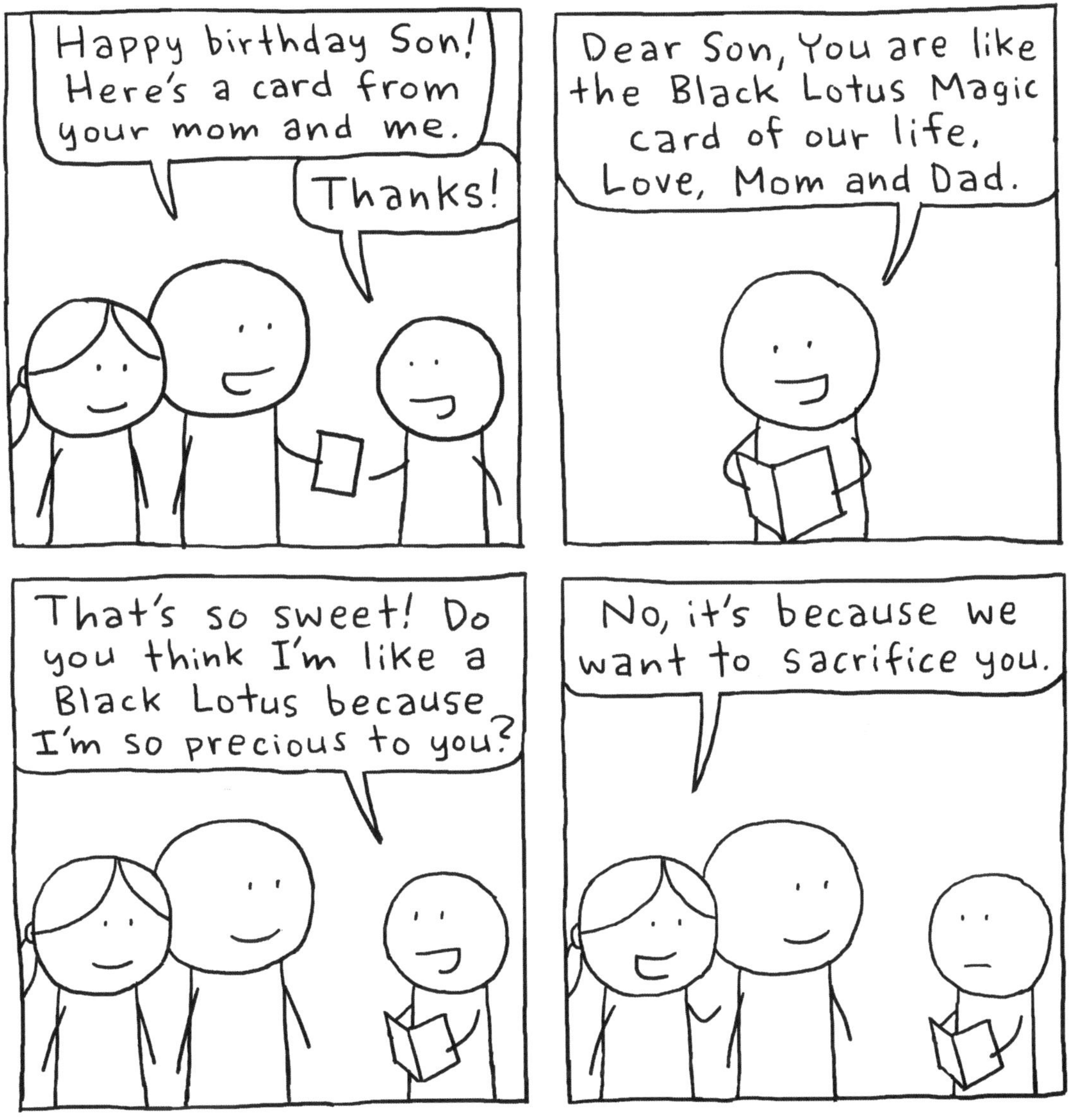
Happy birthday Son! Here's a card from your mom and me.
Thanks!
Dear Son, You are like the Black Lotus Magic card of our life. Love, Mom and Dad.
That's so sweet! Do you think I'm like a Black Lotus because I'm so precious to you?
No, it's because we want to sacrifice you.

Most people are trichromatic. We have three different cone cells in our eye to perceive colors.

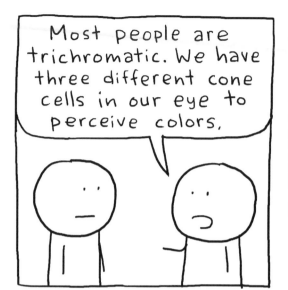

But some women are tetrachromatic and have four different cone cells. They can distinguish between two colors that look identical to the rest of us.

I wonder if that could be useful.

Hmm...

Why didn't you mulligan that land light hand?

I could tell from my sleeves that I was drawing a land next.

But your sleeves are all the same!

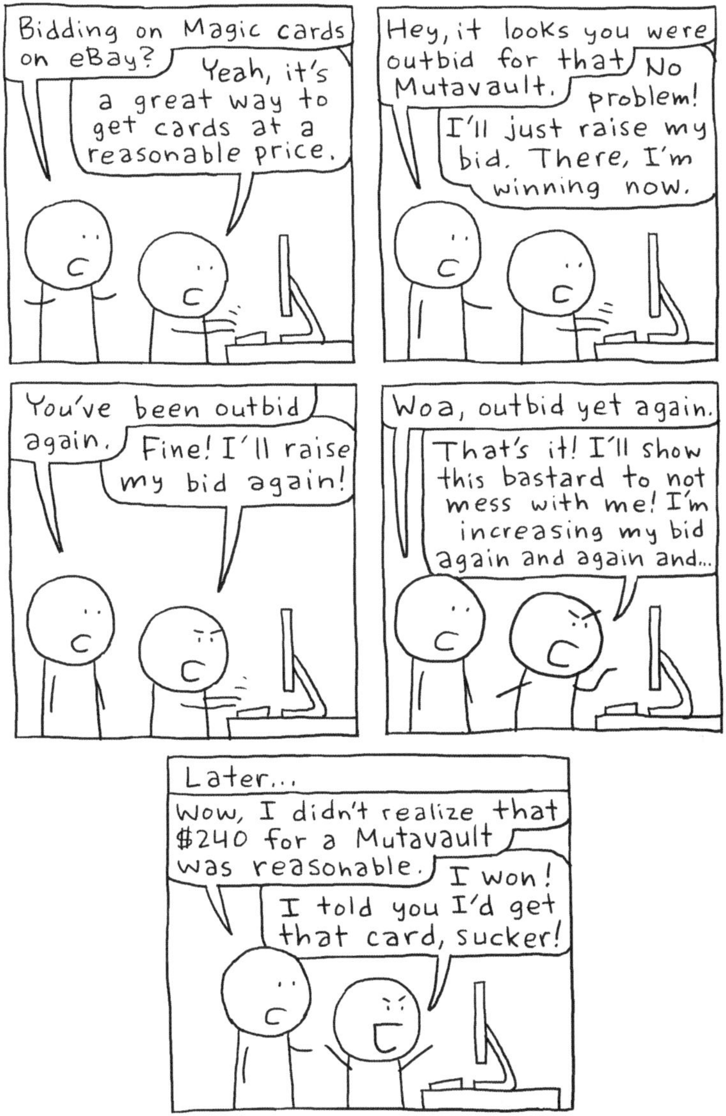
Bidding on Magic cards on eBay?
Yeah, it's a great way to get cards at a reasonable price.
Hey, it looks you were outbid for that Mutavault.
No problem! I'll just raise my bid. There, I'm winning now.
You've been outbid again.
Fine! I'll raise my bid again!
Woa, outbid yet again.
That's it! I'll show this bastard to not mess with me! I'm increasing my bid again and again and...
Later...
Wow, I didn't realize that $240 for a Mutavault was reasonable.
I won! I told you I'd get that card, sucker!

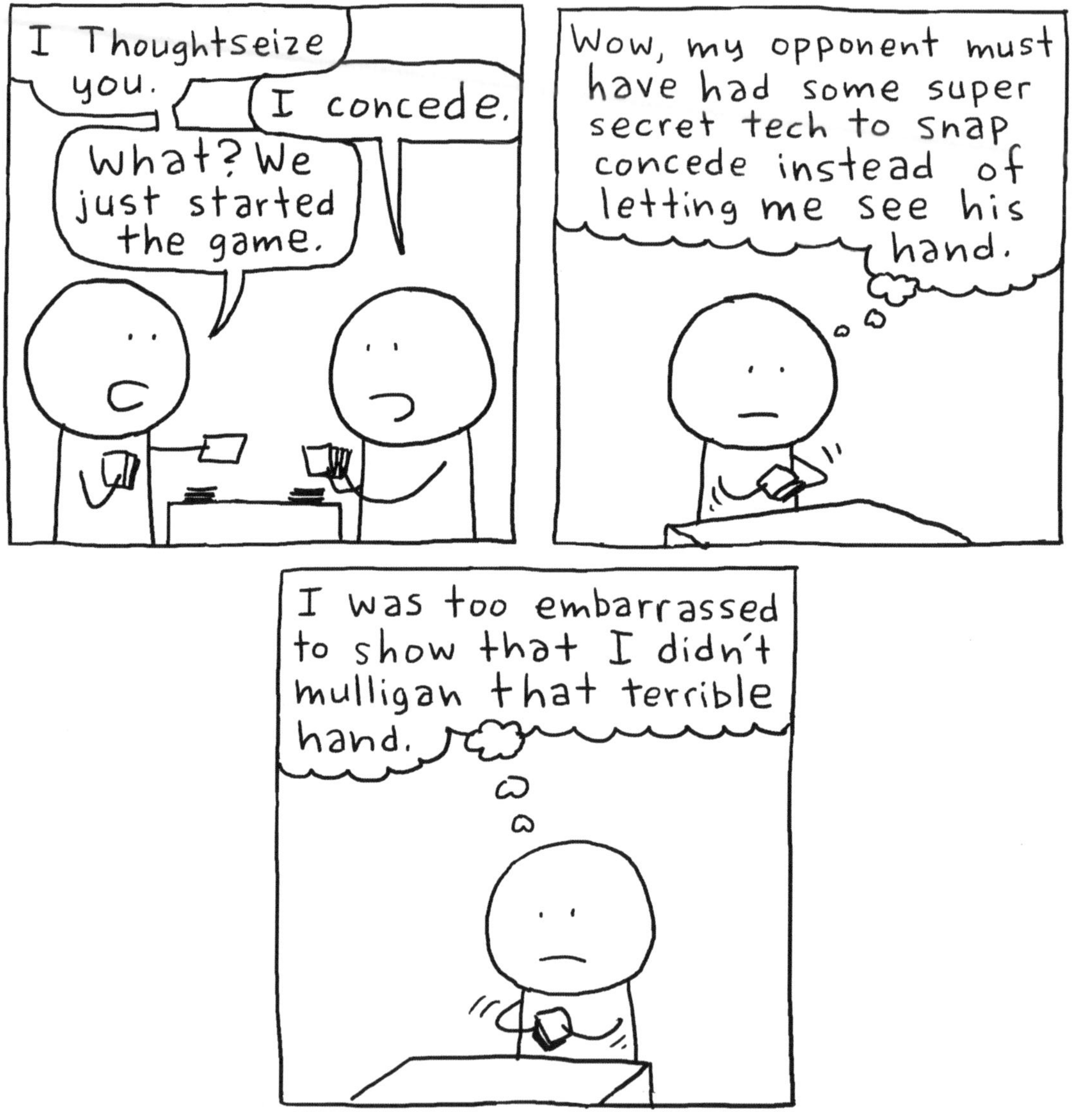
I Thoughtseize you.
What? We just started the game.
I concede.
Wow, my opponent must have had some super secret tech to snap concede instead of letting me see his hand.
I was too embarrassed to show that I didn't mulligan that terrible hand.

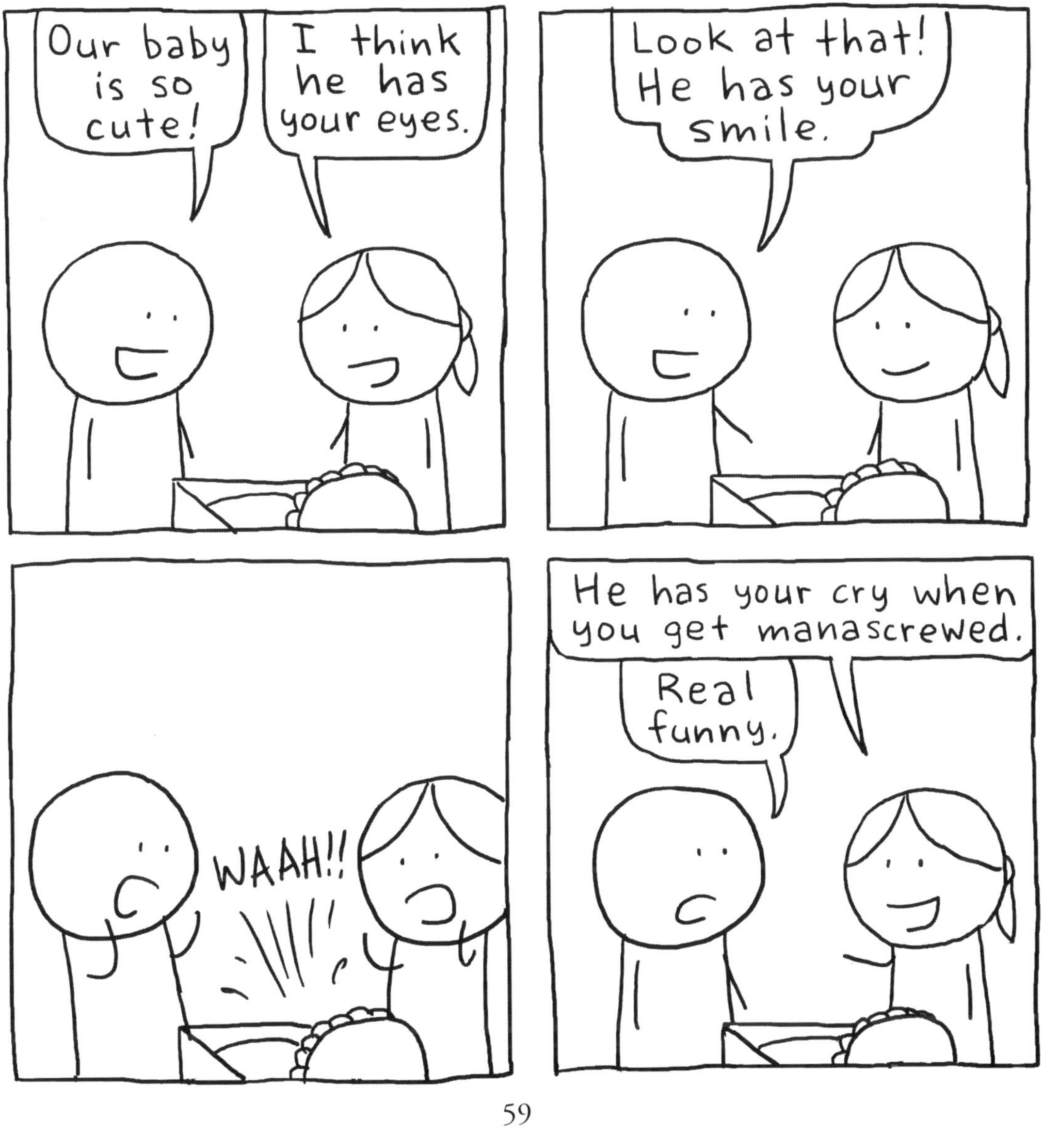
Our baby is so cute!
I think he has your eyes.
Look at that! He has your smile.
WAAH!!
He has your cry when you get manascrewed.
Real funny.

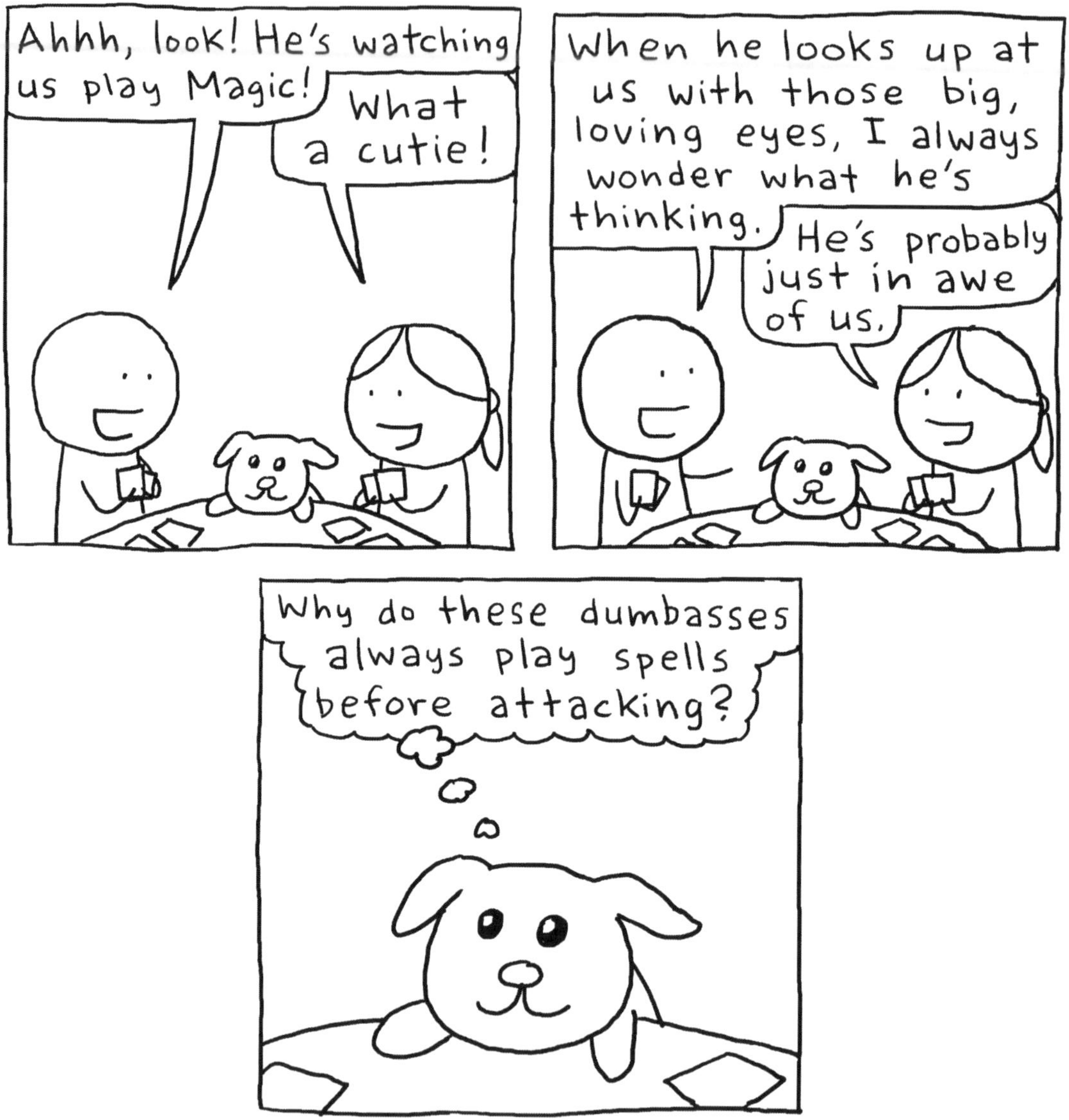
Ahhh, look! He's watching us play Magic!
What a cutie!
When he looks up at us with those big, loving eyes, I always wonder what he's thinking.
He's probably just in awe of us.
Why do these dumbasses always play spells before attacking?

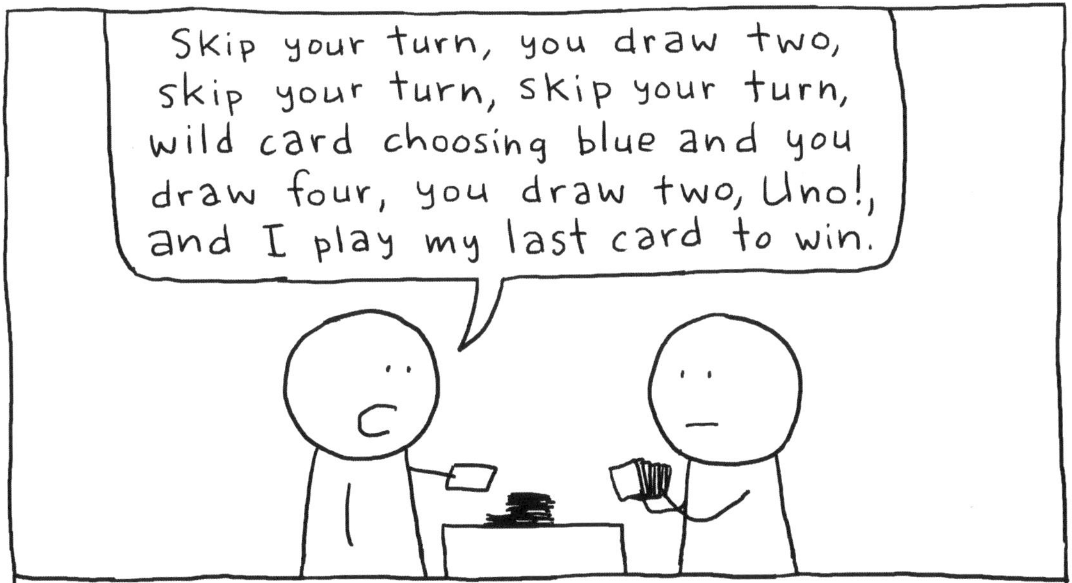
Skip your turn, you draw two, skip your turn, skip your turn, wild card choosing blue and you draw four, you draw two, Uno!, and I play my last card to win.

When Vintage Magic players play Uno.

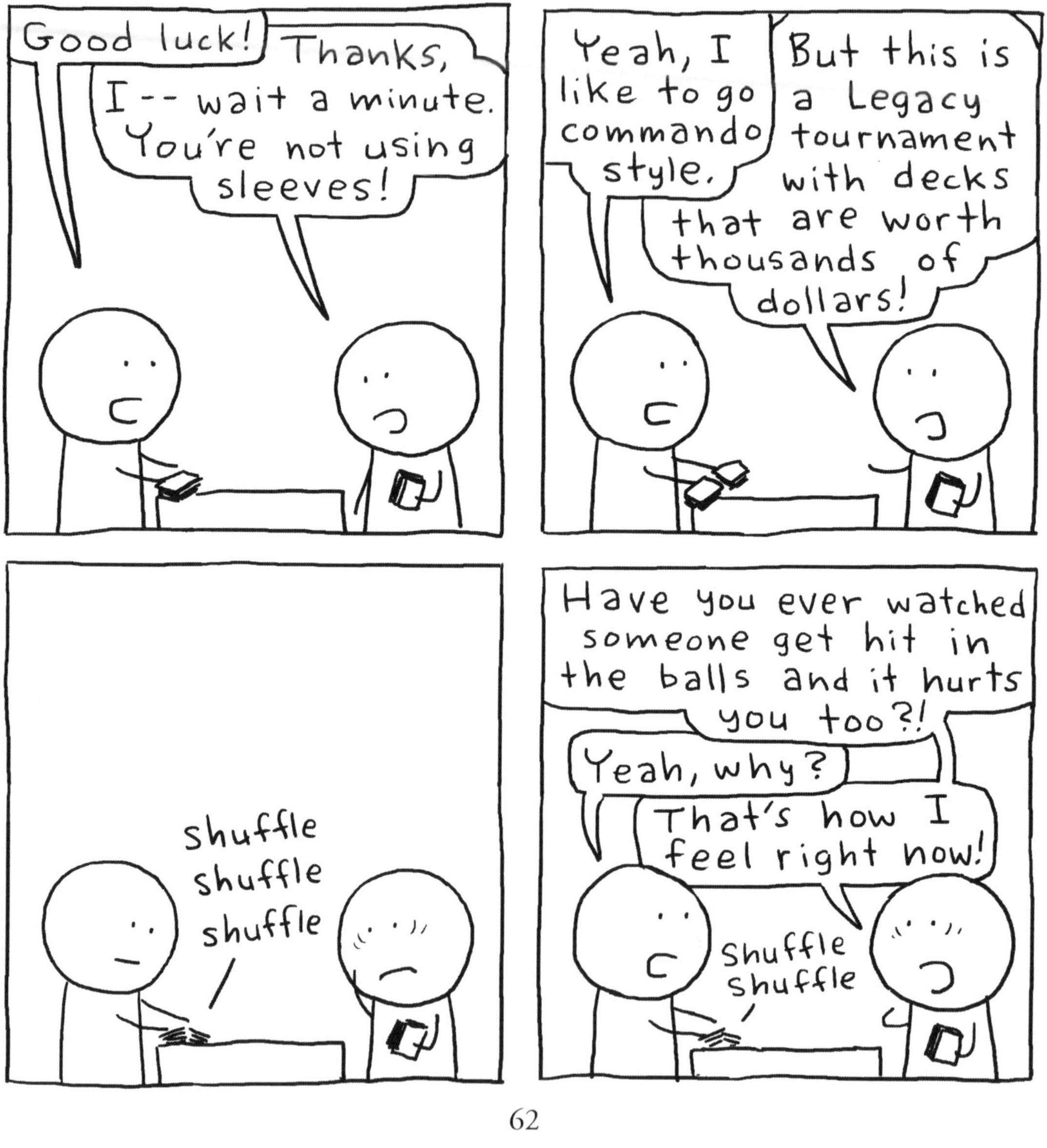
Good luck!
Thanks, I -- wait a minute. You're not using sleeves!
Yeah, I like to go commando style.
But this is a Legacy tournament with decks that are worth thousands of dollars!
shuffle shuffle shuffle
Have you ever watched someone get hit in the balls and it hurts you too?!
Yeah, why?
That's how I feel right now!
shuffle shuffle

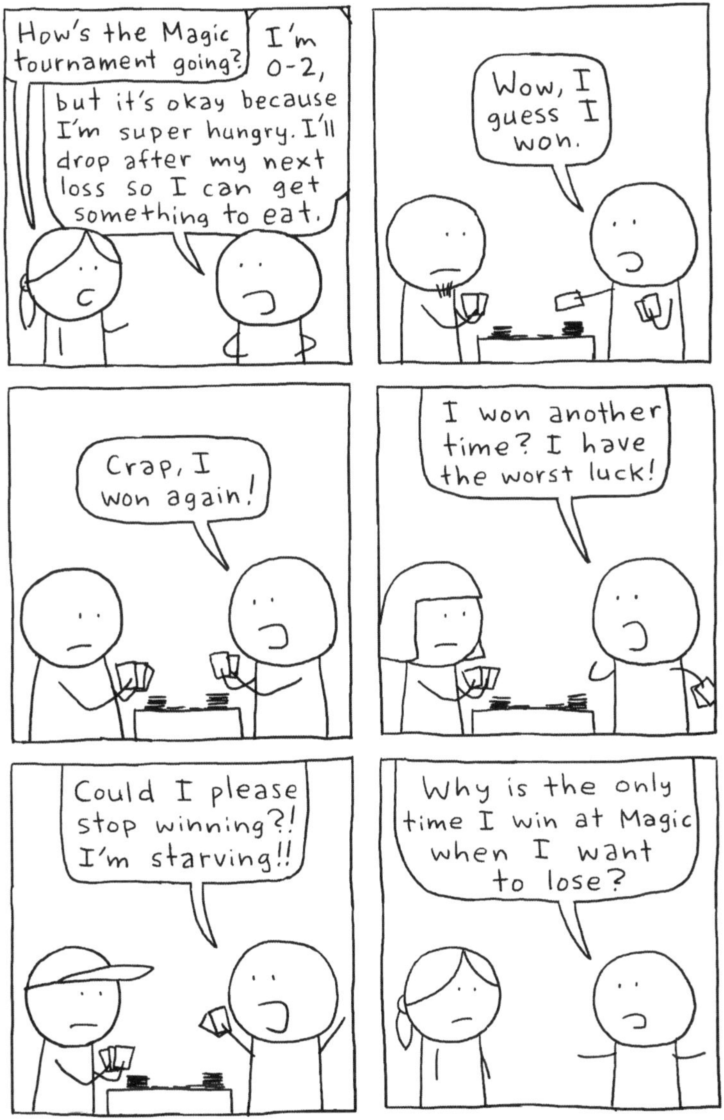
How's the Magic tournament going?
I'm 0-2,
but it's okay because I'm super hungry. I'll drop after my next loss so I can get something to eat.
Wow, I guess I won.
Crap, I won again!
I won another time? I have the worst luck!
Could I please stop winning?! I'm starving!!
Why is the only time I win at Magic when I want to lose?

I heard you play Magic cards. Is that true?
Yeah, but it's for medicinal purposes only.

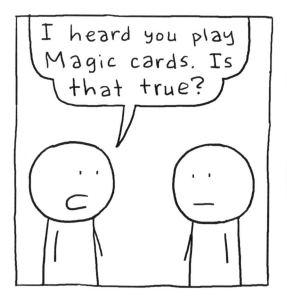

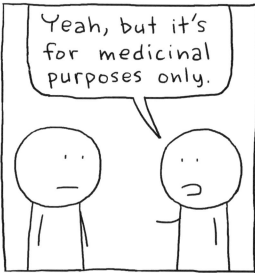

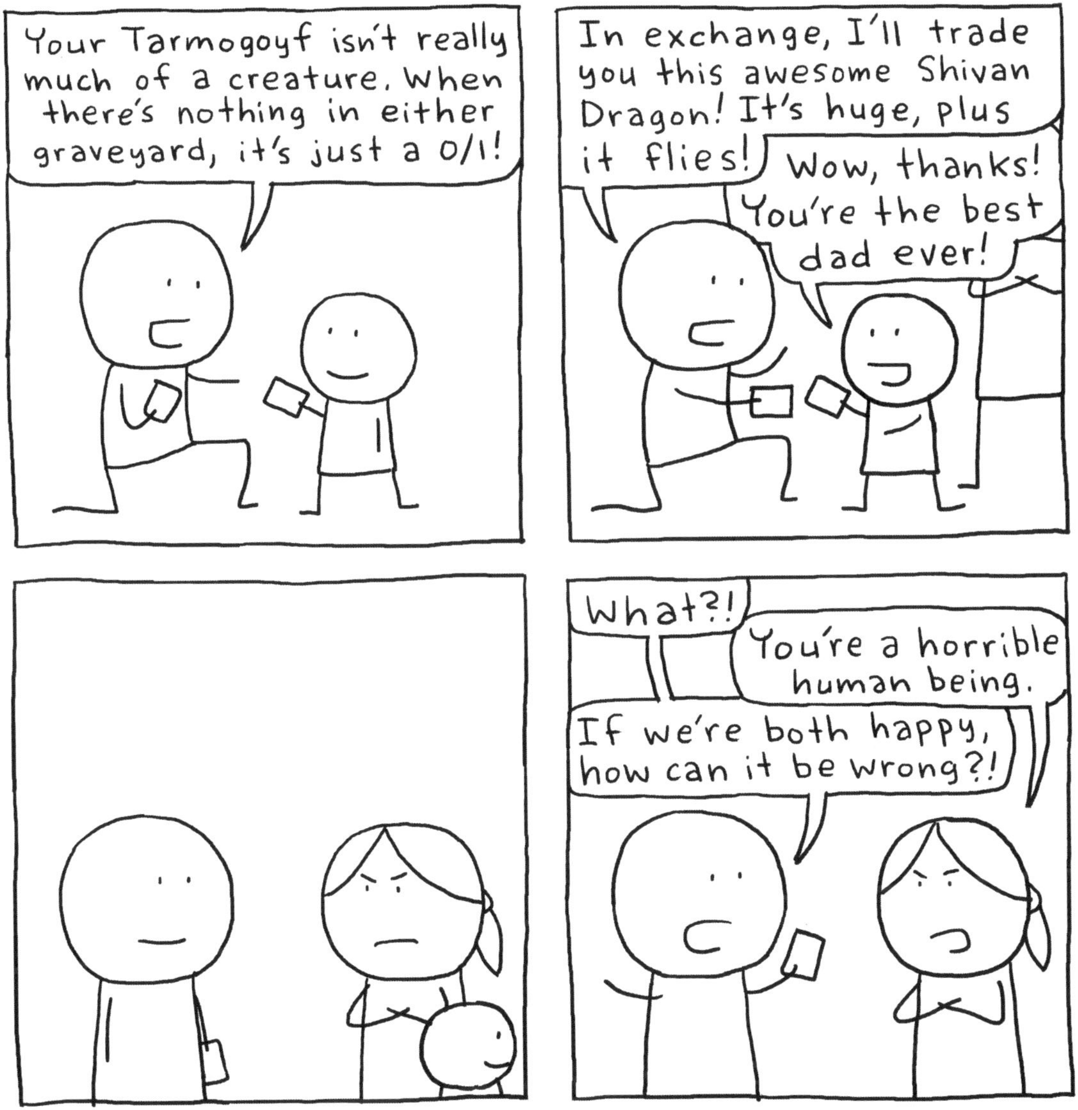
Your Tarmogoyf isn't really much of a creature. When there's nothing in either graveyard, it's just a 0/1!
In exchange, I'll trade you this awesome Shivan Dragon! It's huge, plus it flies!
Wow, thanks! You're the best dad ever!
What?!
You're a horrible human being.
If we're both happy, how can it be wrong?!

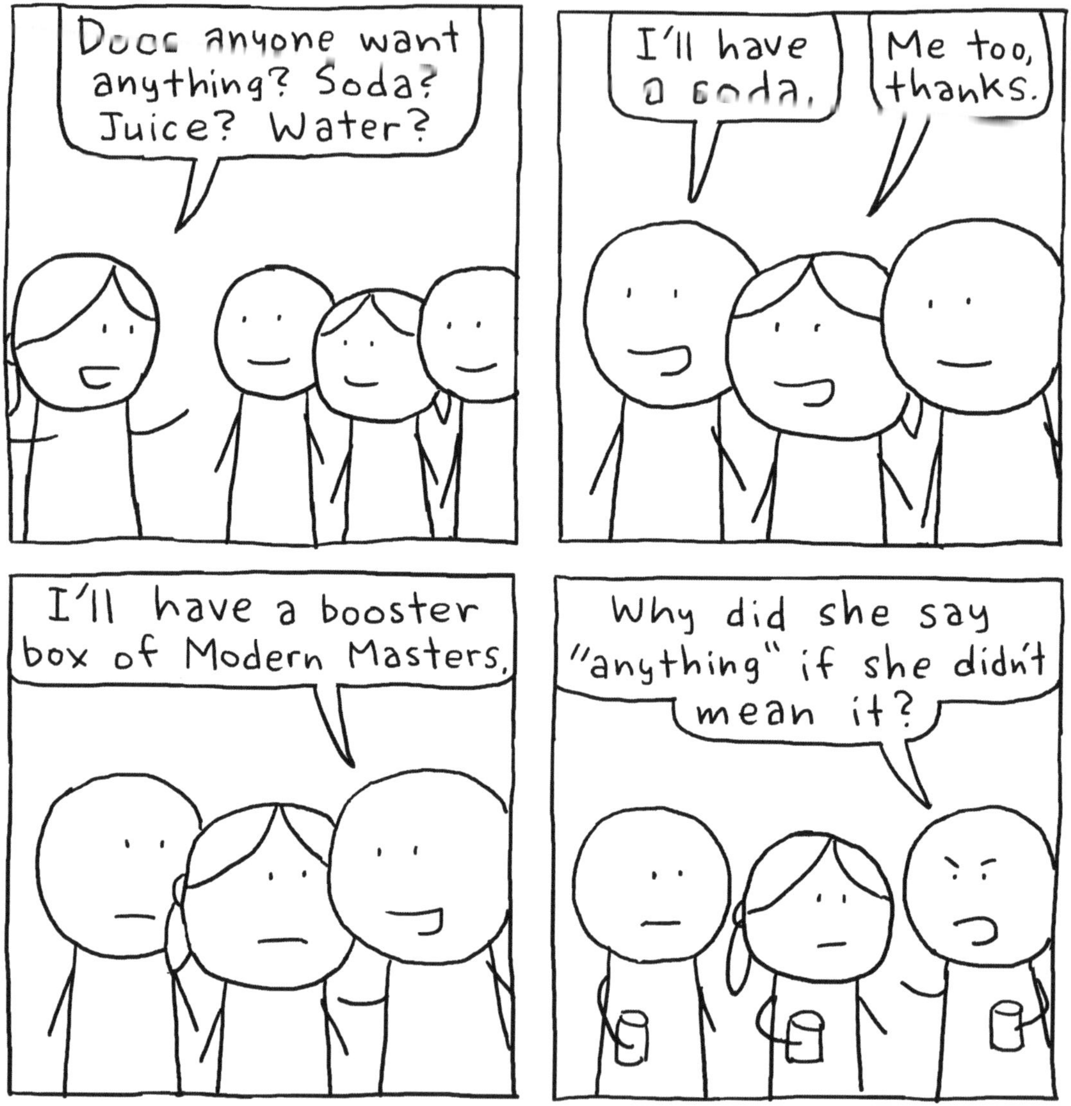
Does anyone want anything? Soda? Juice? Water?
I'll have a soda.
Me too, thanks.
I'll have a booster box of Modern Masters.
Why did she say "anything" if she didn't mean it?

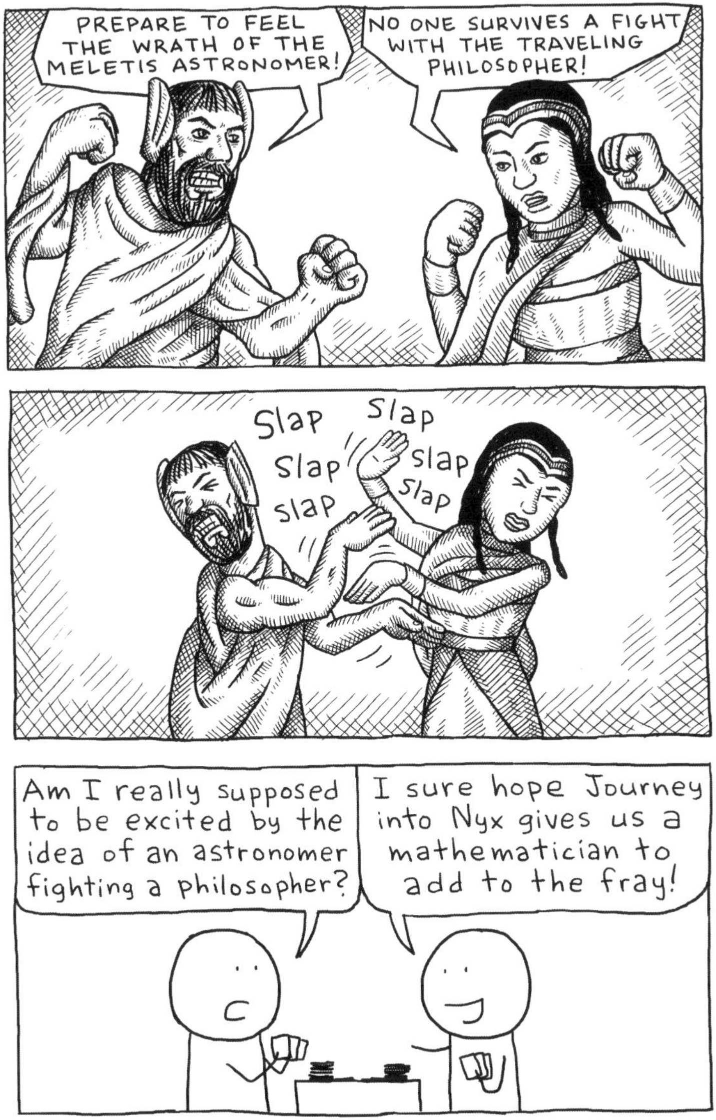
PREPARE TO FEEL THE WRATH OF THE MELETIS ASTRONOMER!
NO ONE SURVIVES A FIGHT WITH THE TRAVELING PHILOSOPHER!
Slap Slap Slap slap slap Slap
Am I really supposed to be excited by the idea of an astronomer fighting a philosopher?
I sure hope Journey into Nyx gives us a mathematician to add to the fray!

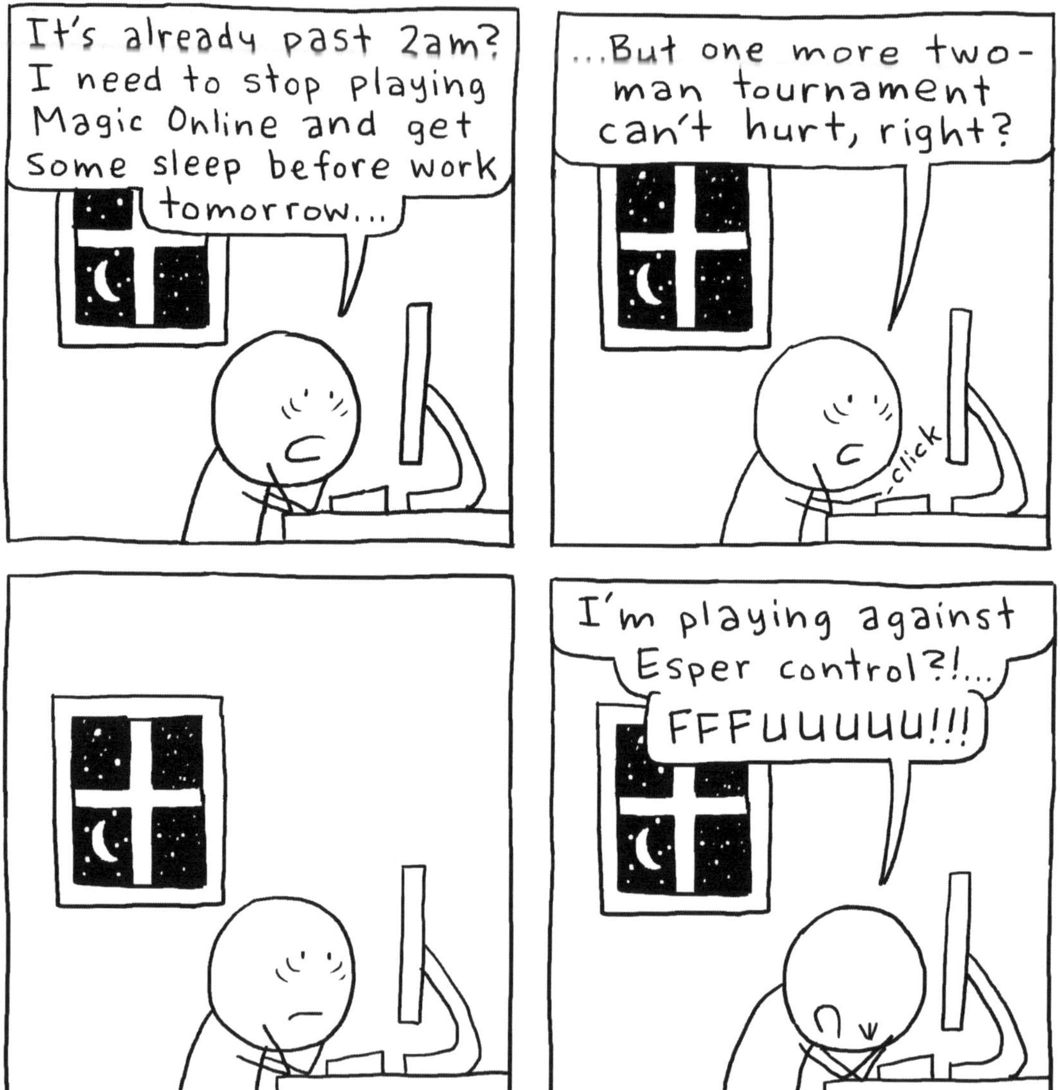
It's already past 2am? I need to stop playing Magic Online and get some sleep before work tomorrow...
...But one more two-man tournament can't hurt, right?
click
I'm playing against Esper control?!...
FFFuuuuu!!!

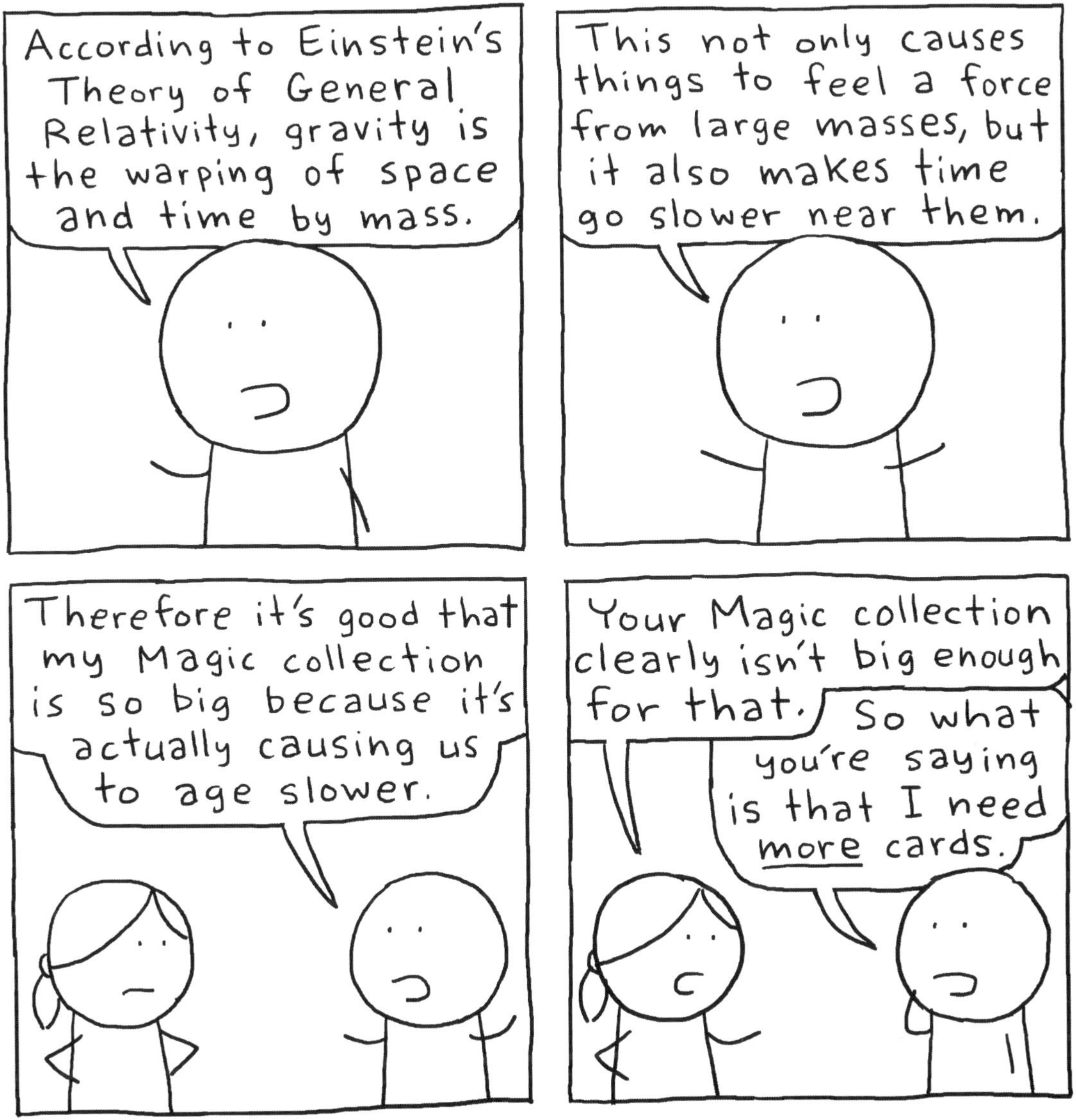
According to Einstein's Theory of General Relativity, gravity is the warping of space and time by mass.
This not only causes things to feel a force from large masses, but it also makes time go slower near them.
Therefore it's good that my Magic collection is so big because it's actually causing us to age slower.
Your Magic collection clearly isn't big enough for that.
So what you're saying is that I need more cards.

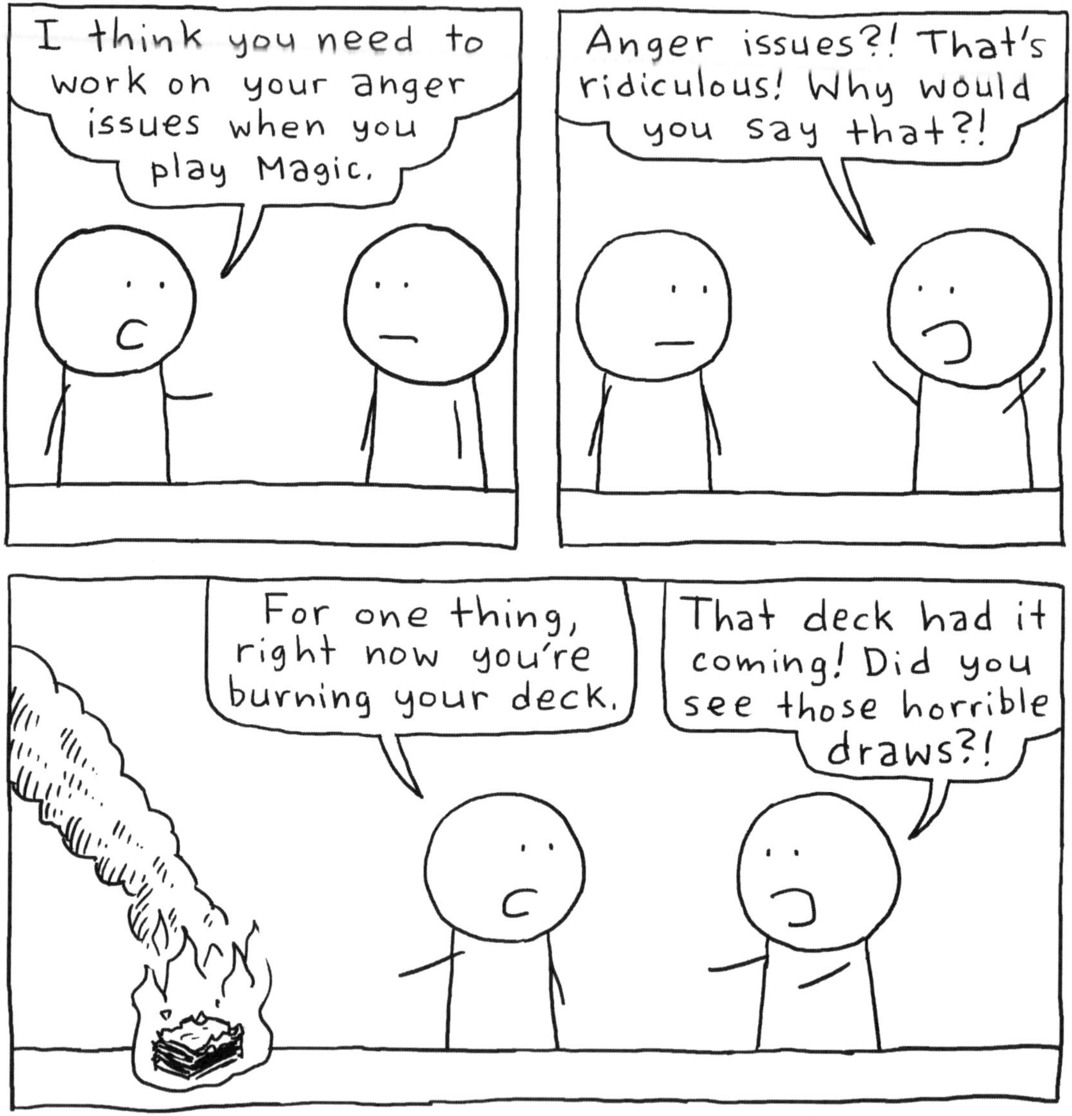
I think you need to work on your anger issues when you play Magic.
Anger issues?! That's ridiculous! Why would you say that?!
For one thing, right now you're burning your deck.
That deck had it coming! Did you see those horrible draws?!

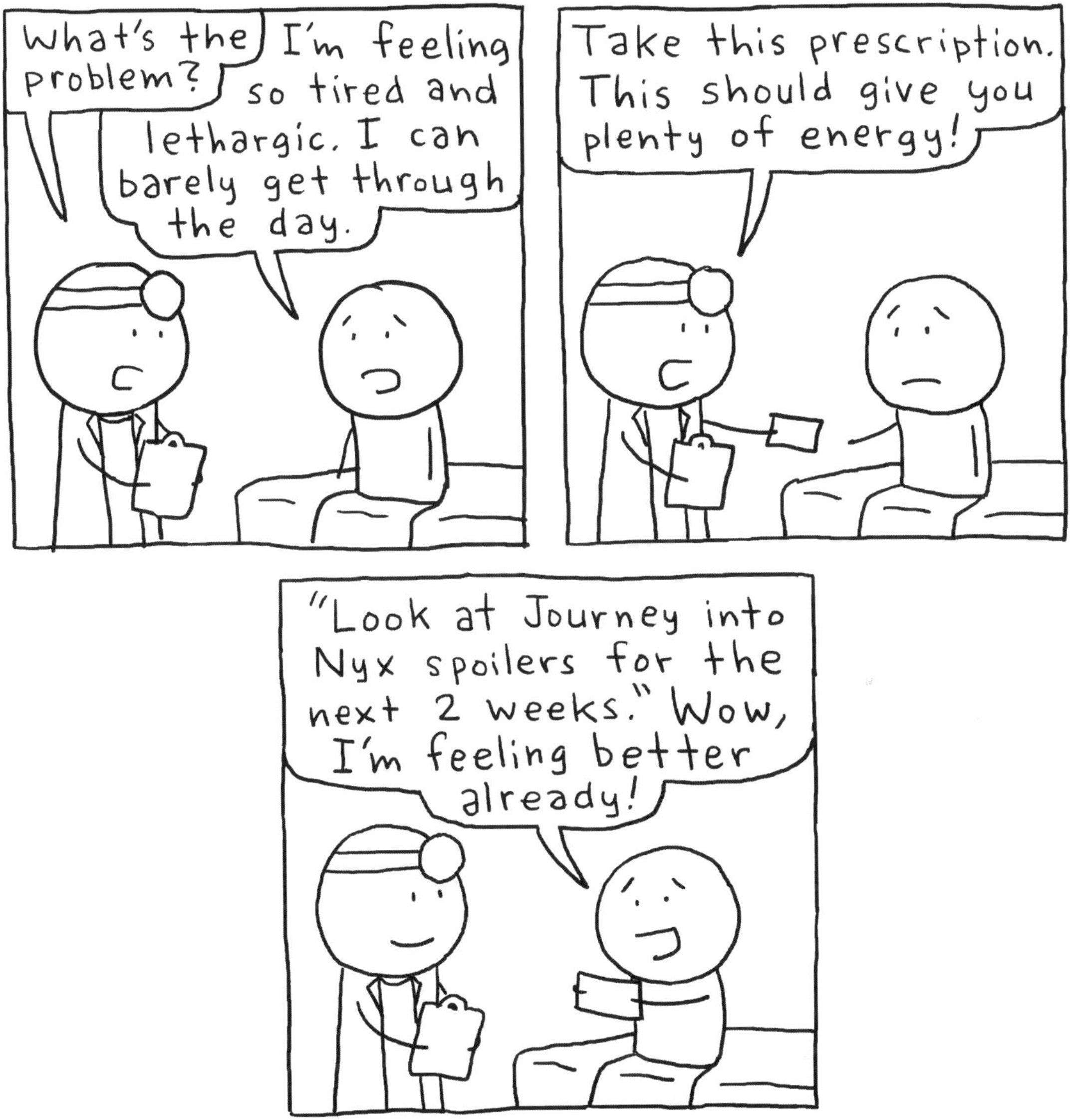
What's the problem?
I'm feeling so tired and lethargic. I can barely get through the day.
Take this prescription. This should give you plenty of energy!
"Look at Journey into Nyx spoilers for the next 2 weeks." Wow, I'm feeling better already!

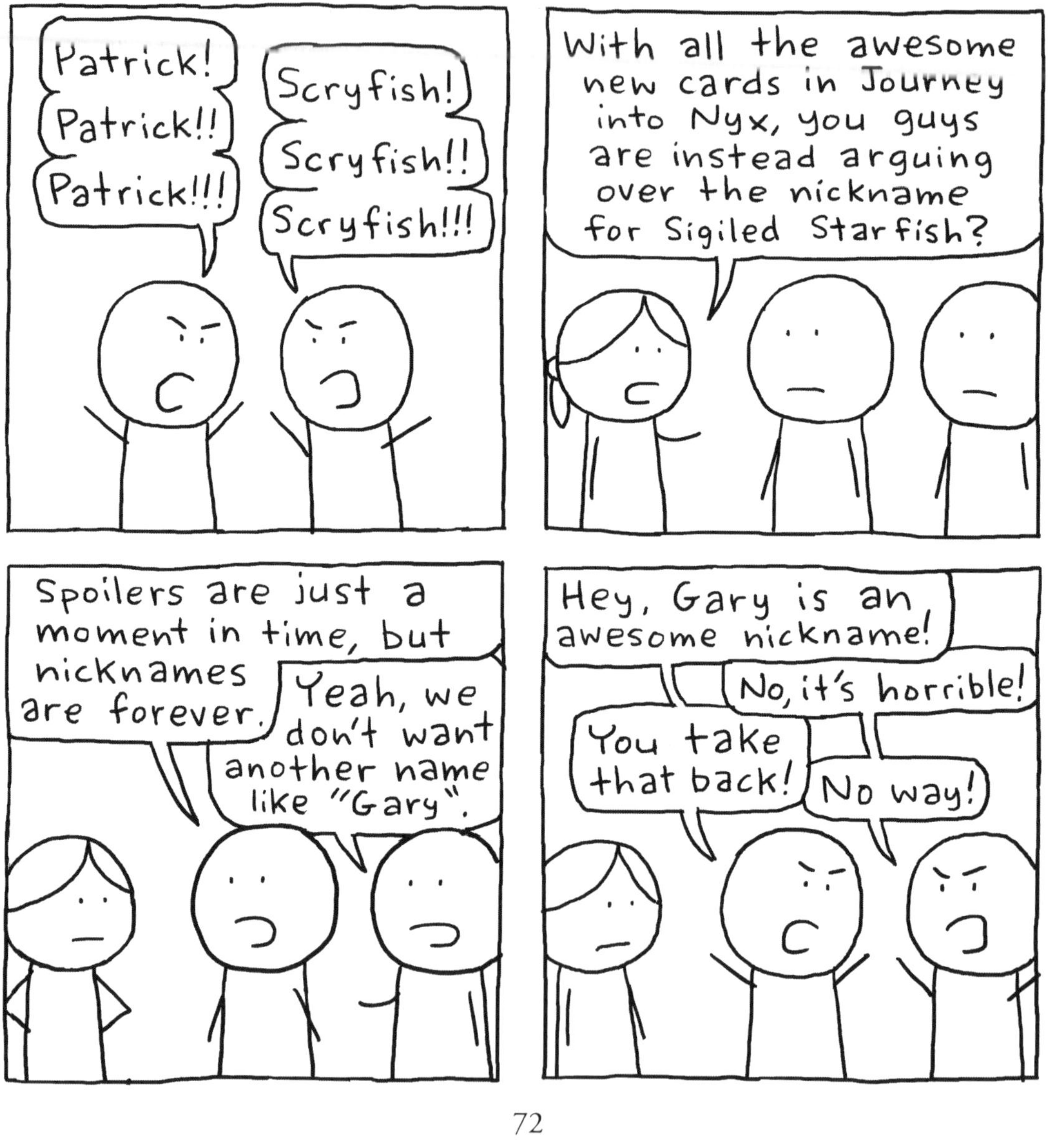
Patrick!
Patrick!!
Patrick!!!
Scryfish!
Scryfish!!
Scryfish!!!
With all the awesome new cards in Journey into Nyx, you guys are instead arguing over the nickname for Sigiled Starfish?
Spoilers are just a moment in time, but nicknames are forever.
Yeah, we don't want another name like "Gary".
Hey, Gary is an awesome nickname!
No, it's horrible!
You take that back!
No way!

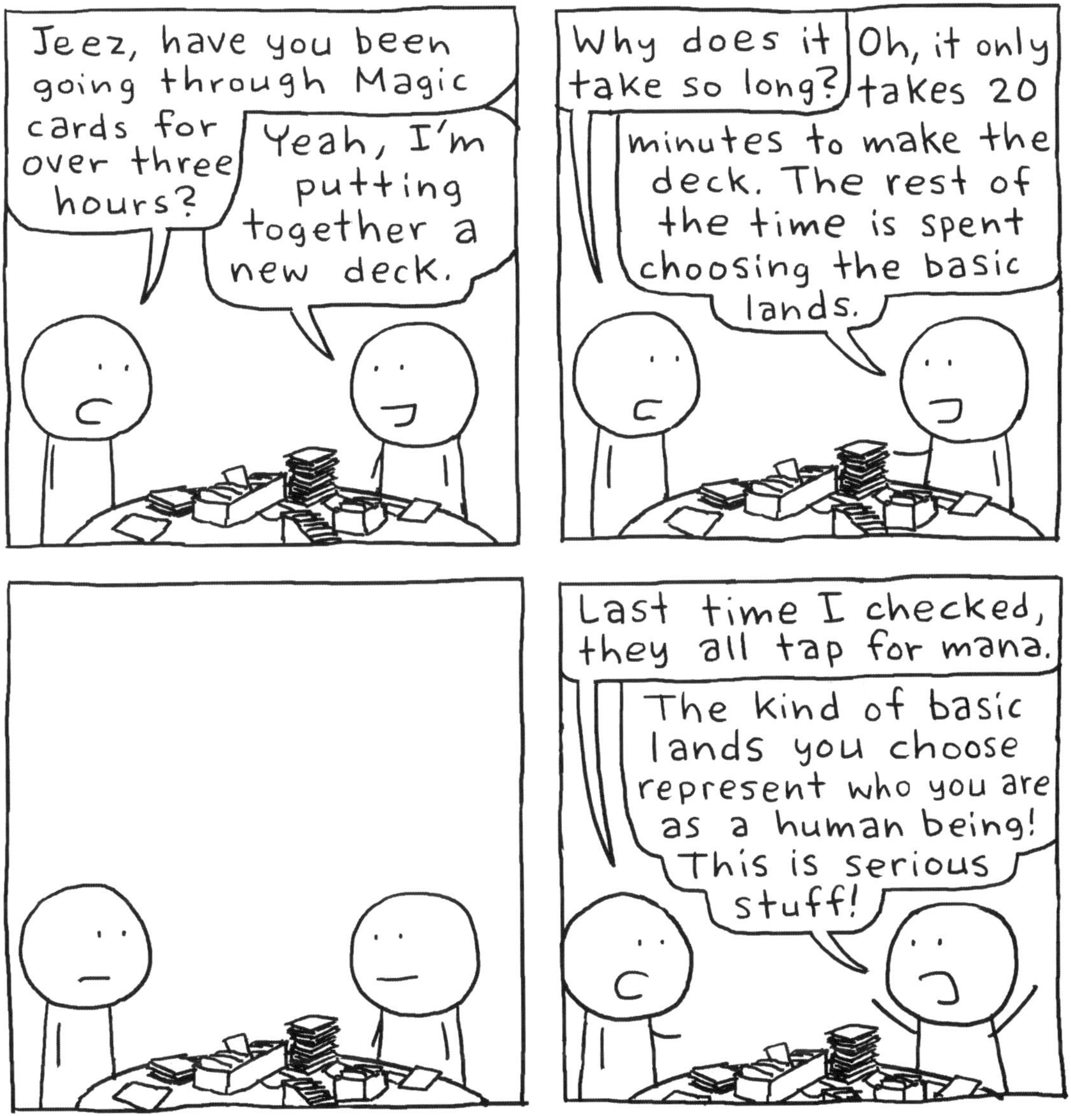
Jeez, have you been going through Magic cards for over three hours?
Yeah, I'm putting together a new deck.
Why does it take so long?
Oh, it only takes 20 minutes to make the deck. The rest of the time is spent choosing the basic lands.
Last time I checked, they all tap for mana.
The kind of basic lands you choose represent who you are as a human being! This is serious stuff!

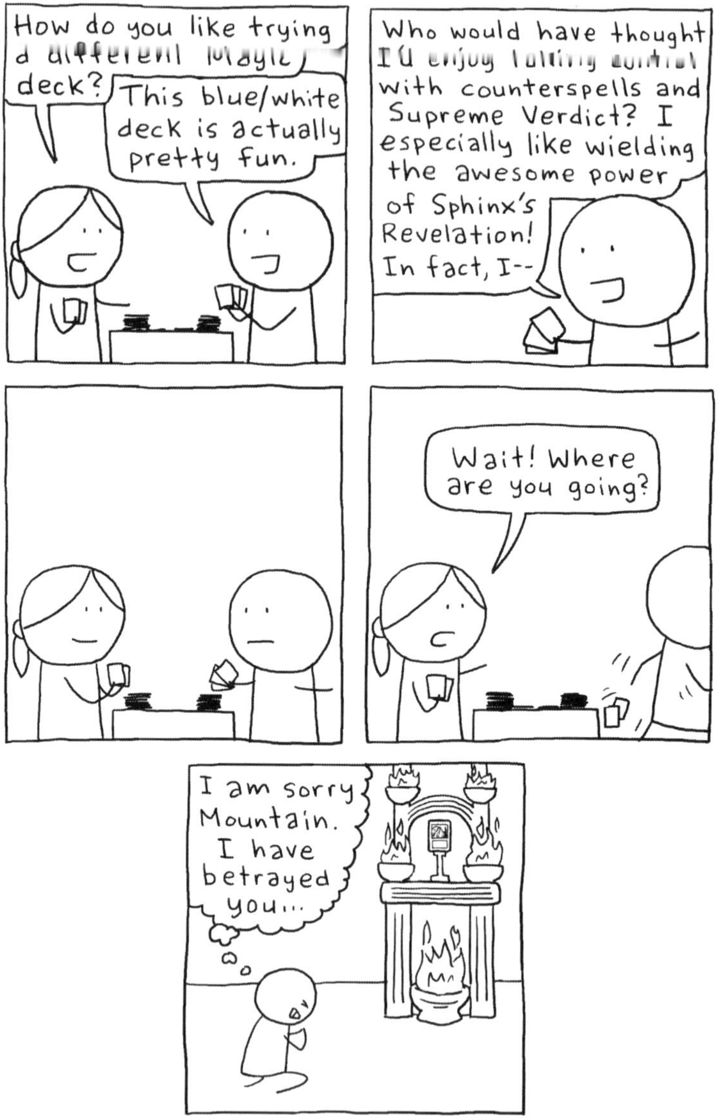
How do you like trying
deck?
This blue/white deck is actually pretty fun.
Who would have thought
with counterspells and Supreme Verdict? I especially like wielding the awesome power of Sphinx's Revelation! In fact, I--
Wait! Where are you going?
I am sorry Mountain. I have betrayed you...

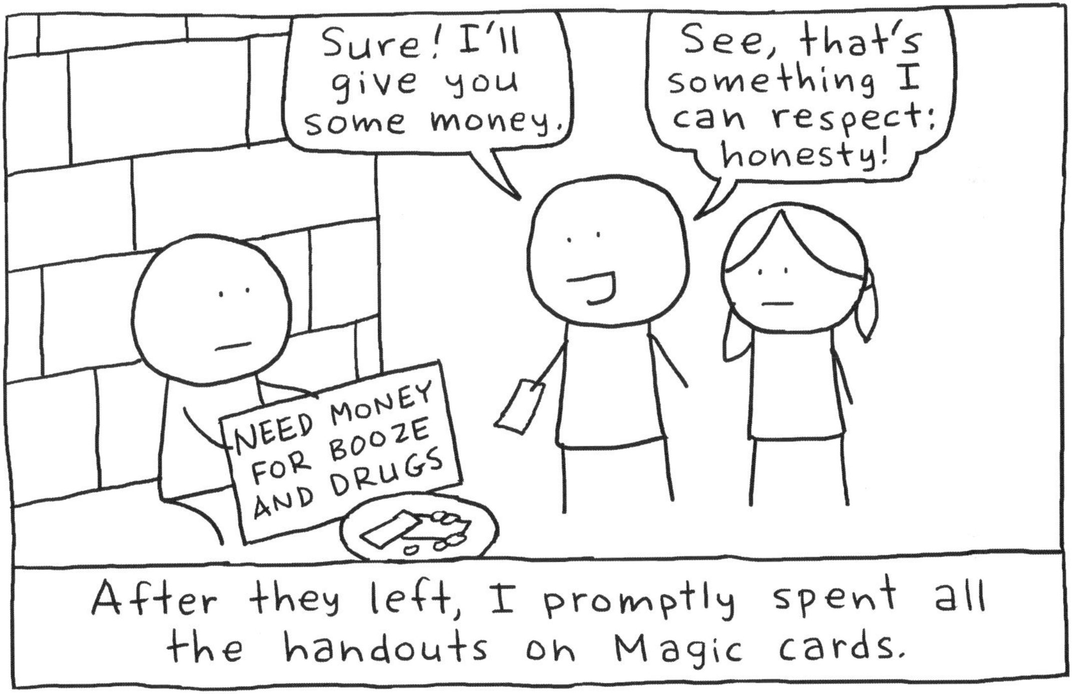
Sure! I'll give you some money.
See, that's something I can respect: honesty!
NEED MONEY FOR BOOZE AND DRUGS
After they left, I promptly spent all the handouts on Magic cards.

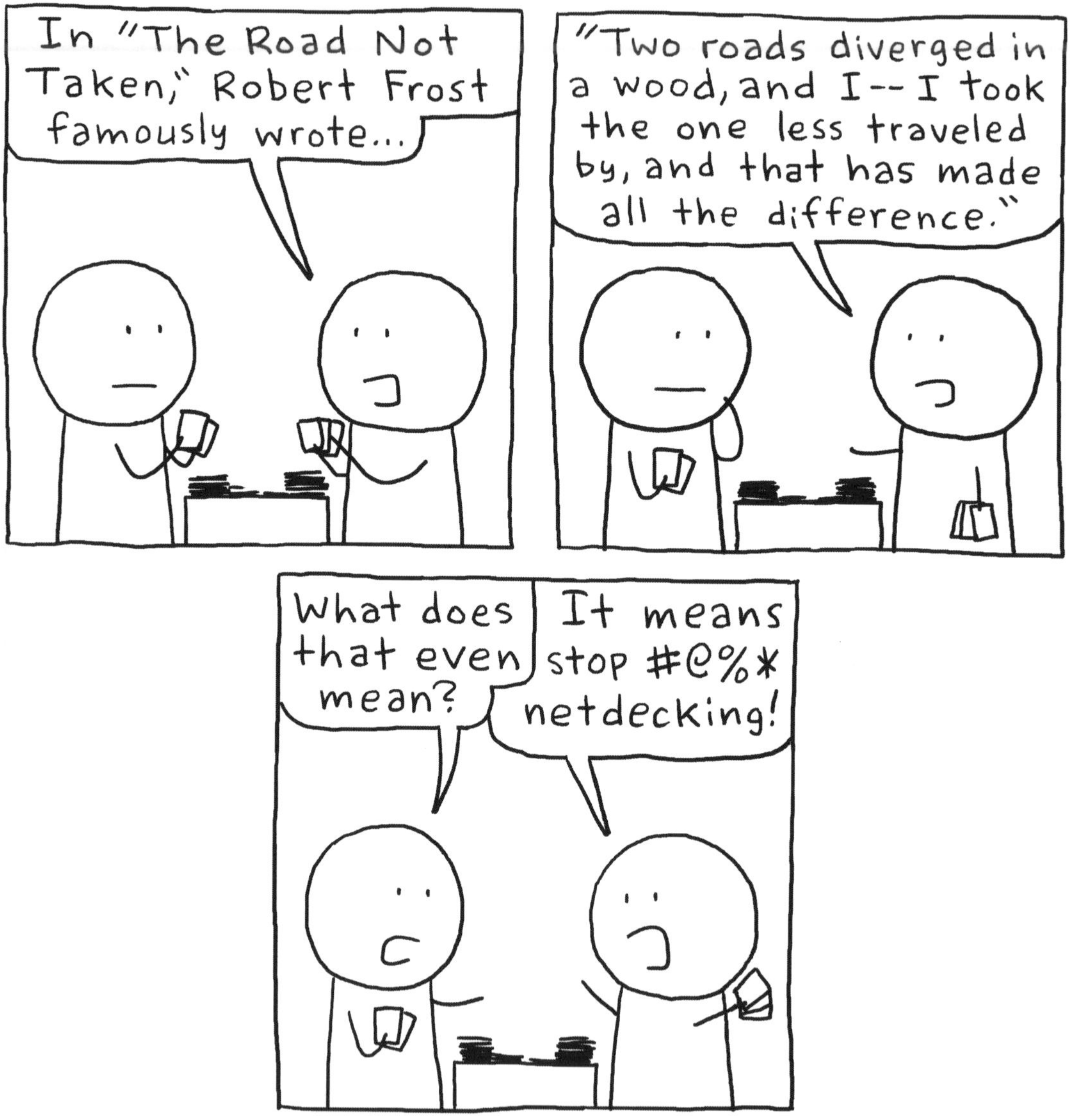
In "The Road Not Taken," Robert Frost famously wrote...
"Two roads diverged in a wood, and I-- I took the one less traveled by, and that has made all the difference."
What does that even mean?
It means stop #@%* netdecking!

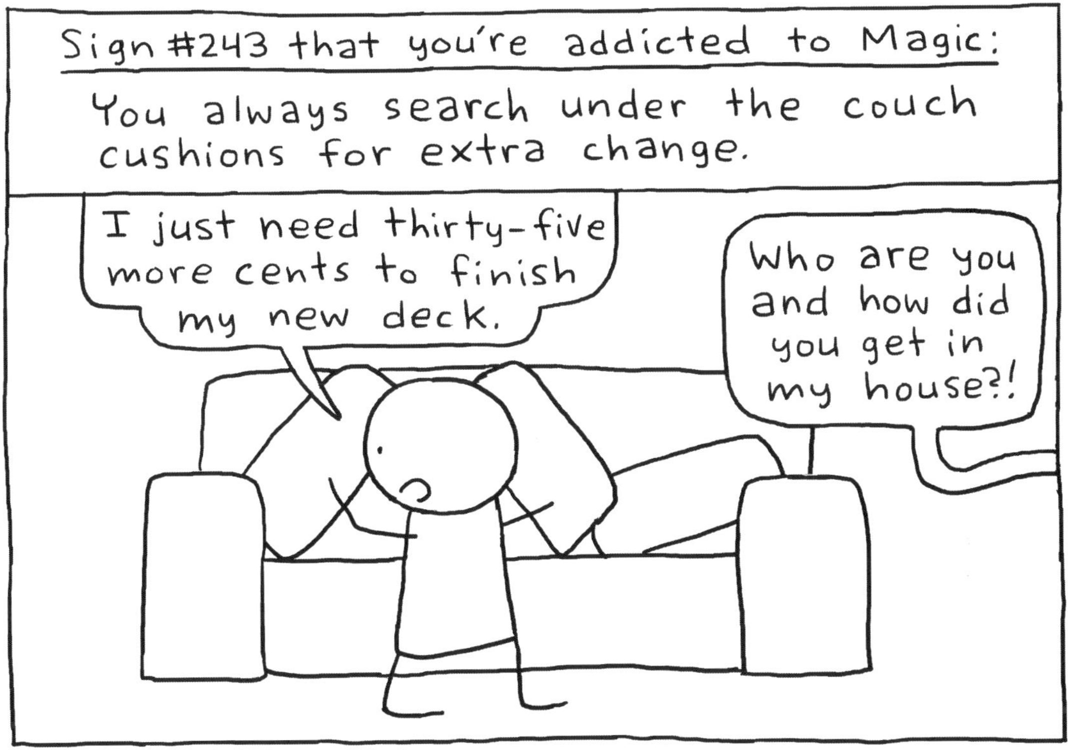
Sign #243 that you're addicted to Magic:
You always search under the couch cushions for extra change.
I just need thirty-five more cents to finish my new deck.
Who are you and how did you get in my house?!

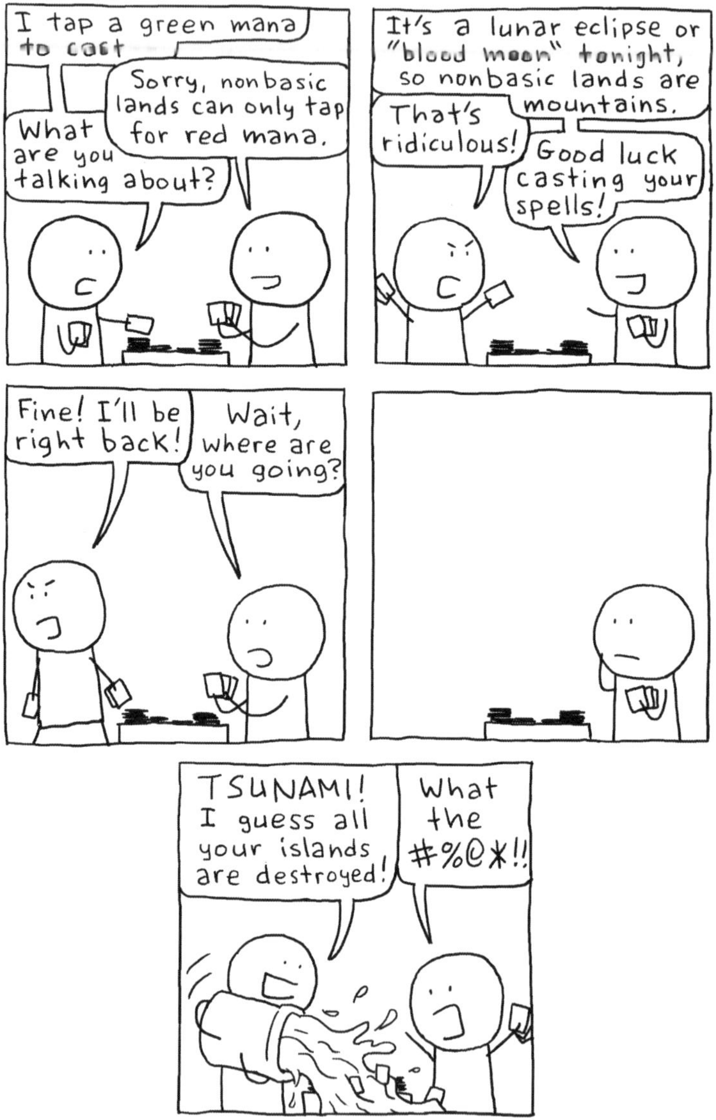
I tap a green mana to cast
What are you talking about?
Sorry, nonbasic lands can only tap for red mana.
It's a lunar eclipse or "blood moon" tonight, so nonbasic lands are mountains.
That's ridiculous!
Good luck casting your spells!
Fine! I'll be right back!
Wait, where are you going?
TSUNAMI! I guess all your islands are destroyed!
What the #%@*!!

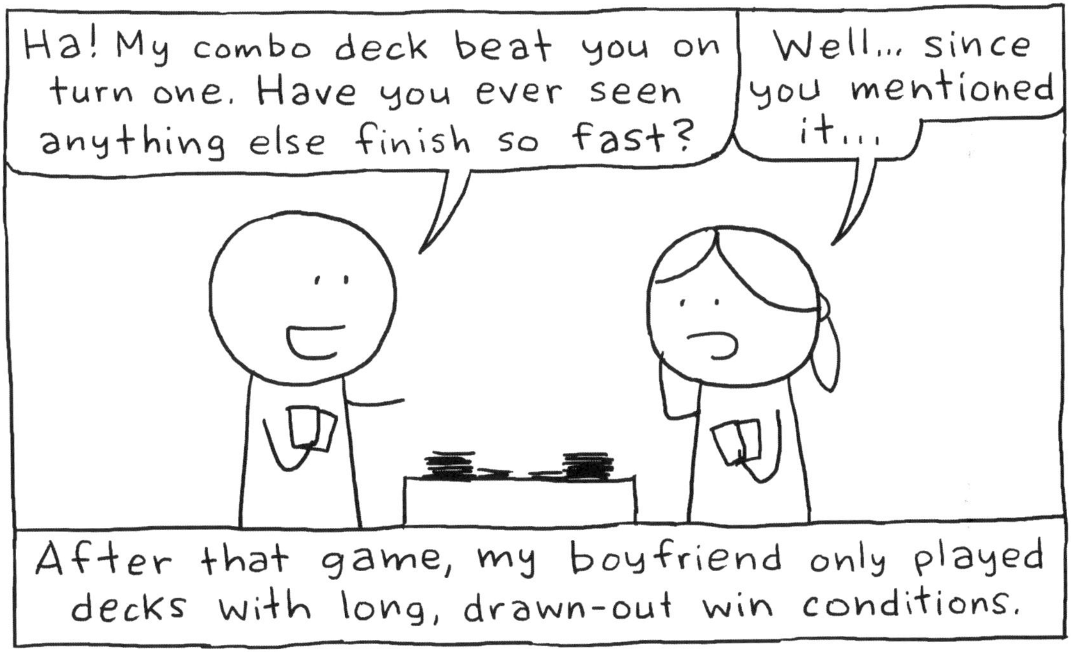
Ha! My combo deck beat you on turn one. Have you ever seen anything else finish so fast?
Well... since you mentioned it...
After that game, my boyfriend only played decks with long, drawn-out win conditions.

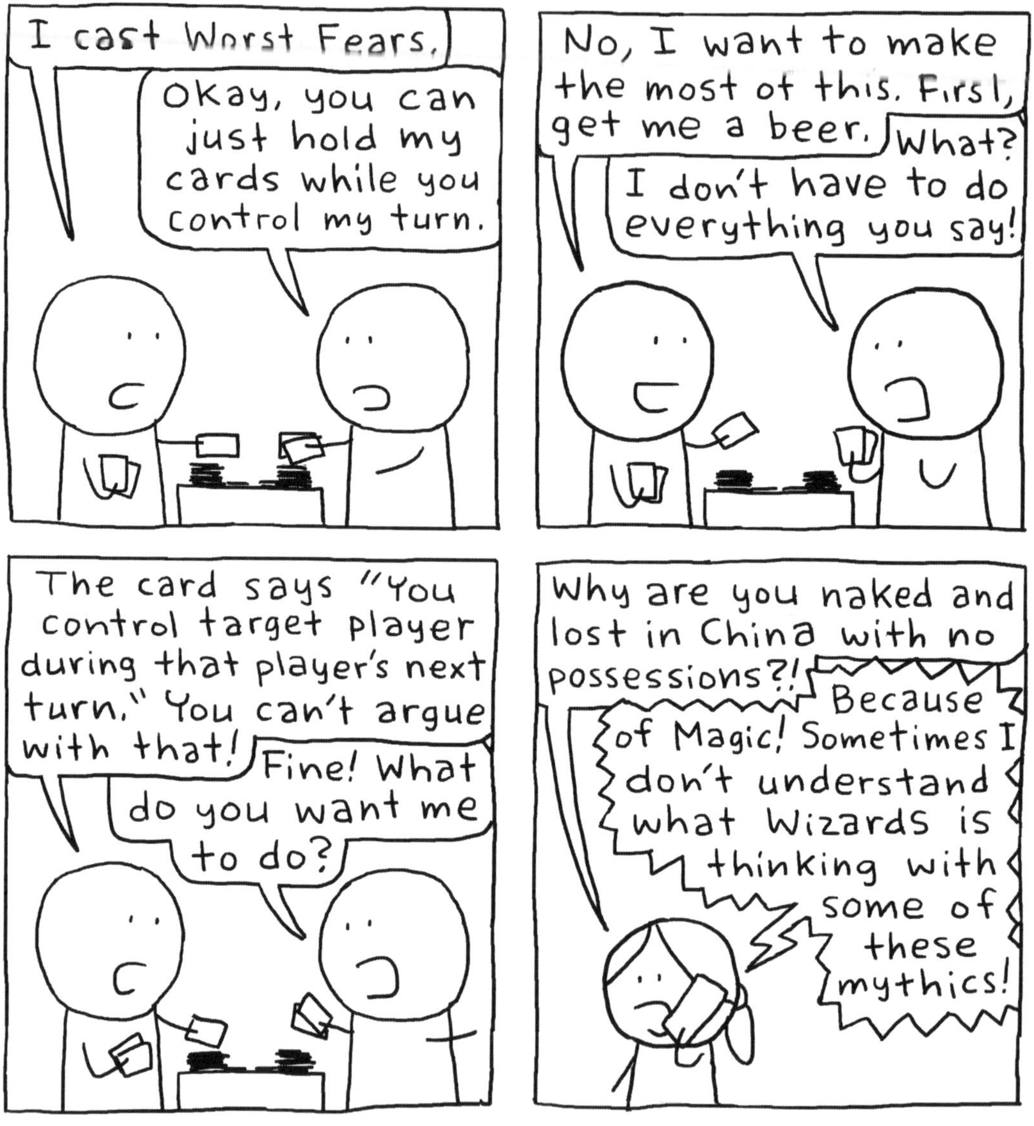
I cast Worst Fears.
Okay, you can just hold my cards while you control my turn.
No, I want to make the most of this. First, get me a beer.
What? I don't have to do everything you say!
The card says "You control target player during that player's next turn." You can't argue with that!
Fine! What do you want me to do?
Why are you naked and lost in China with no possessions?!
Because of Magic! Sometimes I don't understand what Wizards is thinking with some of these mythics!

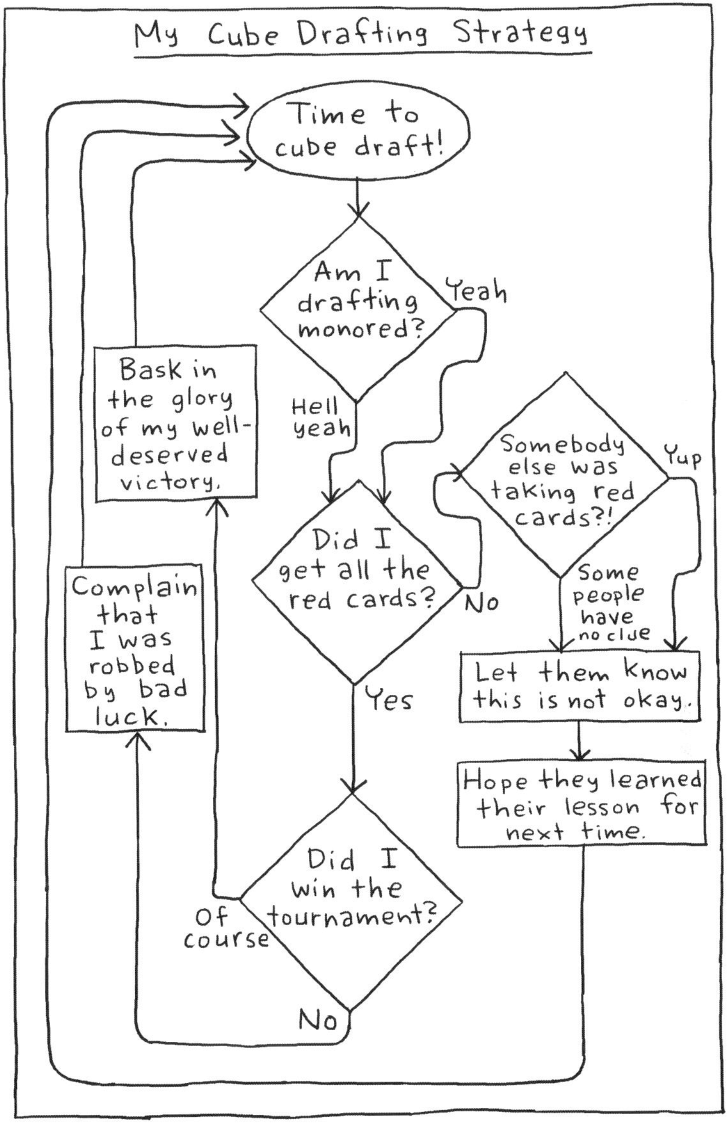
My Cube Drafting Strategy
Time to cube draft!
Am I drafting monored?
Yeah
Hell yeah
Did I get all the red cards?
No
Somebody else was taking red cards?!
Yup
Some people have no clue
Let them know this is not okay.
Hope they learned their lesson for next time.
Yes
Did I win the tournament?
Of course
No
Bask in the glory of my well-deserved victory.
Complain that I was robbed by bad luck.

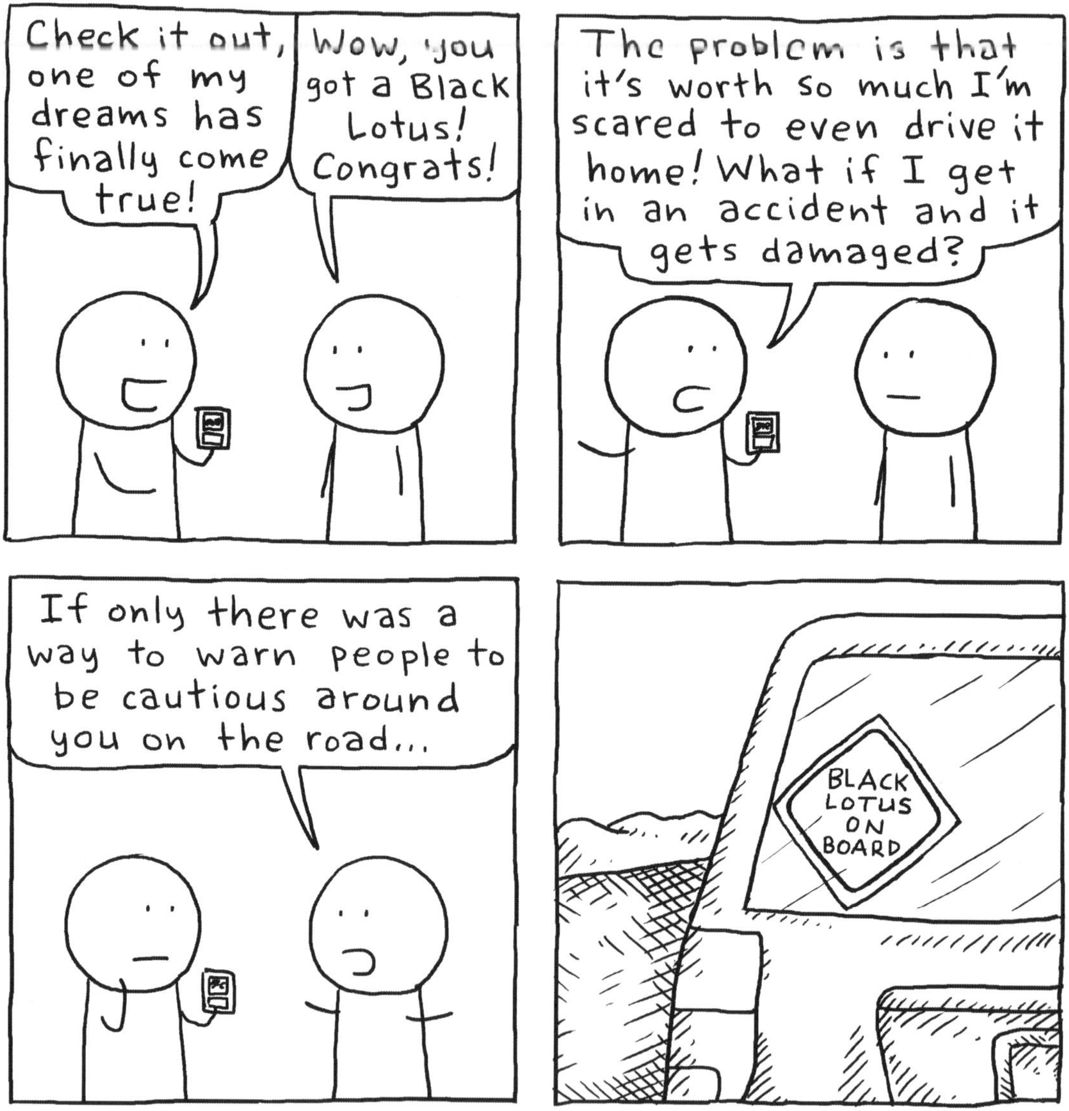
Check it out, one of my dreams has finally come true!
Wow, you got a Black Lotus! Congrats!
The problem is that it's worth so much I'm scared to even drive it home! What if I get in an accident and it gets damaged?
If only there was a way to warn people to be cautious around you on the road...
BLACK LOTUS ON BOARD

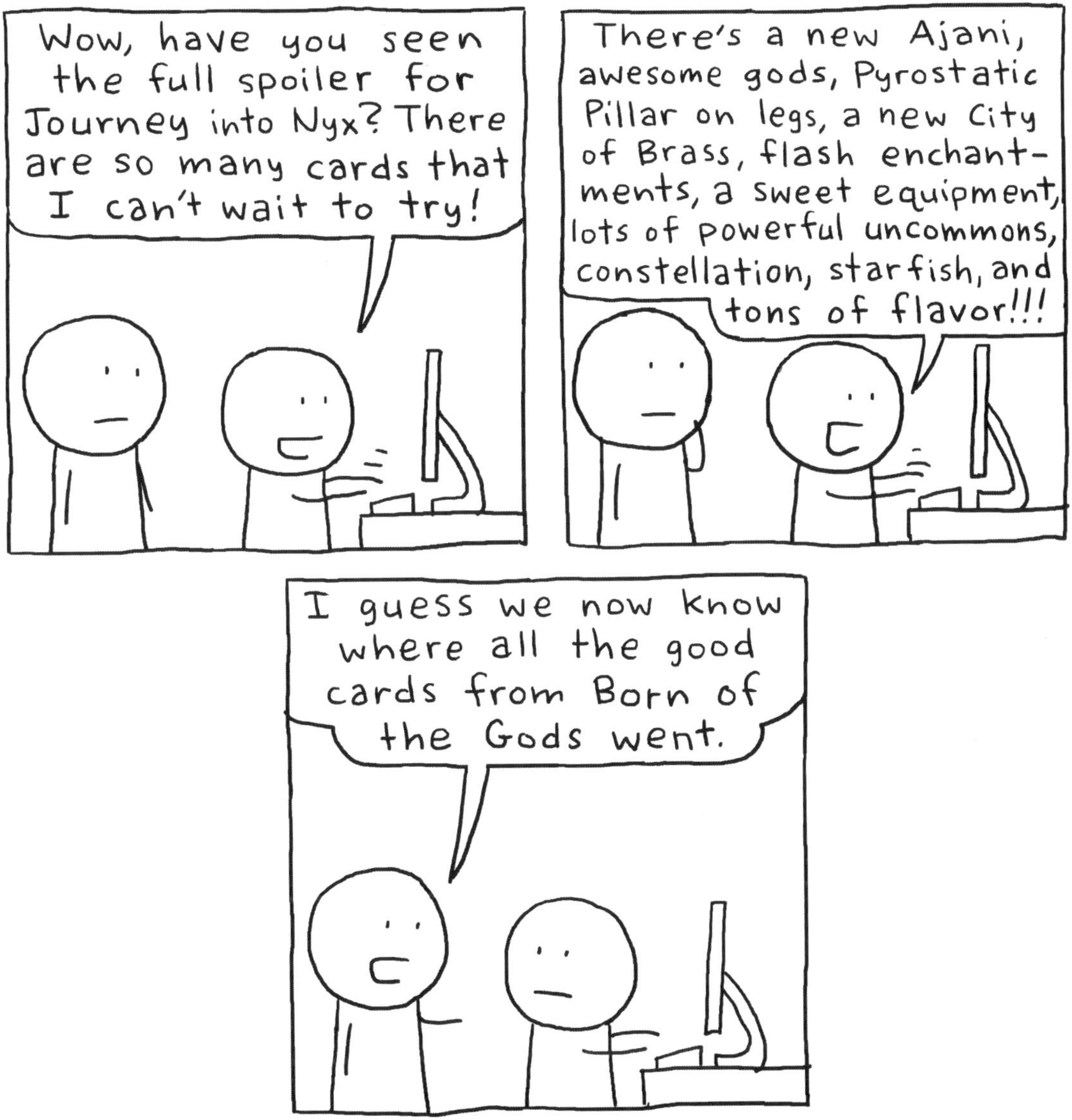
Wow, have you seen the full spoiler for Journey into Nyx? There are so many cards that I can't wait to try!
There's a new Ajani, awesome gods, Pyrostatic Pillar on legs, a new City of Brass, flash enchantments, a sweet equipment, lots of powerful uncommons, constellation, starfish, and tons of flavor!!!
I guess we now know where all the good cards from Born of the Gods went.

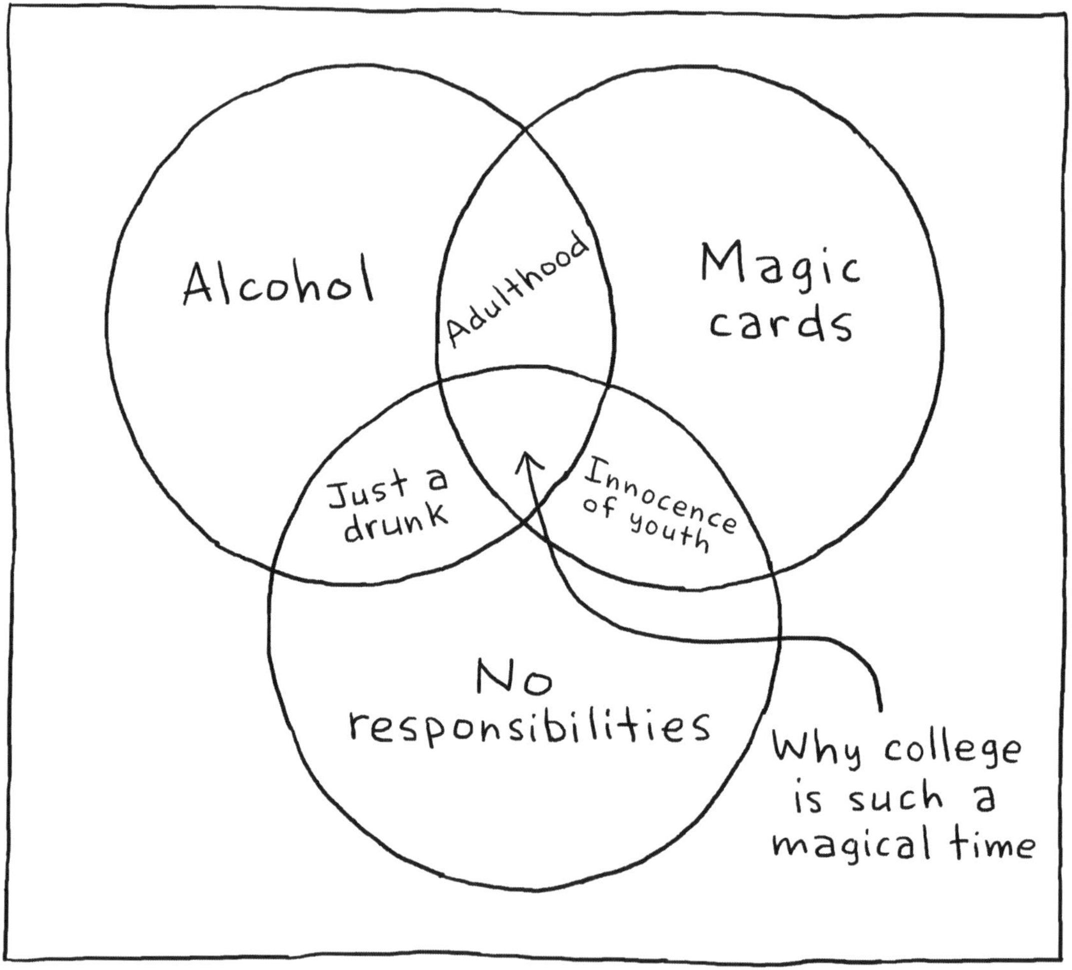
Alcohol
Magic cards
No responsibilities
Adulthood
Just a drunk
Innocence of youth
Why college is such a magical time

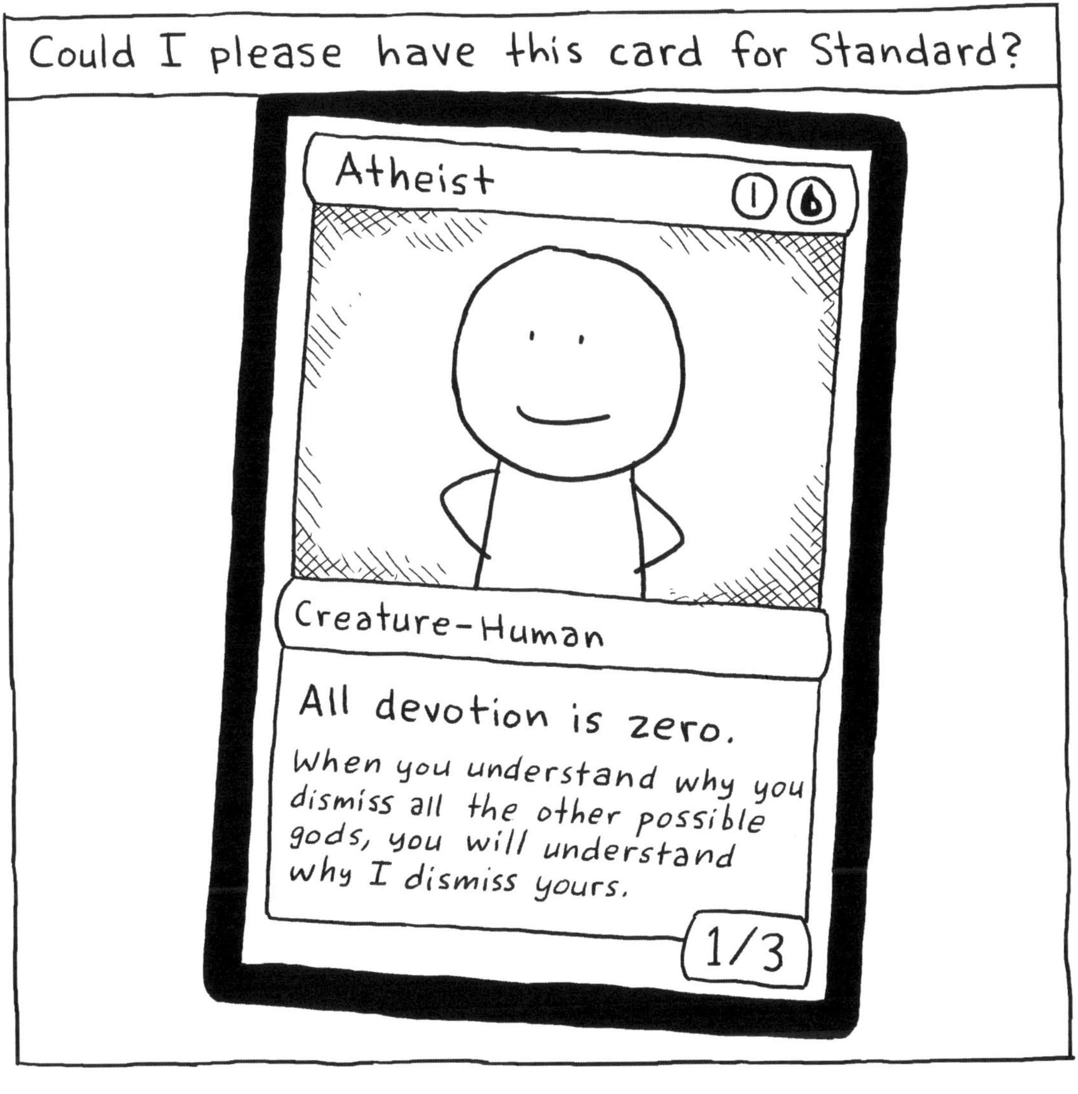

Could I please have this card for Standard?
Atheist
1
Creature-Human
All devotion is zero.
When you understand why you dismiss all the other possible gods, you will understand why I dismiss yours.
1/3

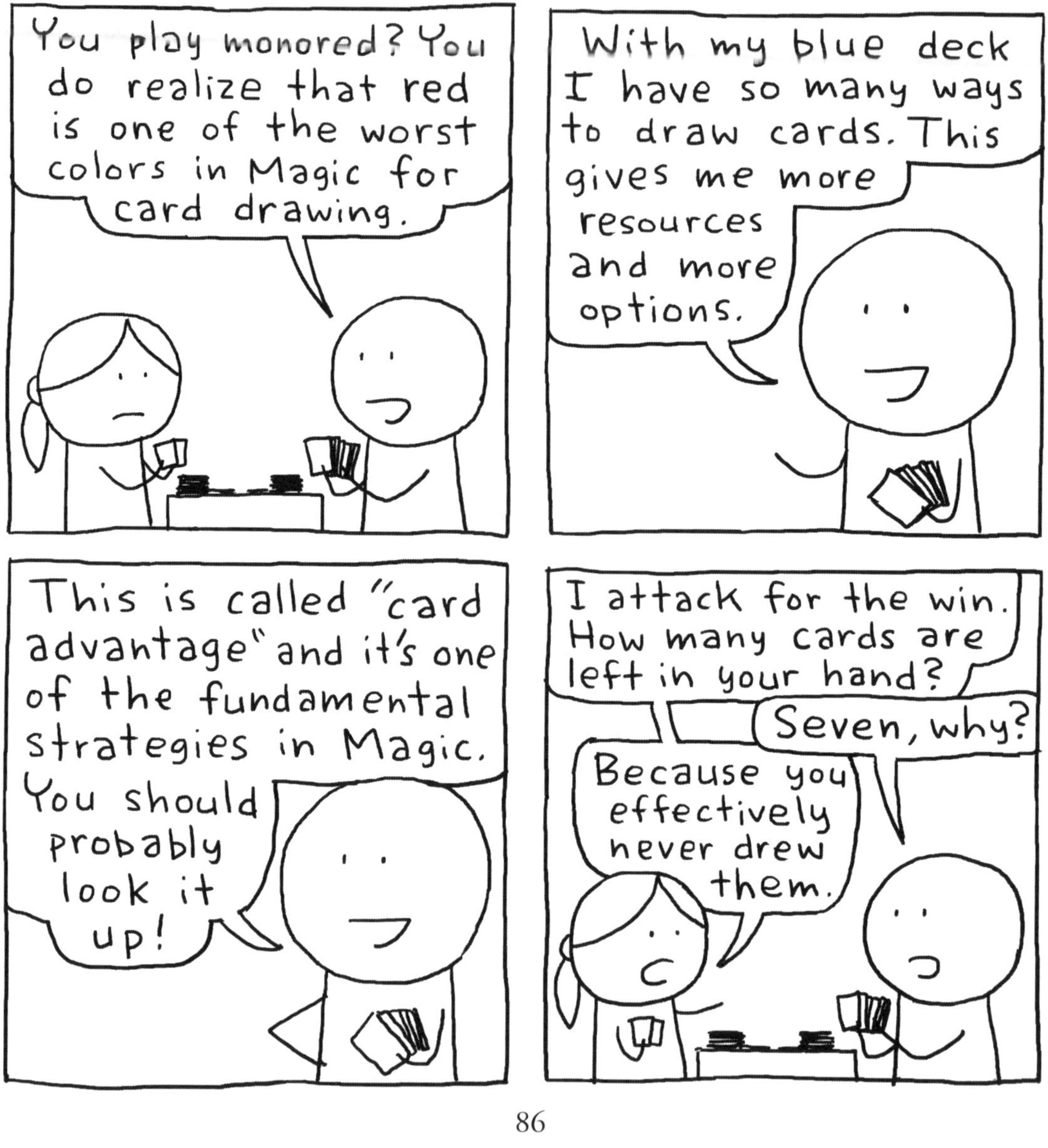
You play monored? You do realize that red is one of the worst colors in Magic for card drawing.
With my blue deck I have so many ways to draw cards. This gives me more resources and more options.
This is called "card advantage" and it's one of the fundamental strategies in Magic.
You should probably look it up!
I attack for the win. How many cards are left in your hand?
Seven, why?
Because you effectively never drew them.

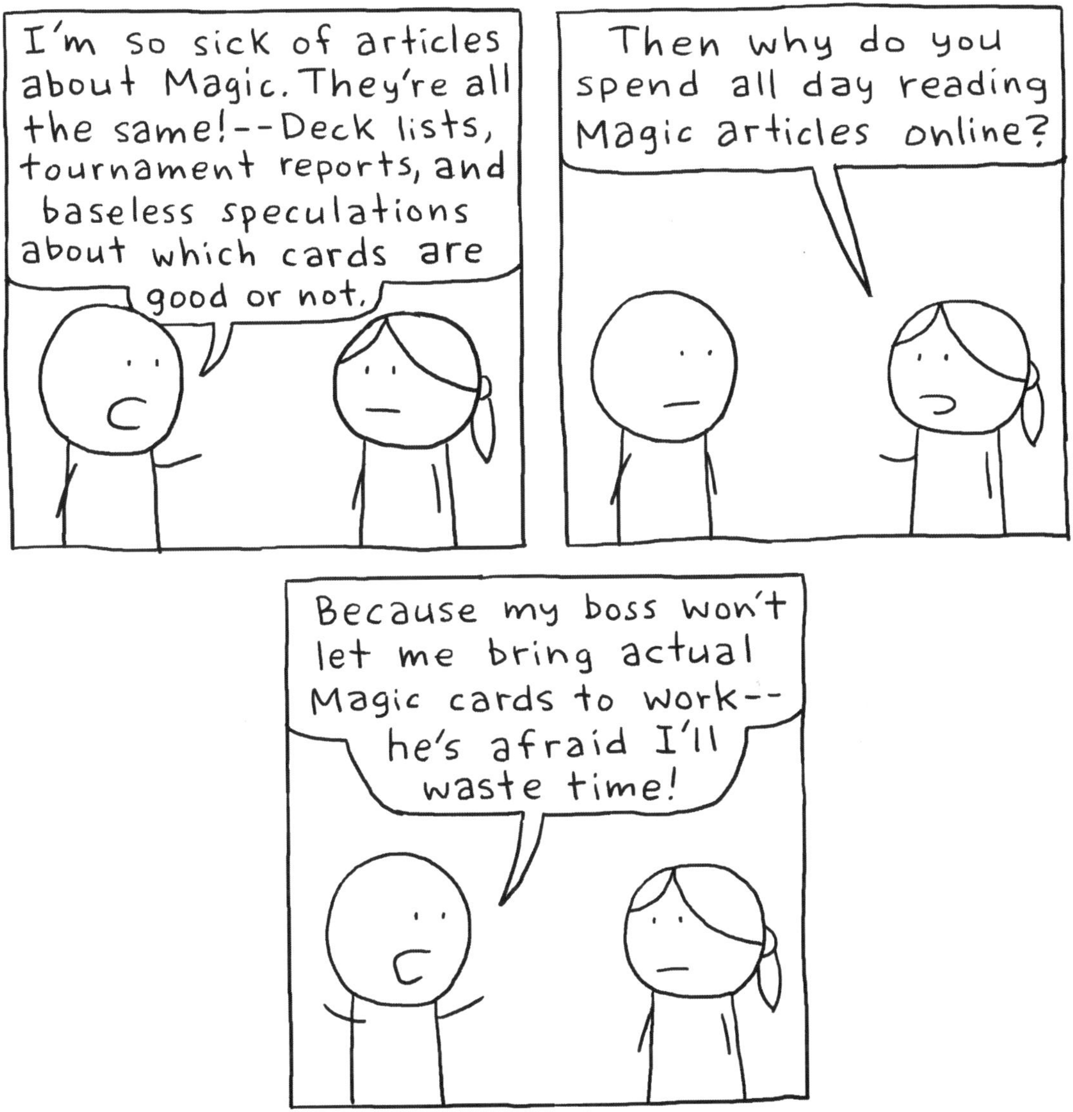

I'm so sick of articles about Magic. They're all the same!--Deck lists, tournament reports, and baseless speculations about which cards are good or not.
Then why do you spend all day reading Magic articles online?
Because my boss won't let me bring actual Magic cards to work--he's afraid I'll waste time!

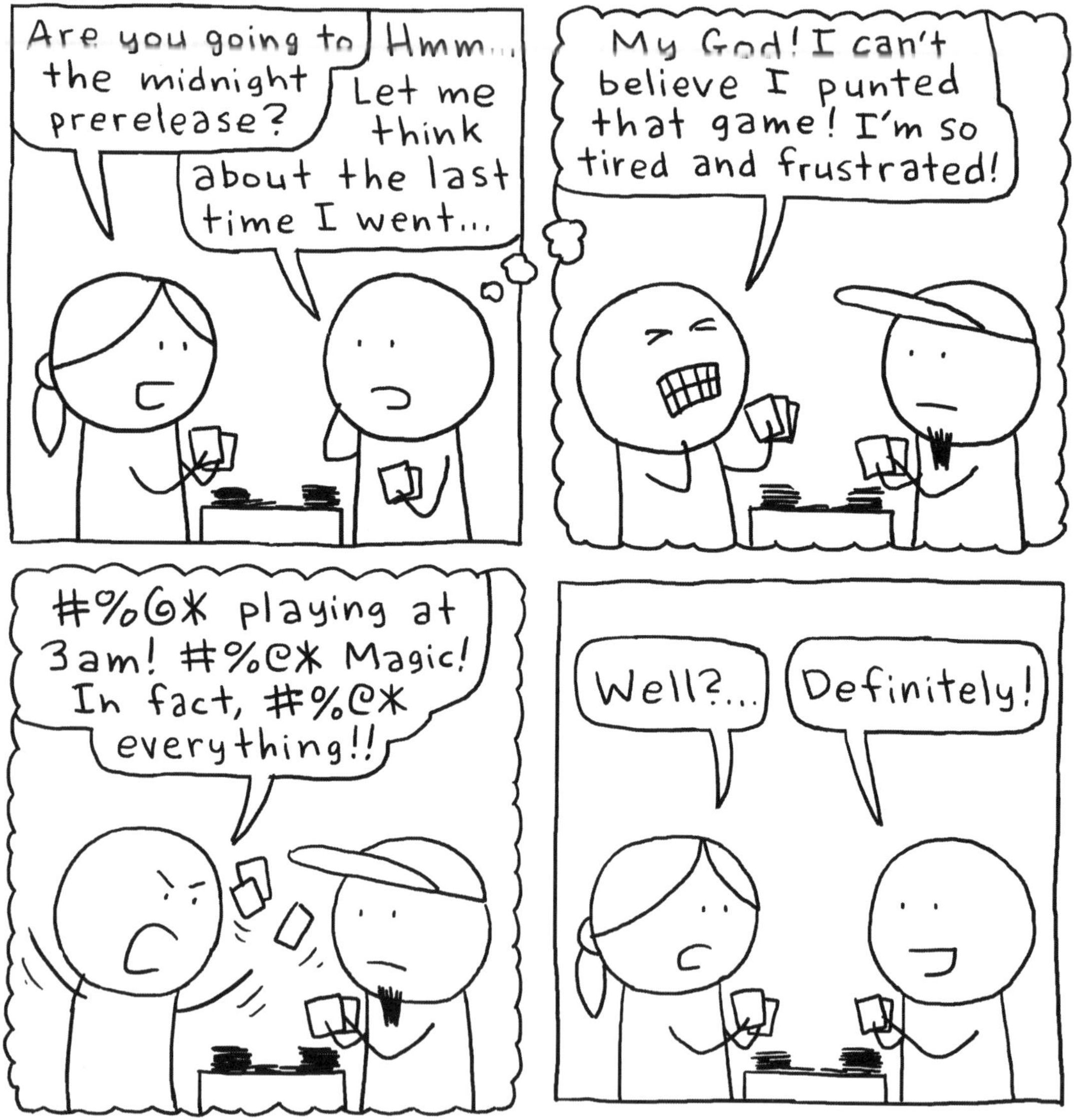
Are you going to the midnight prerelease?
Hmm... Let me think about the last time I went...
My God! I can't believe I punted that game! I'm so tired and frustrated!
#%@* playing at 3am! #%@* Magic! In fact, #%@* everything!!
Well?...
Definitely!

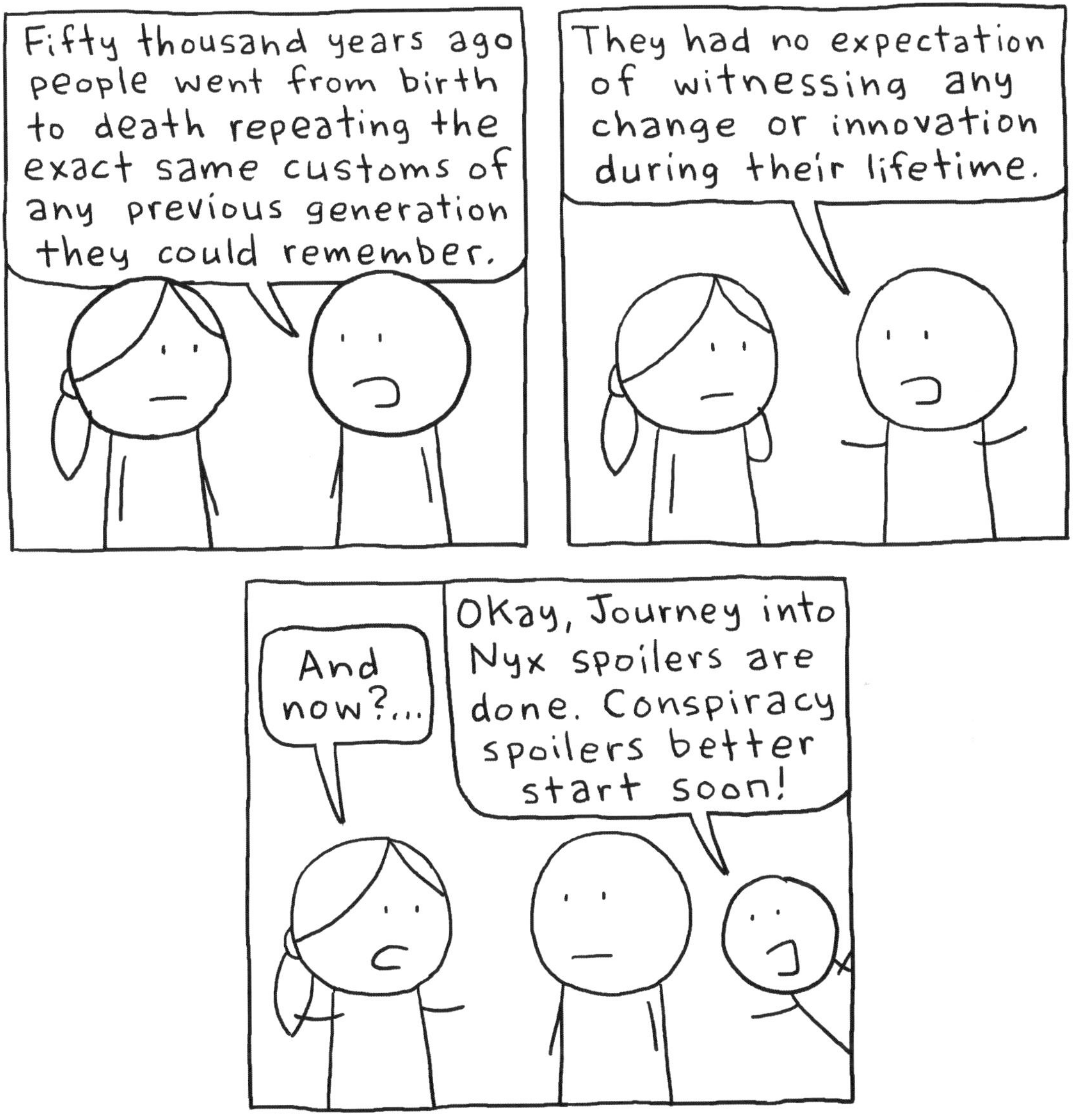

Fifty thousand years ago people went from birth to death repeating the exact same customs of any previous generation they could remember.
They had no expectation of witnessing any change or innovation during their lifetime.
And now?...
Okay, Journey into Nyx spoilers are done. Conspiracy spoilers better start soon!

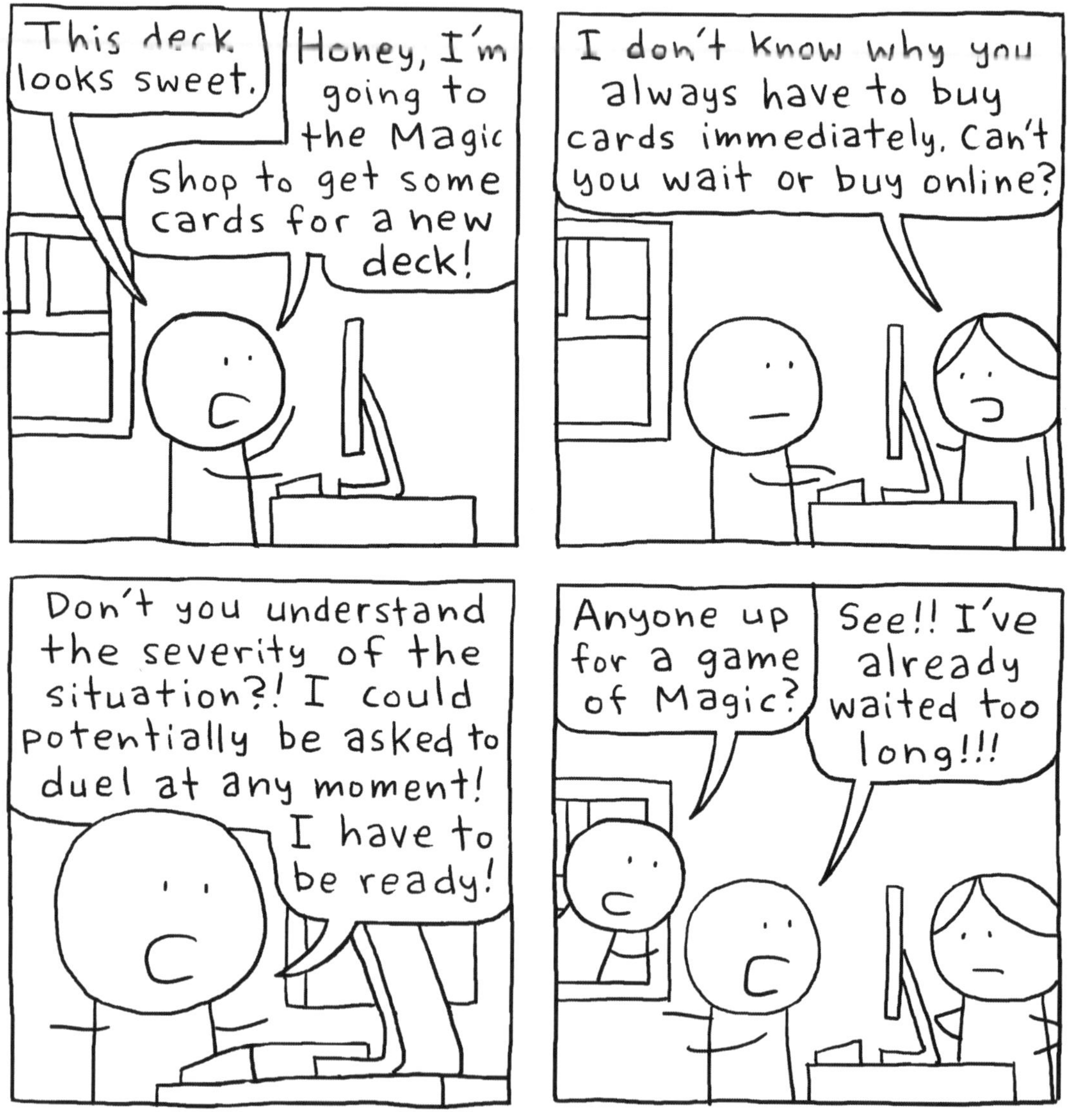
This deck looks sweet.
Honey, I'm going to the Magic shop to get some cards for a new deck!
I don't know why you always have to buy cards immediately. Can't you wait or buy online?
Don't you understand the severity of the situation?! I could potentially be asked to duel at any moment!
I have to be ready!
Anyone up for a game of Magic?
See!! I've already waited too long!!!

Eventually, I decided it was time for me to join a Magic support group...
My name is Jon, and I have a Magic card problem.
... but I may have sorta misunderstood the purpose of the group.
My problem is that I have so many cards that I don't know how to organize them...
...seriously, does anyone have suggestions?

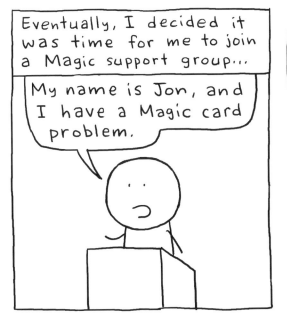

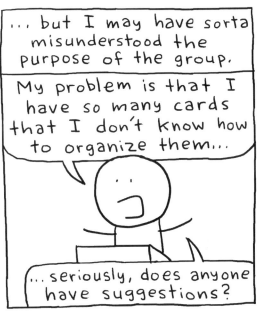

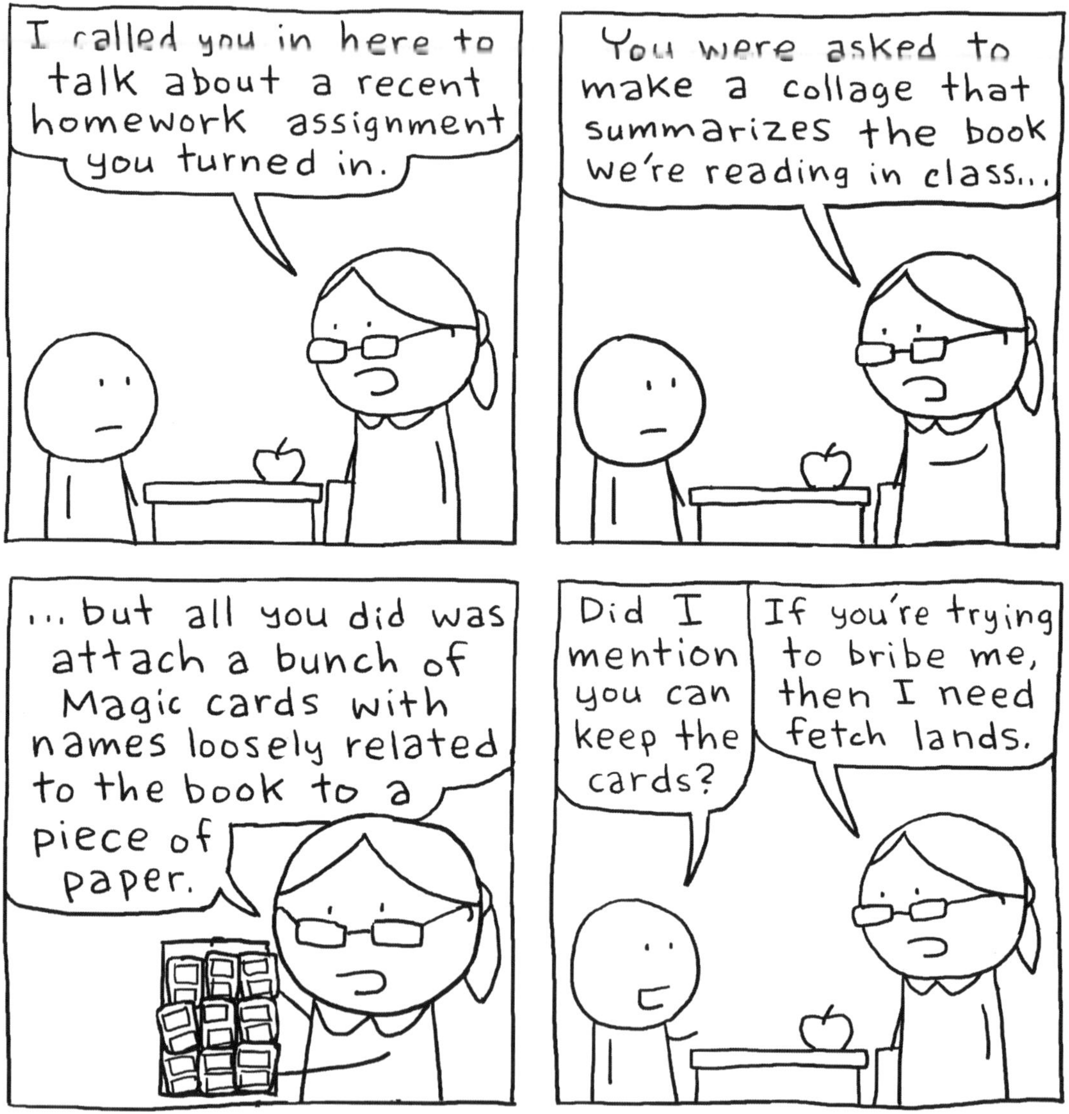
I called you in here to talk about a recent homework assignment you turned in.
You were asked to make a collage that summarizes the book we're reading in class...
...but all you did was attach a bunch of Magic cards with names loosely related to the book to a piece of paper.
Did I mention you can keep the cards?
If you're trying to bribe me, then I need fetch lands.

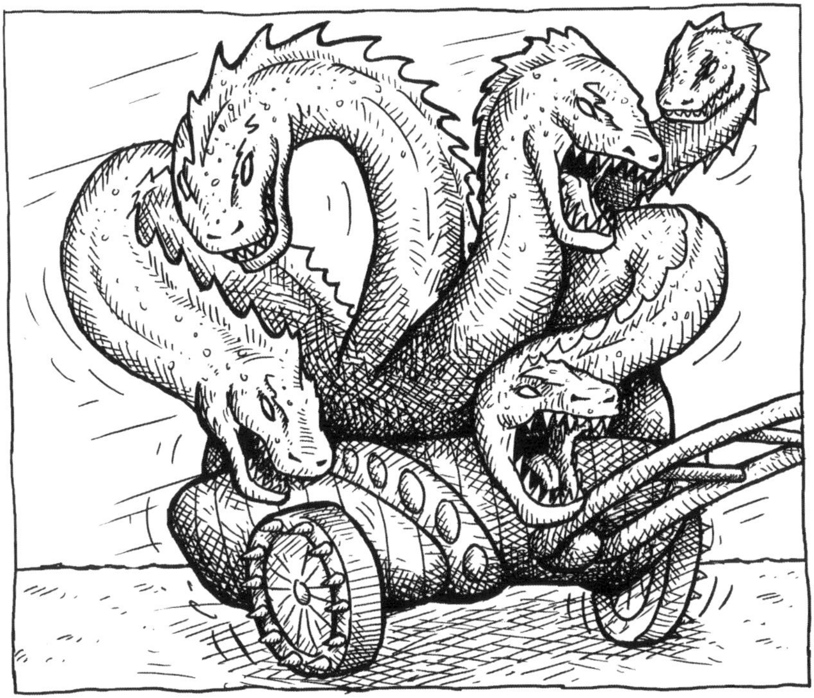

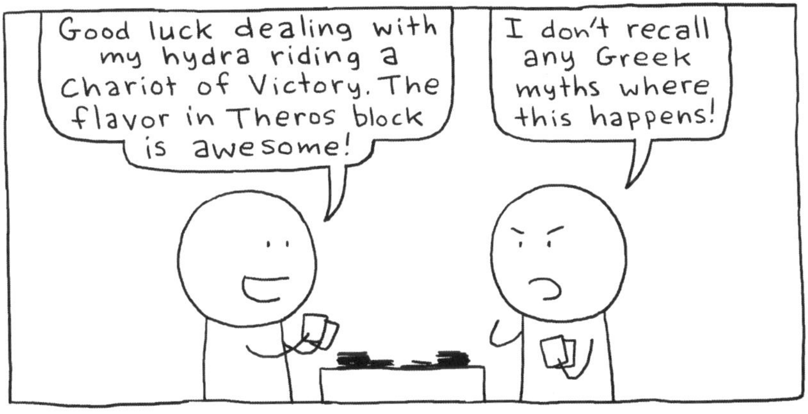
Good luck dealing with my hydra riding a Chariot of Victory. The flavor in Theros block is awesome!
I don't recall any Greek myths where this happens!

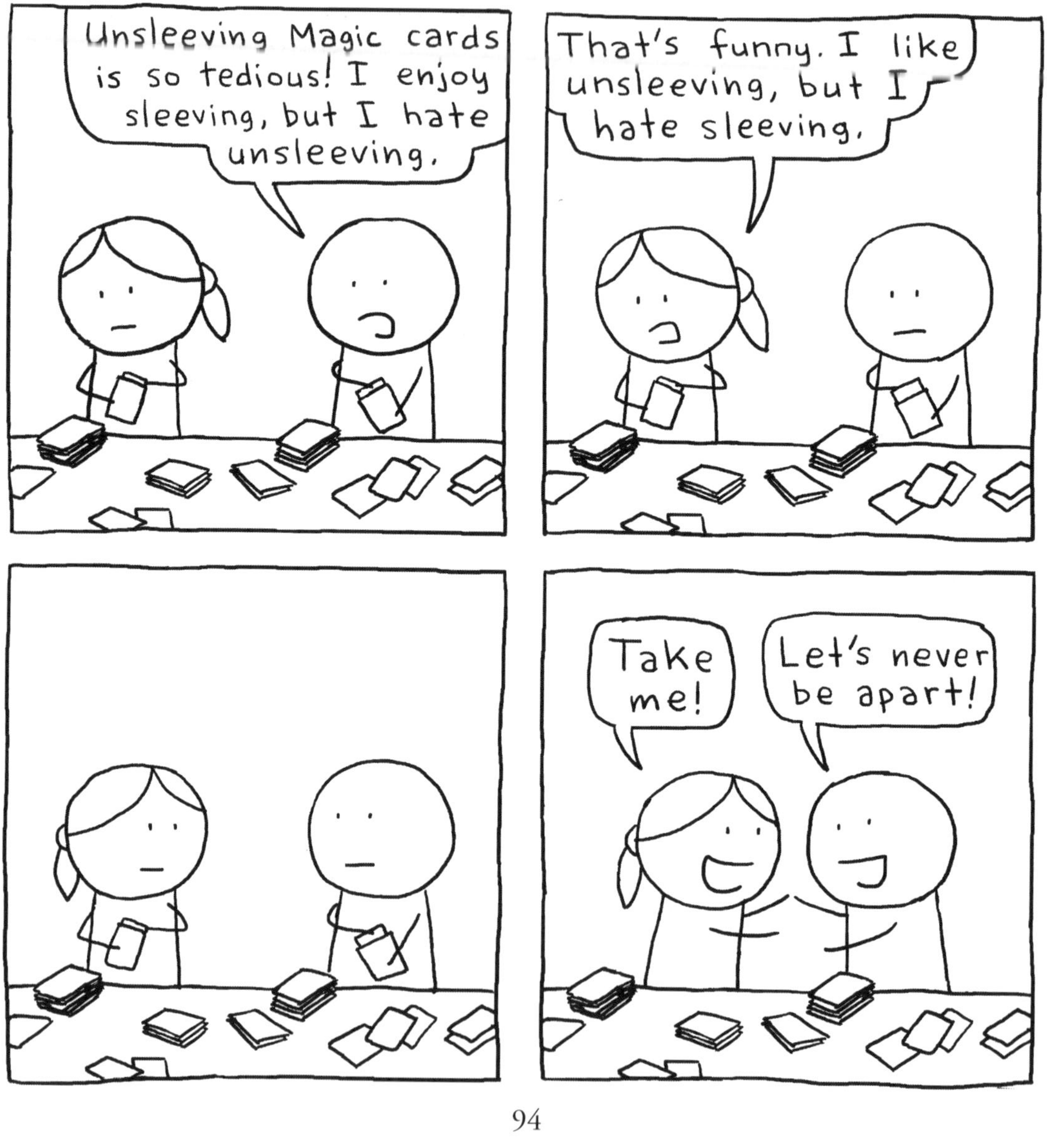
Unsleeving Magic cards is so tedious! I enjoy sleeving, but I hate unsleeving.
That's funny. I like unsleeving, but I hate sleeving.
Take me!
Let's never be apart!

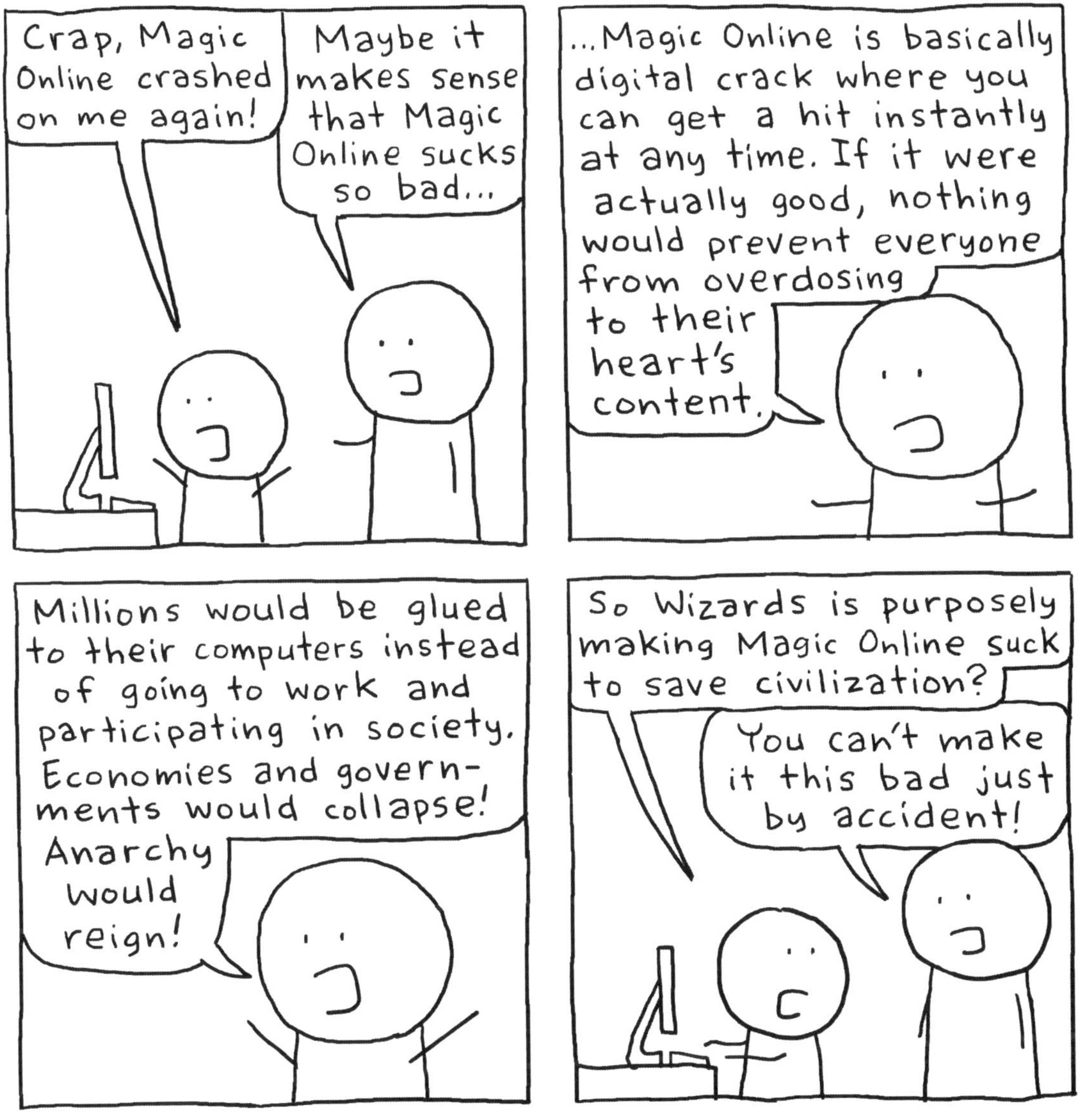
Crap, Magic Online crashed on me again!
Maybe it makes sense that Magic Online sucks so bad...
...Magic Online is basically digital crack where you can get a hit instantly at any time. If it were actually good, nothing would prevent everyone from overdosing
to their heart's content.
Millions would be glued to their computers instead of going to work and participating in society. Economies and governments would collapse!
Anarchy would reign!
So Wizards is purposely making Magic Online suck to save civilization?
You can't make it this bad just by accident!

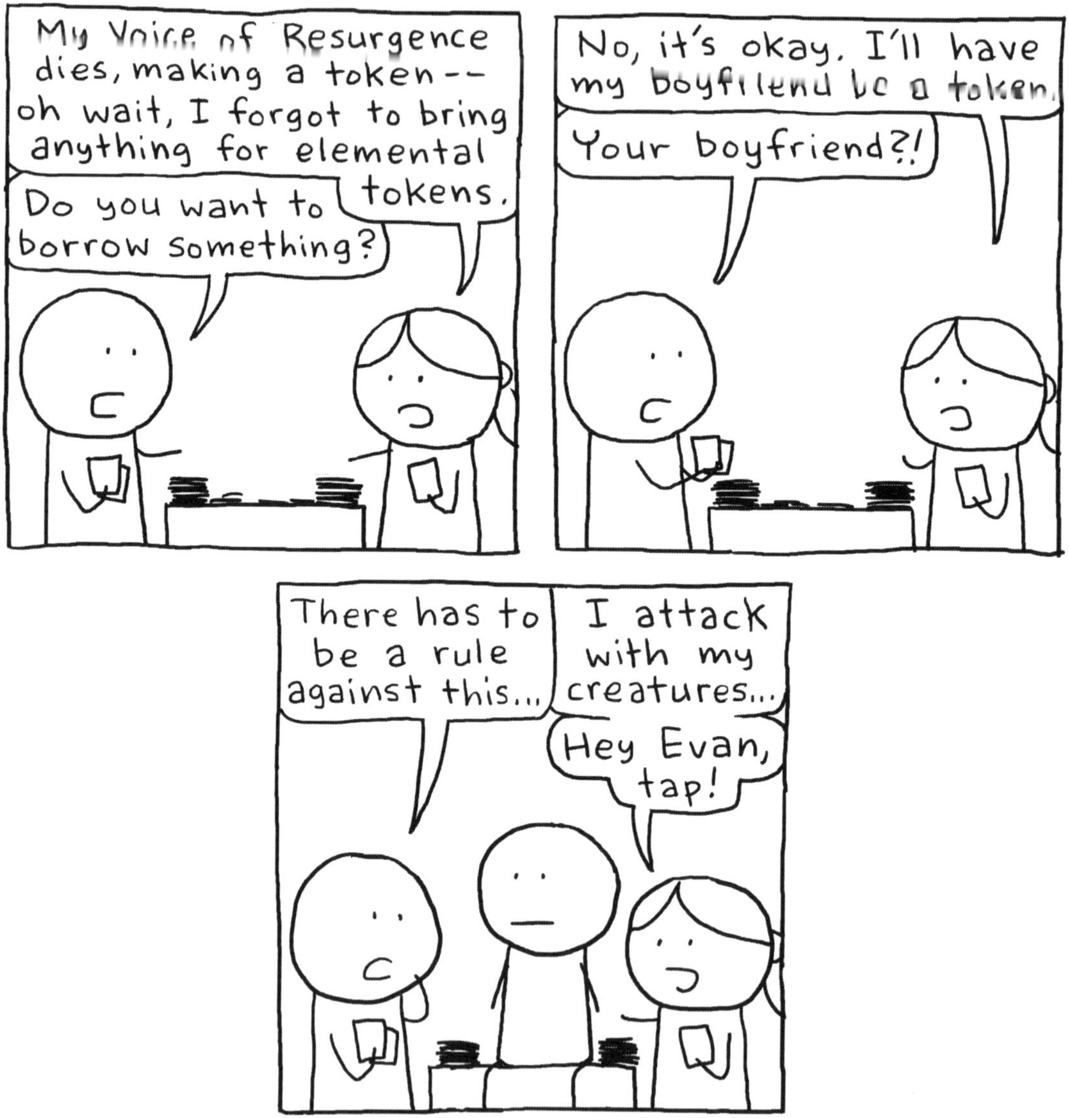
My Voice of Resurgence dies, making a token -- oh wait, I forgot to bring anything for elemental tokens.
Do you want to borrow something?
No, it's okay. I'll have my boyfriend be a token.
Your boyfriend?!
There has to be a rule against this...
I attack with my creatures...
Hey Evan, tap!

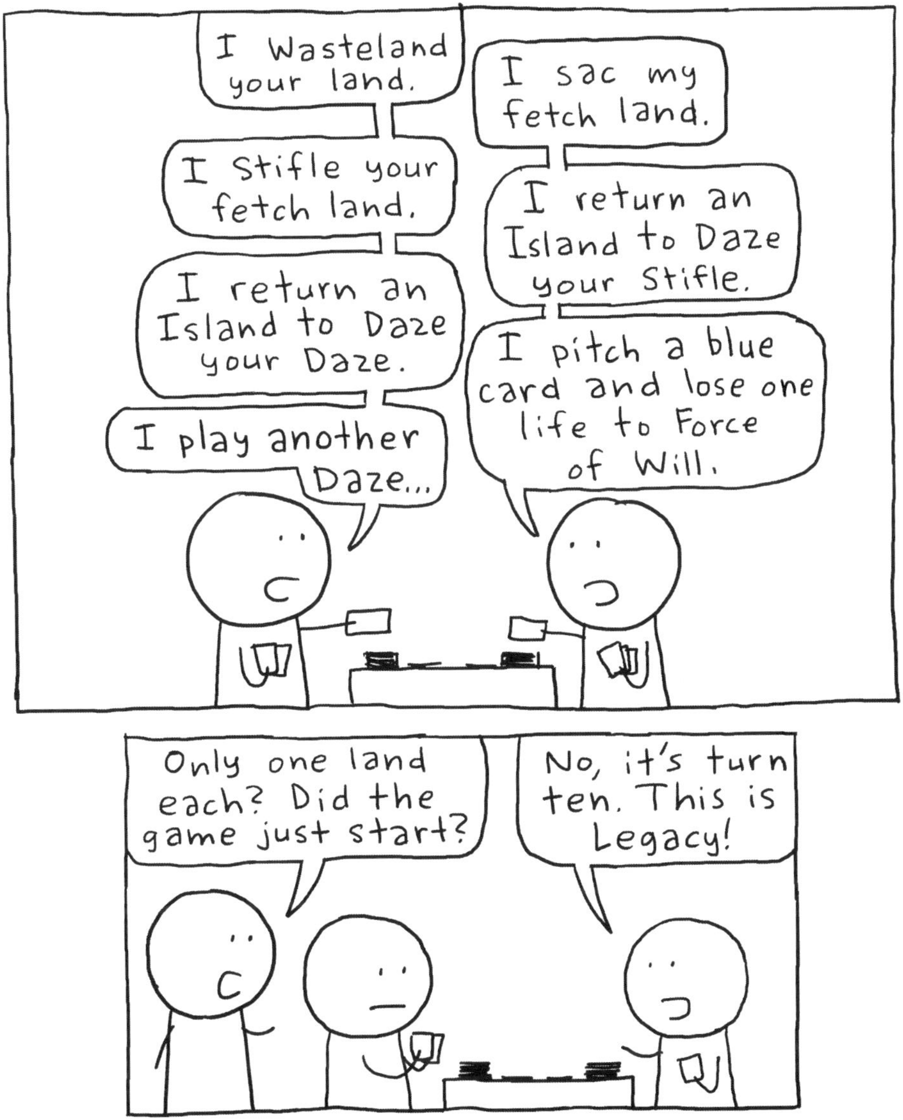
I Wasteland your land.
I sac my fetch land.
I Stifle your fetch land.
I return an Island to Daze your Stifle.
I return an Island to Daze your Daze.
I pitch a blue card and lose one life to Force of Will.
I play another Daze...
Only one land each? Did the game just start?
No, it's turn ten. This is Legacy!

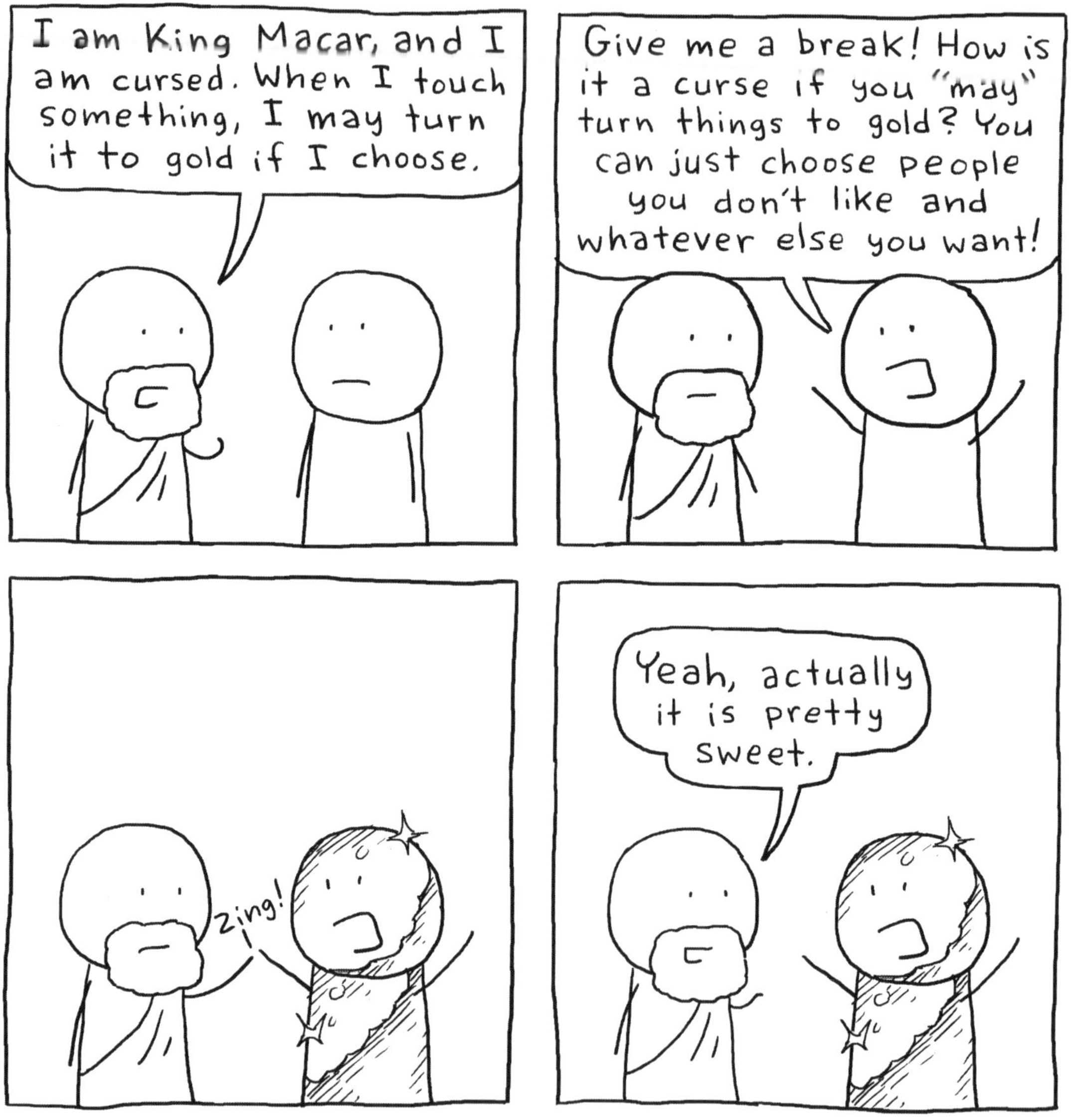
I am King Macar, and I am cursed. When I touch something, I may turn it to gold if I choose.
Give me a break! How is it a curse if you "may" turn things to gold? You can just choose people you don't like and whatever else you want!
zing!
Yeah, actually it is pretty sweet.

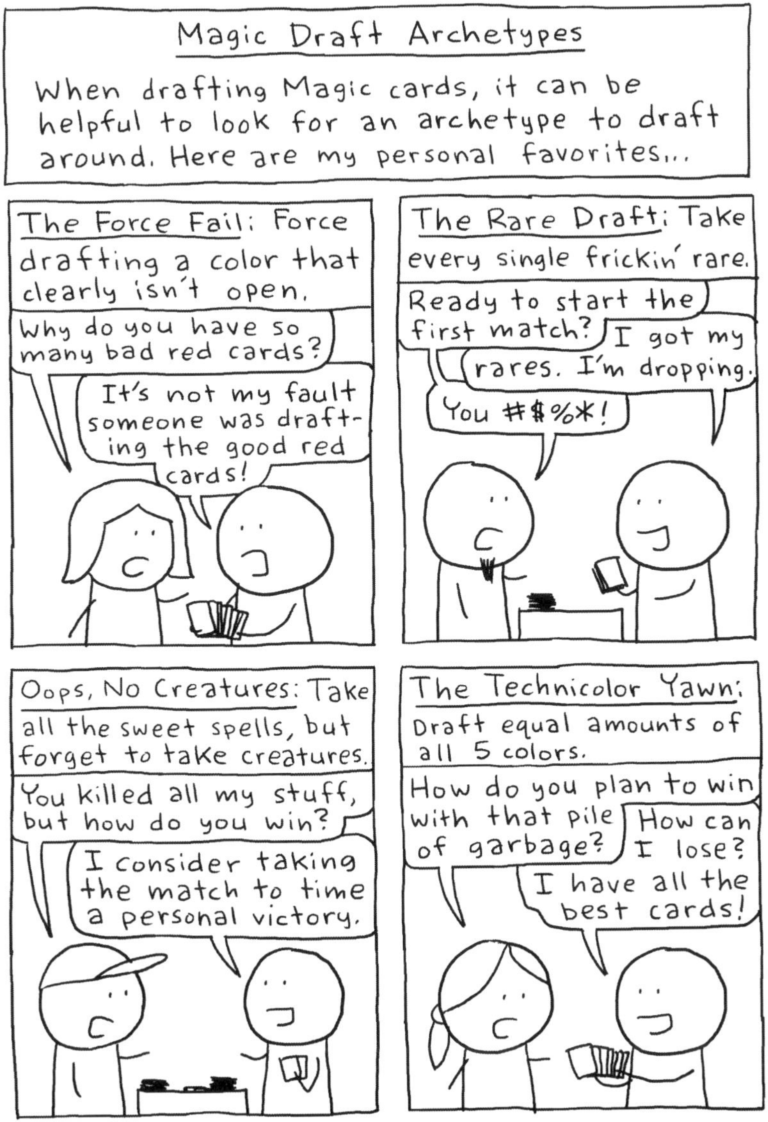
Magic Draft Archetypes
When drafting Magic cards, it can be helpful to look for an archetype to draft around. Here are my personal favorites...
The Force Fail: Force drafting a color that clearly isn't open.
Why do you have so many bad red cards?
It's not my fault someone was drafting the good red cards!
The Rare Draft: Take every single frickin' rare.
Ready to start the first match?
I got my rares. I'm dropping.
You #$%*!
Oops, No Creatures: Take all the sweet spells, but forget to take creatures.
You killed all my stuff, but how do you win?
I consider taking the match to time a personal victory.
The Technicolor Yawn: Draft equal amounts of all 5 colors.
How do you plan to win with that pile of garbage?
How can I lose? I have all the best cards!

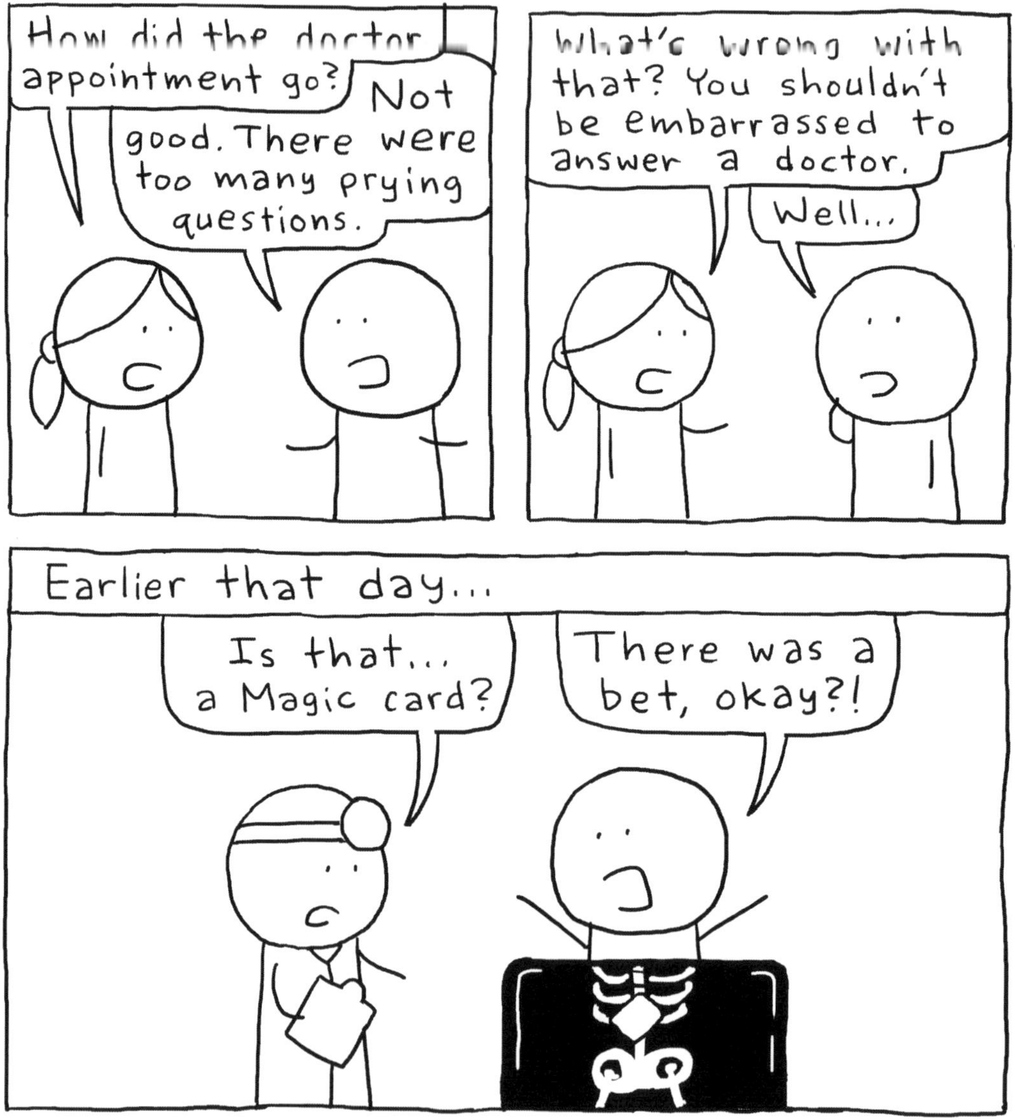
How did the doctor appointment go?
Not good. There were too many prying questions.
What's wrong with that? You shouldn't be embarrassed to answer a doctor.
Well...
Earlier that day...
Is that... a Magic card?
There was a bet, okay?!

Son, there's one piece of advice I hope you always remember-- you can accomplish anything, if you put your mind to it.
Thanks, Mom!
Does that mean I can have a perfect life like Brian Kibler?
No, don't be ridiculous.

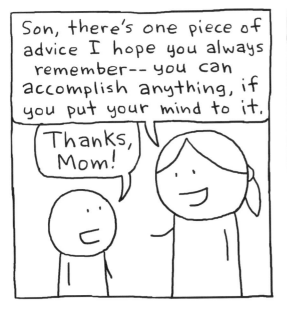

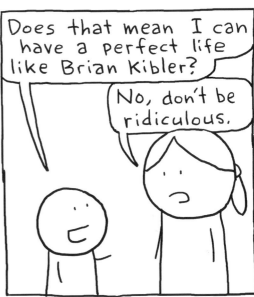

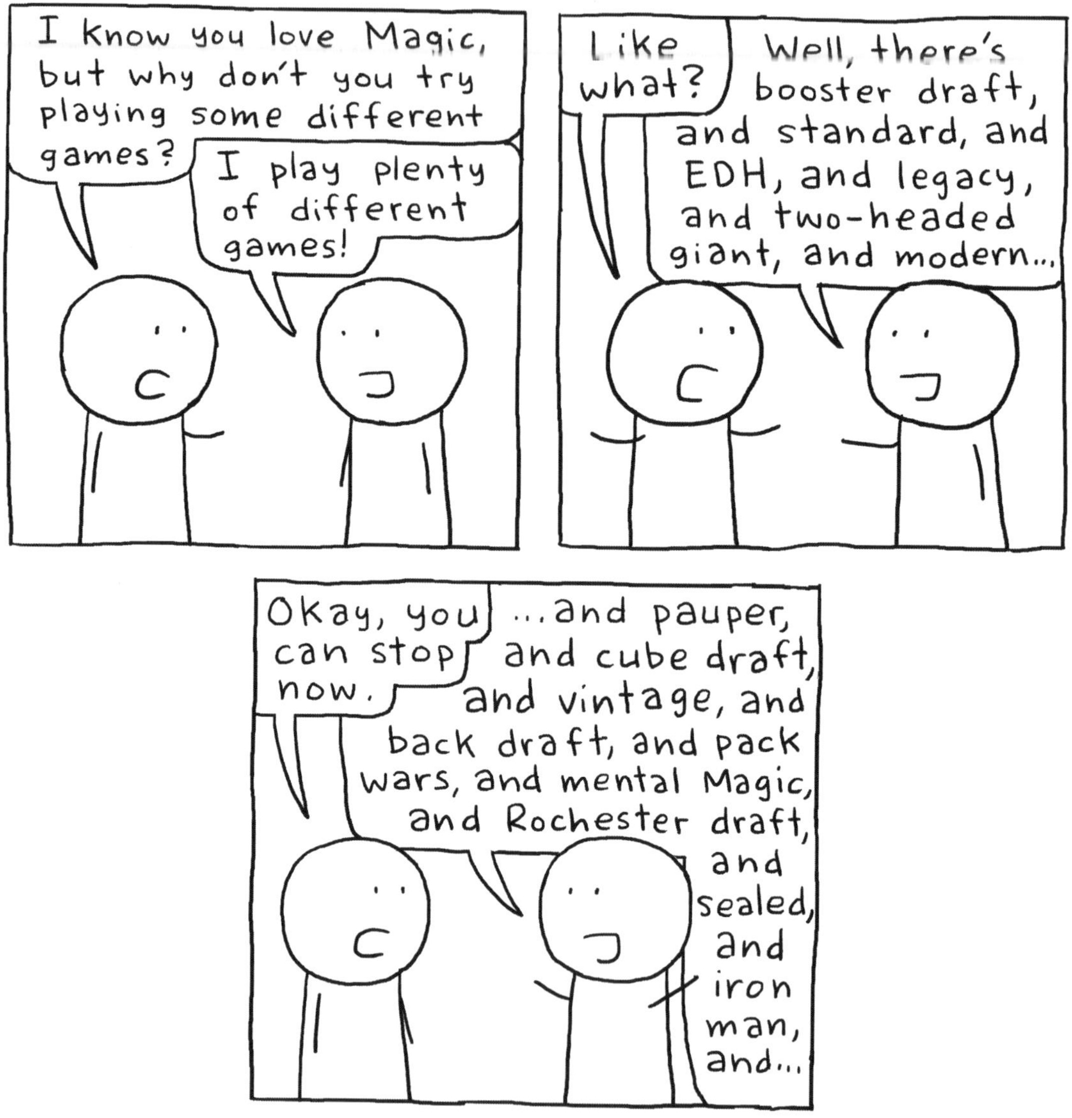
I know you love Magic, but why don't you try playing some different games?
I play plenty of different games!
Like what?
Well, there's booster draft, and standard, and EDH, and legacy, and two-headed giant, and modern...
Okay, you can stop now.
...and pauper, and cube draft, and vintage, and back draft, and pack wars, and mental Magic, and Rochester draft, and sealed, and iron man, and...

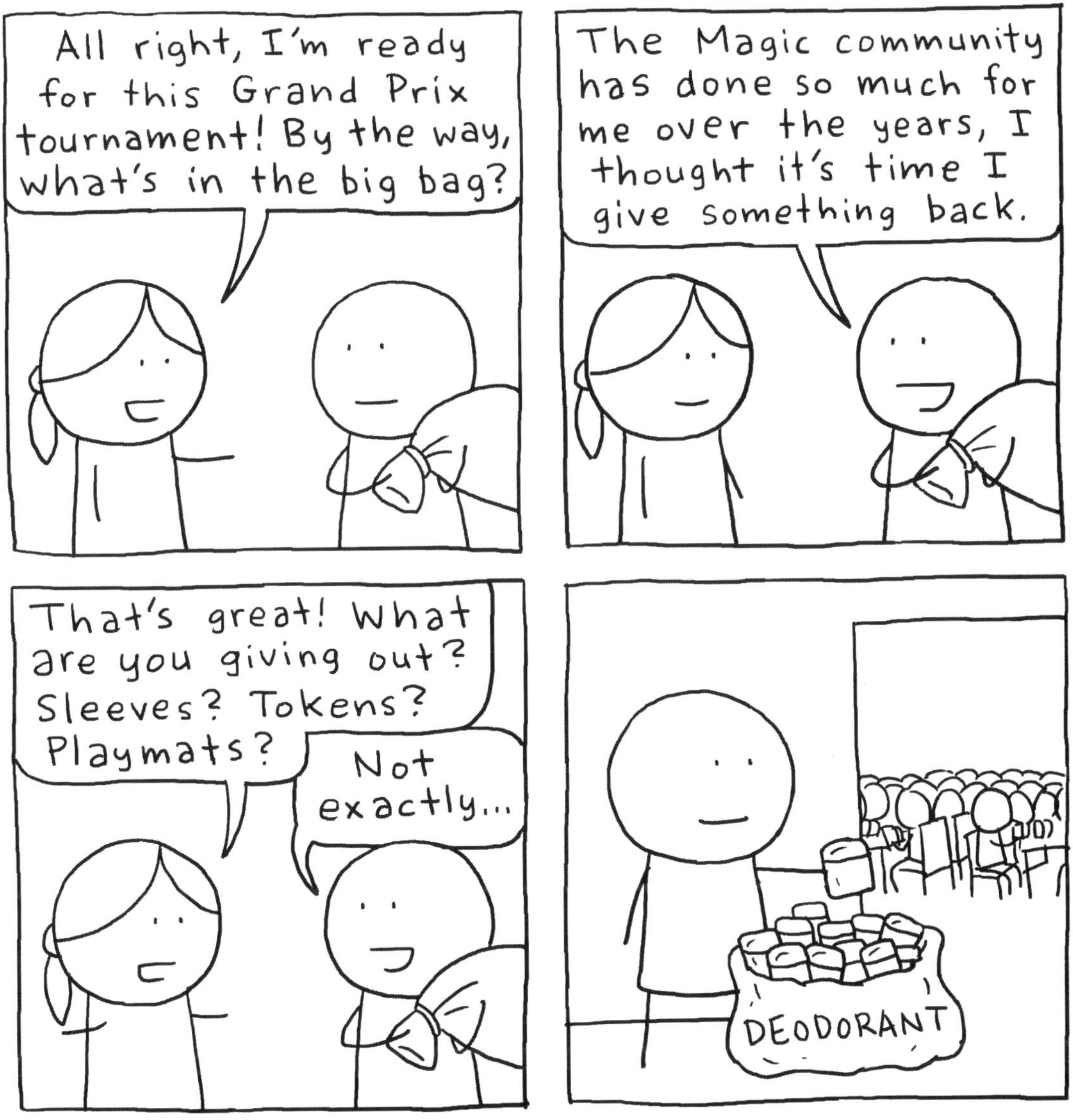
All right, I'm ready for this Grand Prix tournament! By the way, what's in the big bag?
The Magic community has done so much for me over the years, I thought it's time I give something back.
That's great! What are you giving out? Sleeves? Tokens? Playmats?
Not exactly...
DEODORANT

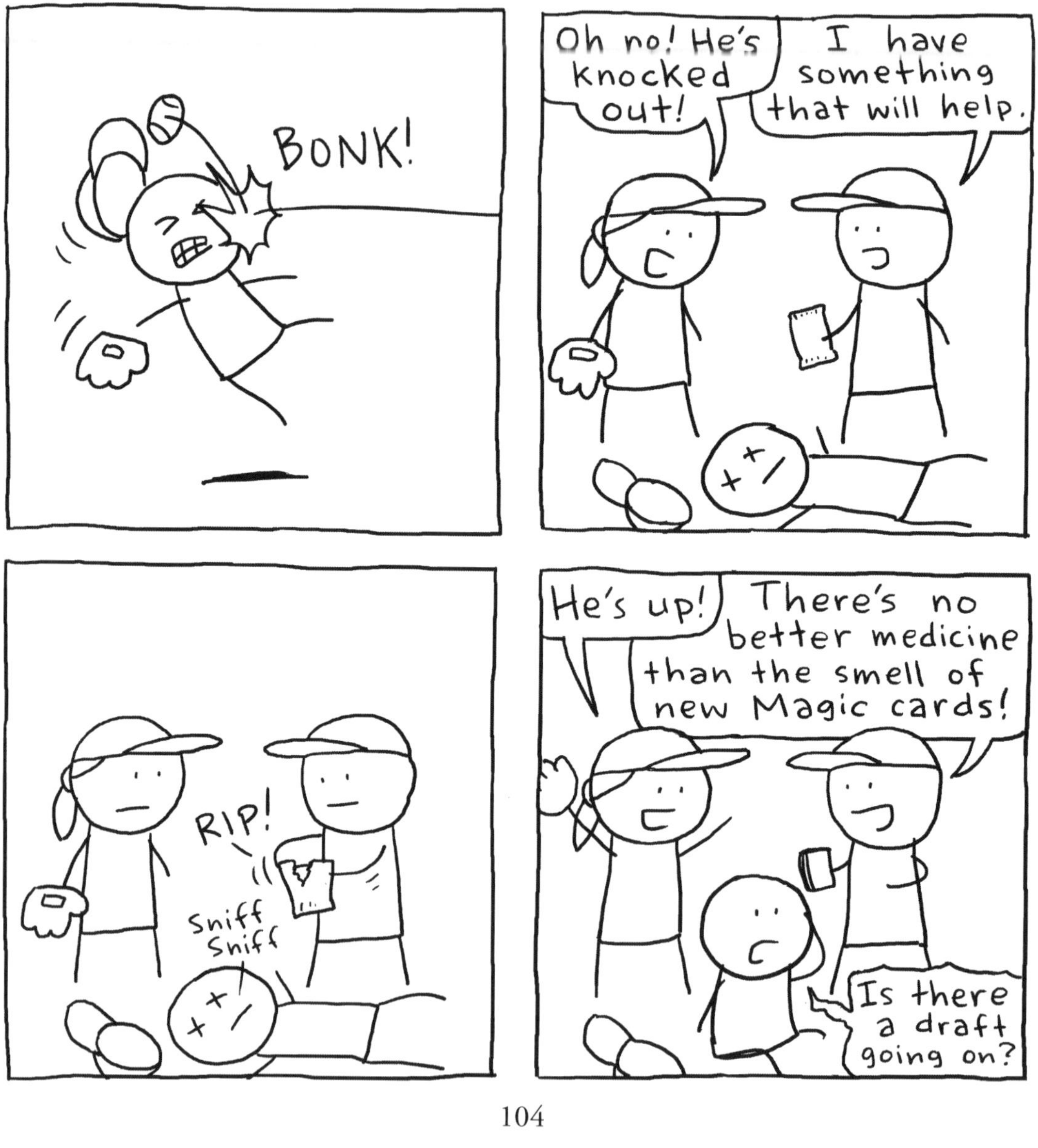
BONK!
Oh no! He's knocked out!
I have something that will help.
RIP!
Sniff Sniff
He's up!
There's no better medicine than the smell of new Magic cards!
Is there a draft going on?

Then...

I can't wait until I'm older and have a job making real money. Then I'll get all the Magic cards I want.

Now...

I wish I had more time to play Magic.

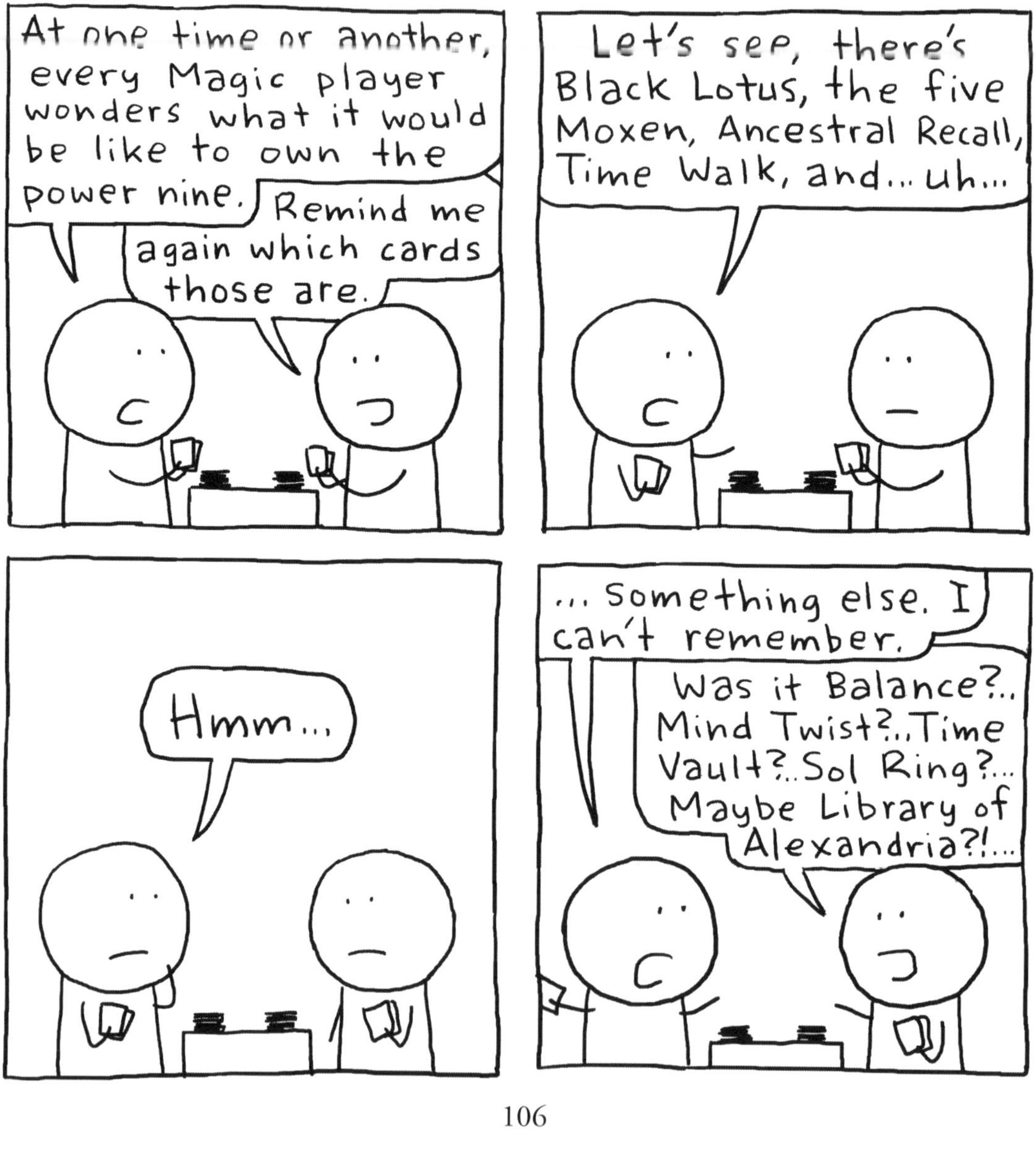
At one time or another, every Magic player wonders what it would be like to own the power nine.
Remind me again which cards those are.
Let's see, there's Black Lotus, the five Moxen, Ancestral Recall, Time Walk, and... uh...
Hmm...
... Something else. I can't remember.
Was it Balance?.. Mind Twist?.. Time Vault?.. Sol Ring?... Maybe Library of Alexandria?!...

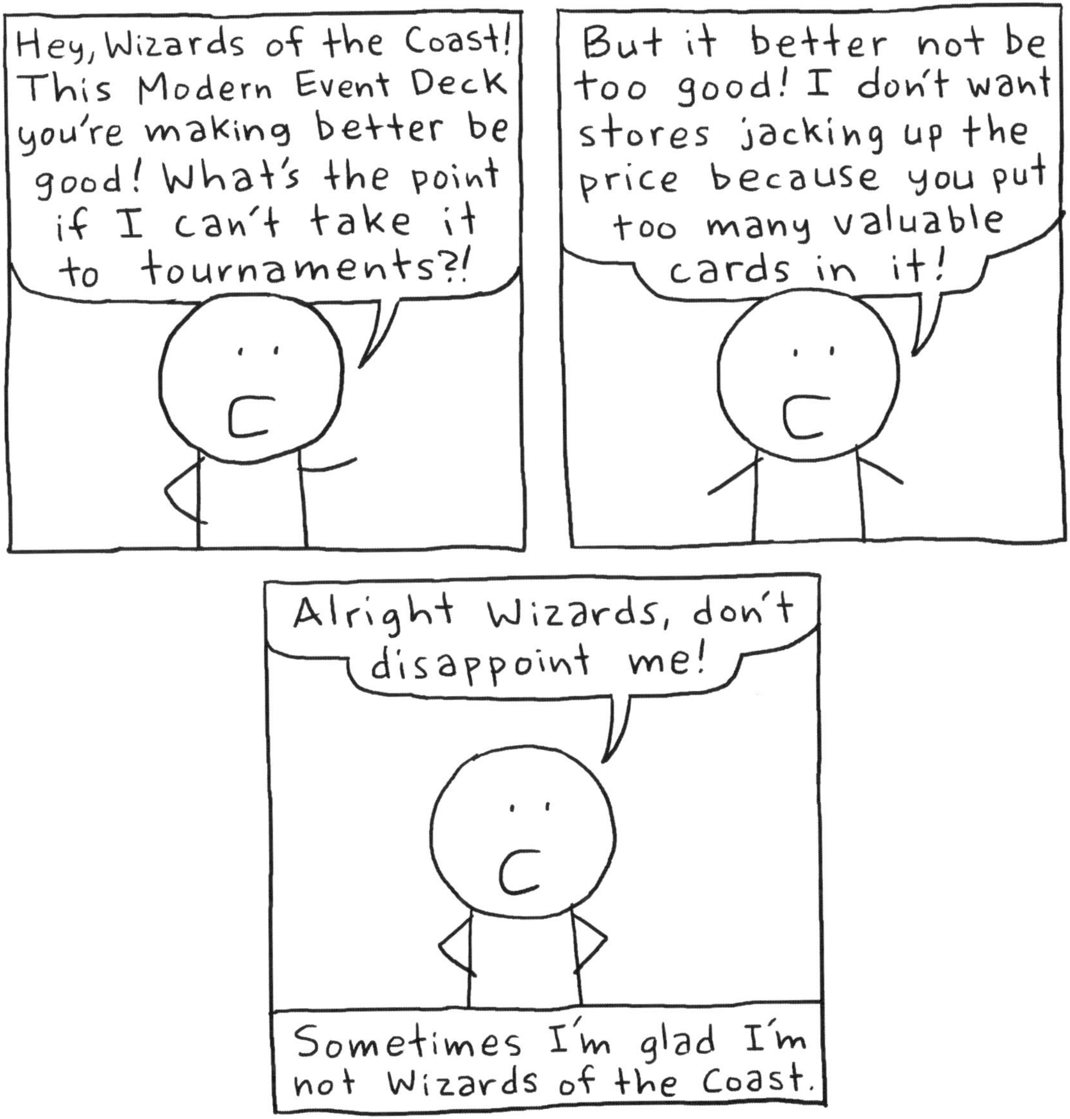
Hey, Wizards of the Coast! This Modern Event Deck you're making better be good! What's the point if I can't take it to tournaments?!
But it better not be too good! I don't want stores jacking up the price because you put too many valuable cards in it!
Alright Wizards, don't disappoint me!
Sometimes I'm glad I'm not Wizards of the Coast.

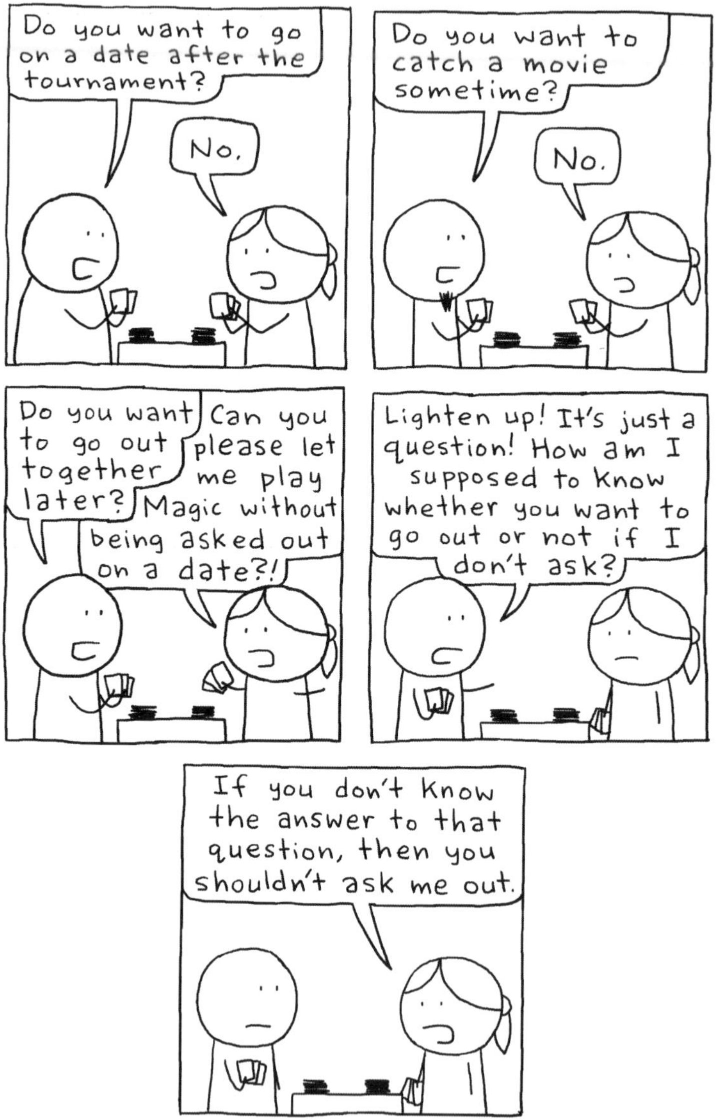
Do you want to go on a date after the tournament?
No.
Do you want to catch a movie sometime?
No.
Do you want to go out together later?
Can you please let me play Magic without being asked out on a date?!
Lighten up! It's just a question! How am I supposed to know whether you want to go out or not if I don't ask?
If you don't know the answer to that question, then you shouldn't ask me out.

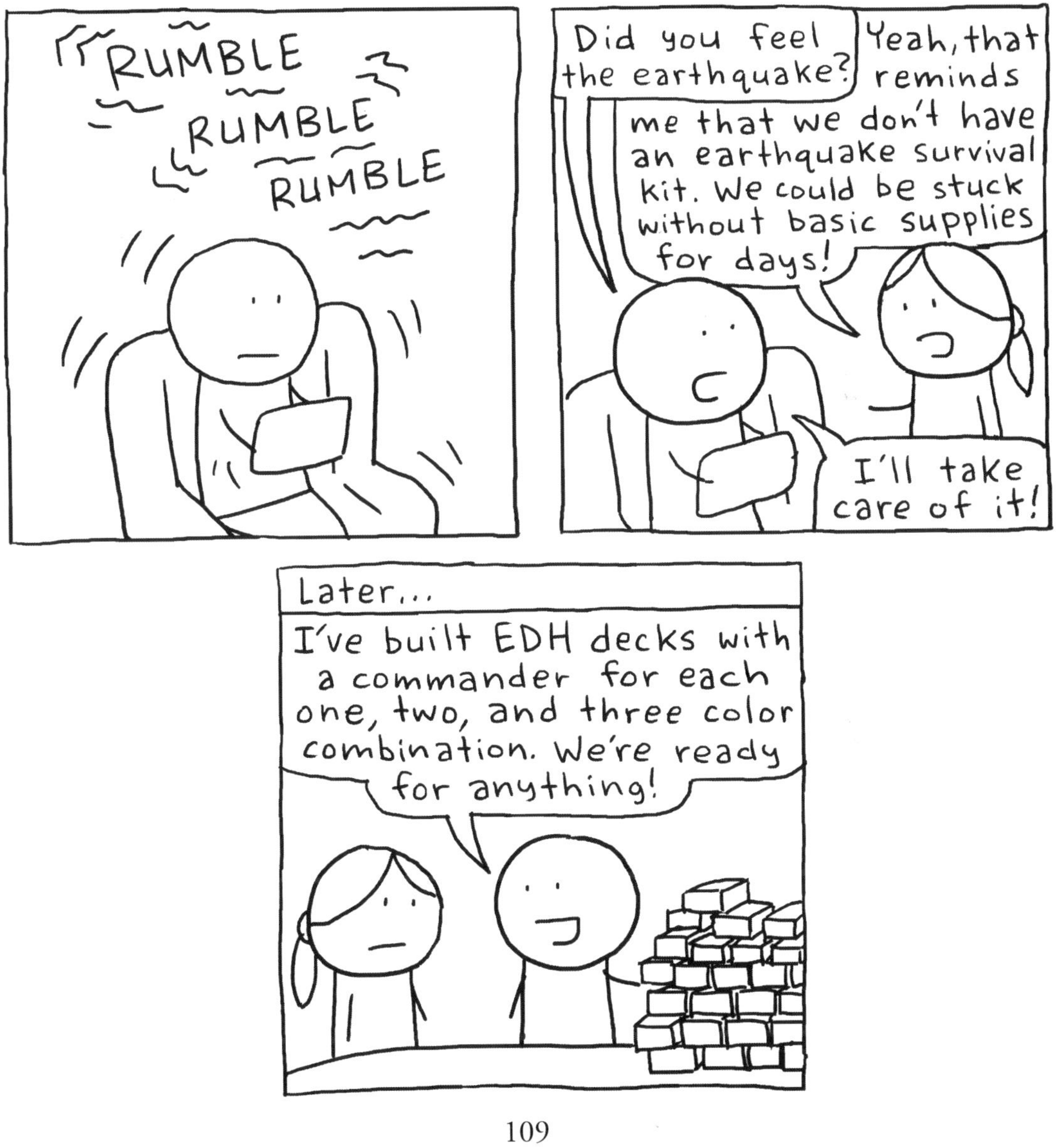
RUMBLE
RUMBLE
RUMBLE
Did you feel the earthquake?
Yeah, that reminds me that we don't have an earthquake survival kit. We could be stuck without basic supplies for days!
I'll take care of it!
Later...
I've built EDH decks with a commander for each one, two, and three color combination. We're ready for anything!

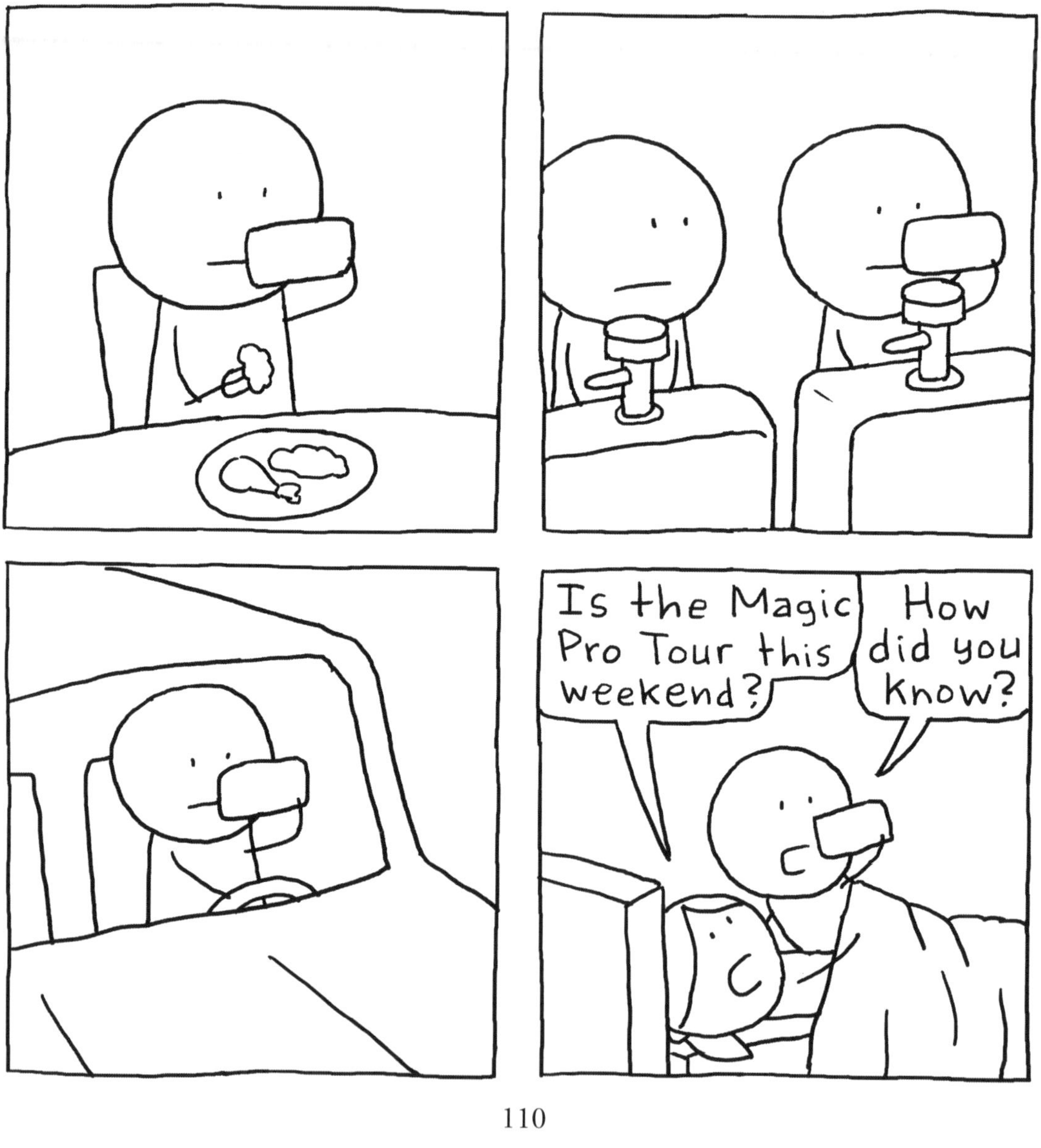
Is the Magic Pro Tour this weekend?
How did you know?

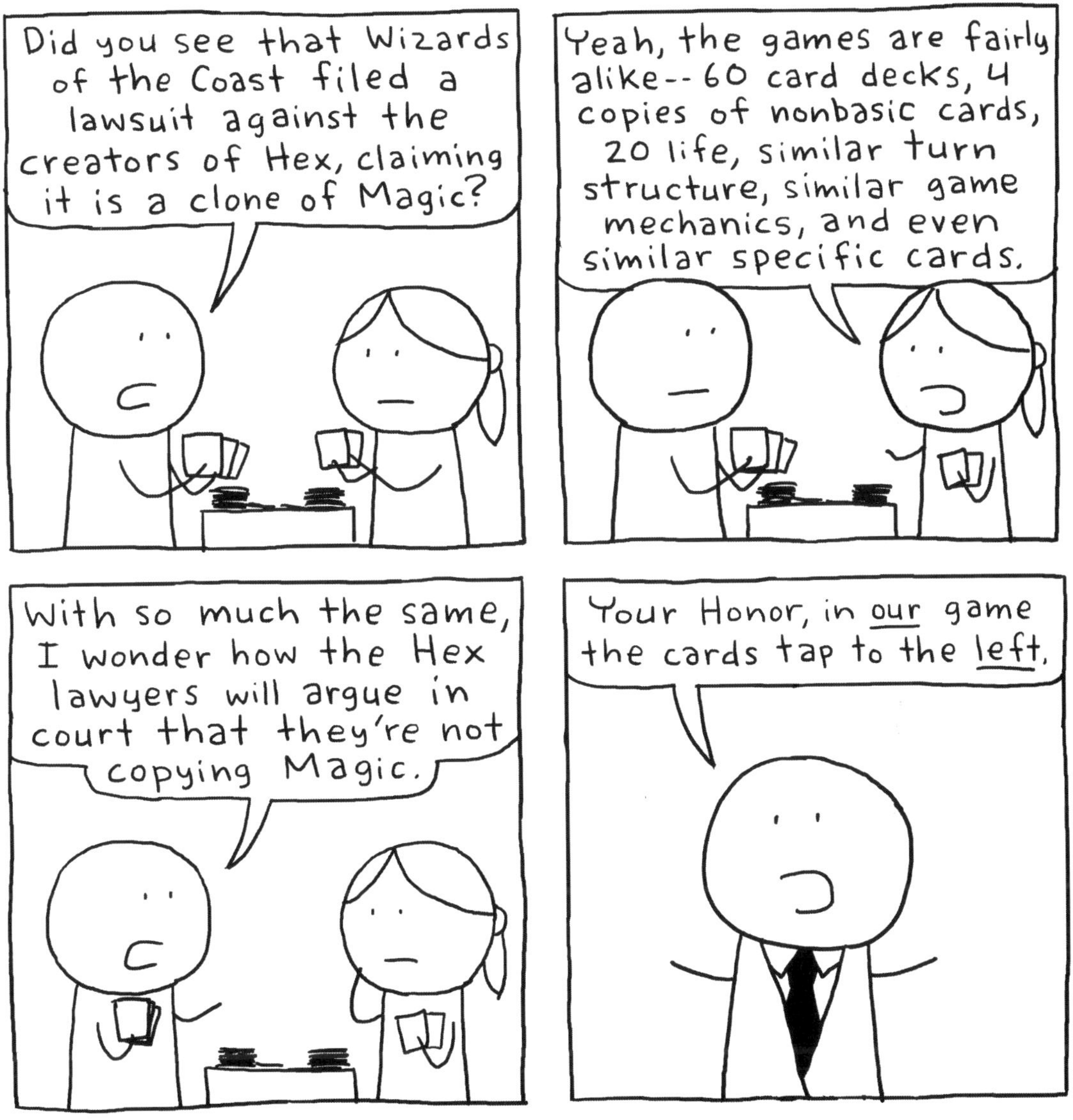
Did you see that Wizards of the Coast filed a lawsuit against the creators of Hex, claiming it is a clone of Magic?
Yeah, the games are fairly alike--60 card decks, 4 copies of nonbasic cards, 20 life, similar turn structure, similar game mechanics, and even similar specific cards.
With so much the same, I wonder how the Hex lawyers will argue in court that they're not copying Magic.
Your Honor, in our game the cards tap to the left.

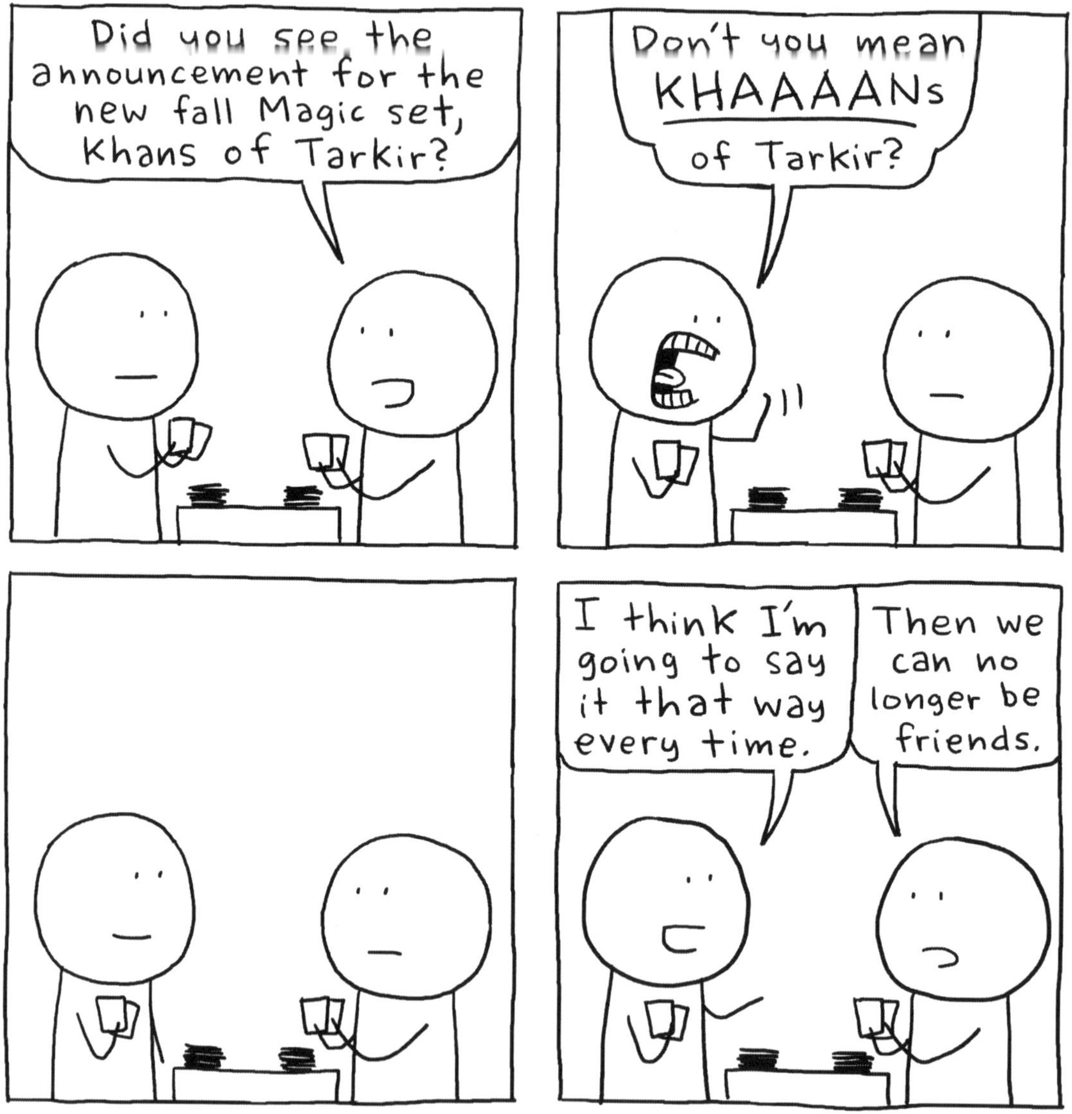
Did you see the announcement for the new fall Magic set, Khans of Tarkir?
Don't you mean KHAAAANs of Tarkir?
I think I'm going to say it that way every time.
Then we can no longer be friends.

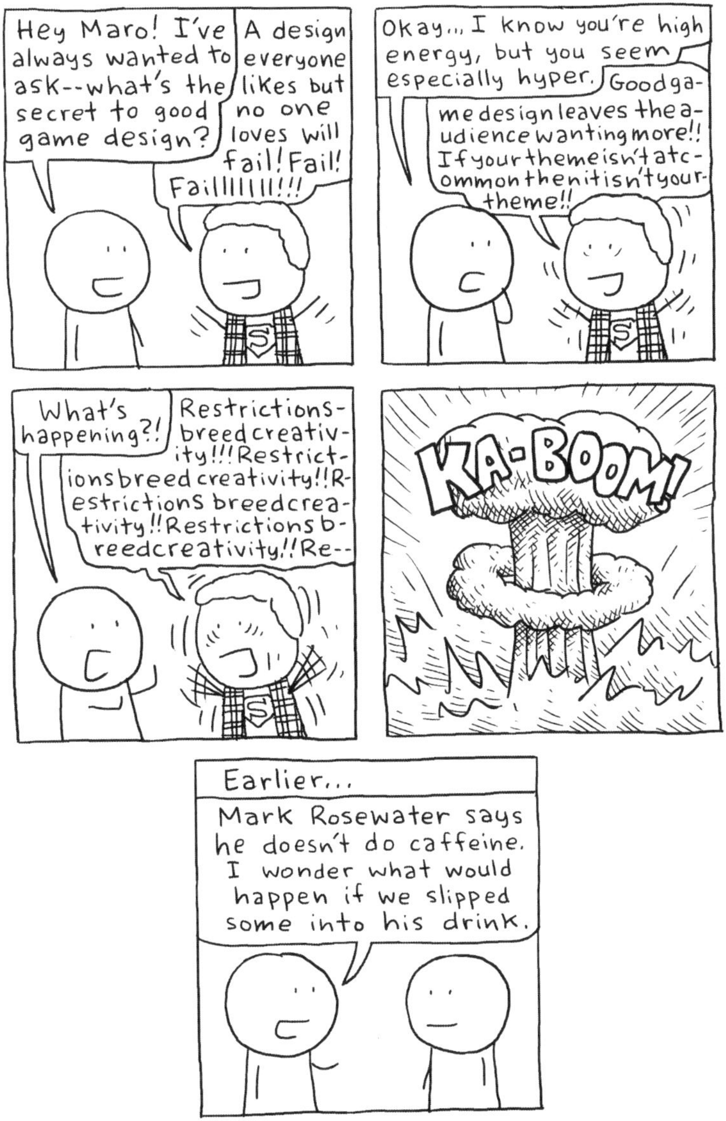
Hey Maro! I've always wanted to ask--what's the secret to good game design?
A design everyone likes but no one loves will fail! Fail! Faillllllll!!!
Okay... I know you're high energy, but you seem especially hyper.
Good game design leaves the audience wanting more!! If your theme isn't atcommon then it isn't your theme!!
What's happening?!
Restrictions breed creativity!!! Restrictions breed creativity!! Restrictions breed creativity!! Restrictions breed creativity!! Re--
KA-BOOM!
Earlier...
Mark Rosewater says he doesn't do caffeine. I wonder what would happen if we slipped some into his drink.

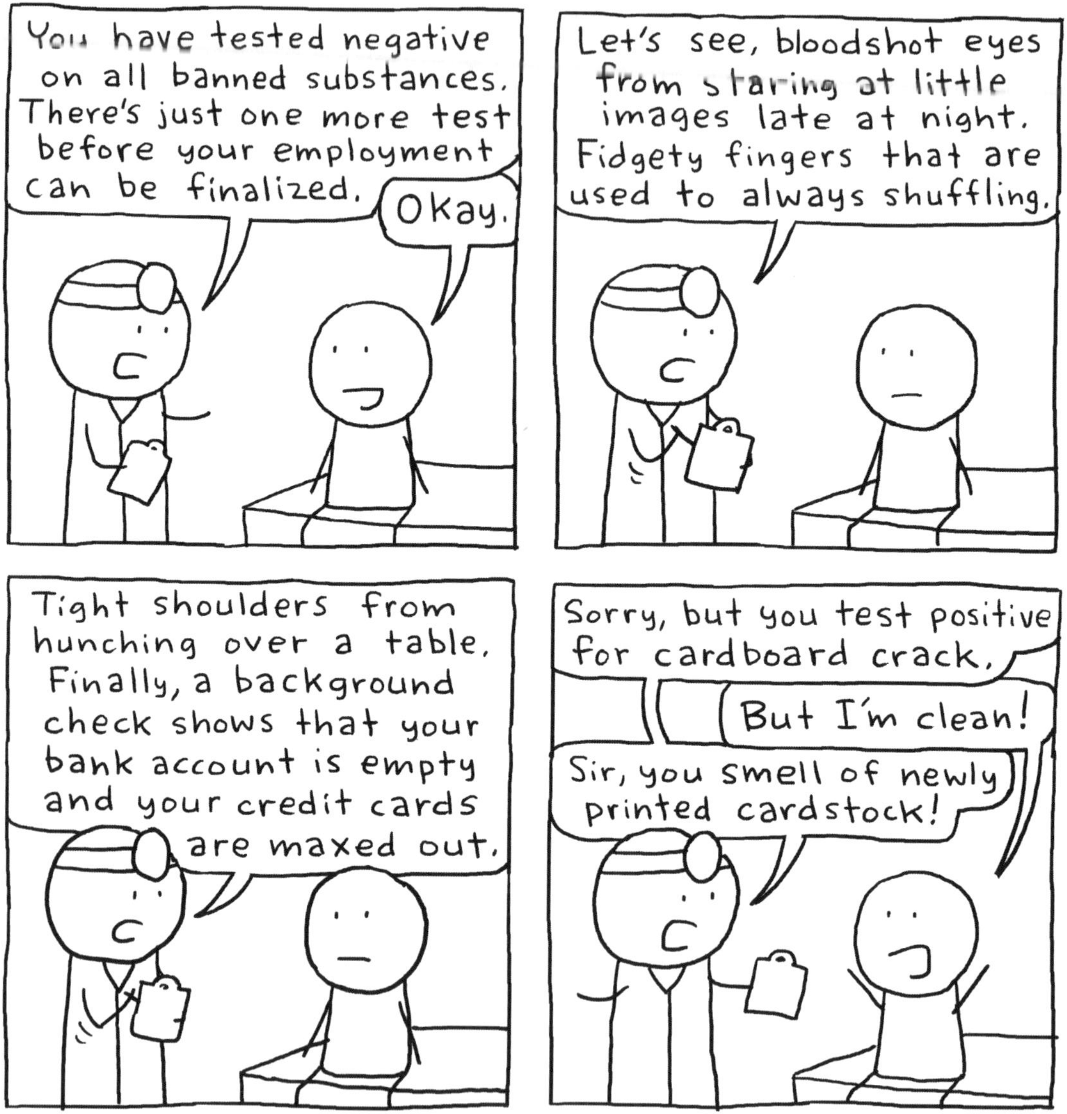
You have tested negative on all banned substances. There's just one more test before your employment can be finalized.
Okay.
Let's see, bloodshot eyes from staring at little images late at night. Fidgety fingers that are used to always shuffling.
Tight shoulders from hunching over a table. Finally, a background check shows that your bank account is empty and your credit cards are maxed out.
Sorry, but you test positive for cardboard crack.
But I'm clean!
Sir, you smell of newly printed cardstock!

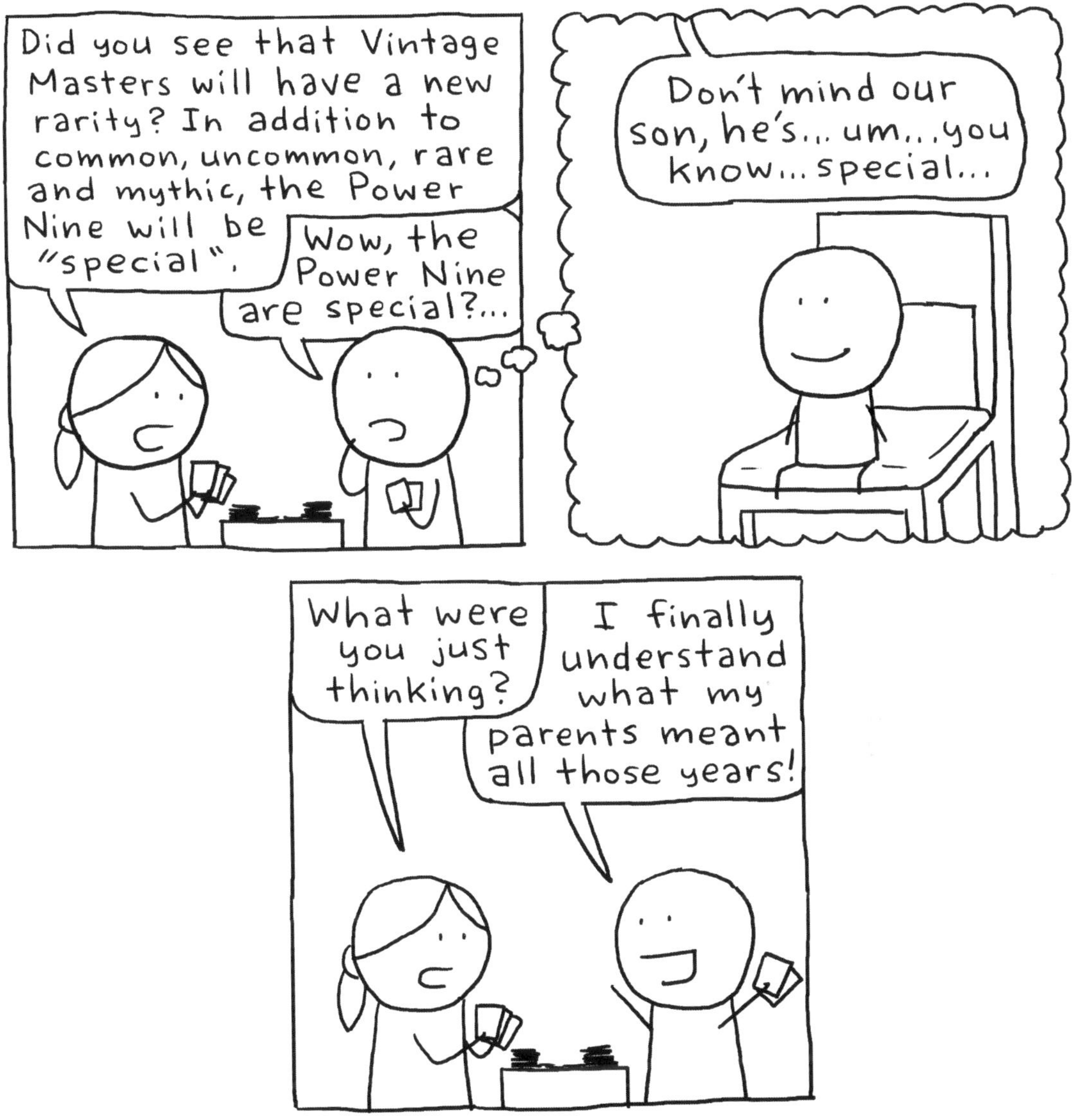
Did you see that Vintage Masters will have a new rarity? In addition to common, uncommon, rare and mythic, the Power Nine will be "special".
Wow, the Power Nine are special?...
Don't mind our son, he's... um... you know... special...
What were you just thinking?
I finally understand what my parents meant all those years!

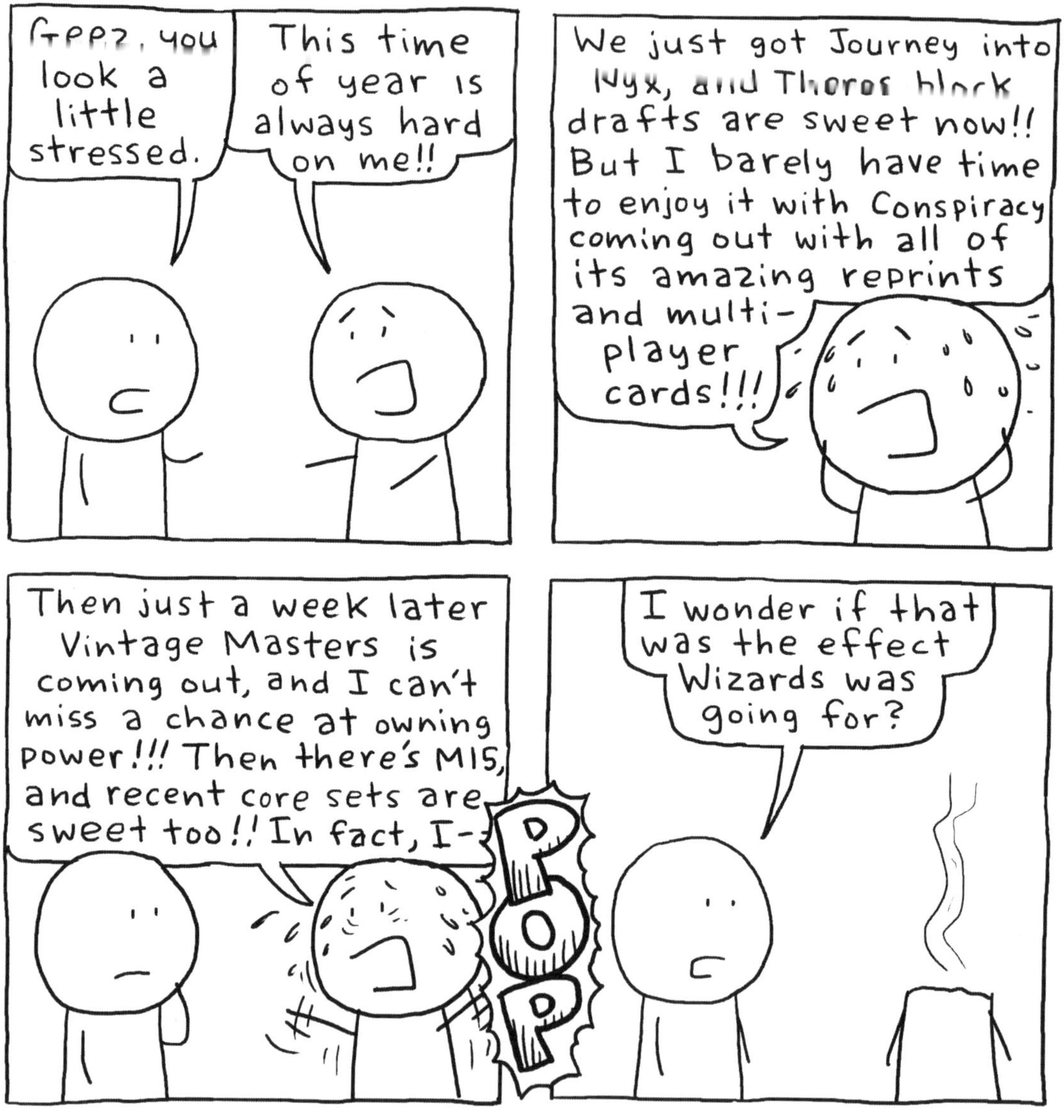
Geez, you look a little stressed.
This time of year is always hard on me!!
We just got Journey into Nyx, and Theros block drafts are sweet now!! But I barely have time to enjoy it with Conspiracy coming out with all of its amazing reprints and multi-player cards!!!
Then just a week later Vintage Masters is coming out, and I can't miss a chance at owning power!!! Then there's M15, and recent core sets are sweet too!! In fact, I--
POP
I wonder if that was the effect Wizards was going for?

Wow, it's beautiful outside today!
We should do something to take advantage of this great weather!
It sure is nice playing Magic with the curtains open!
The Sun's reflection off my sleeves is hurting my eyes.

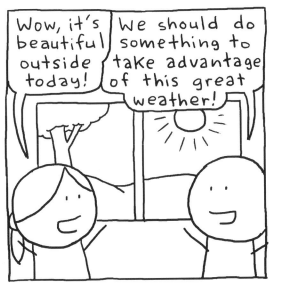

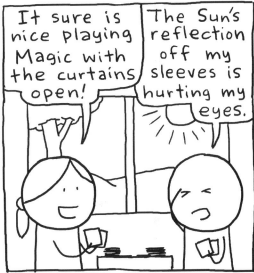

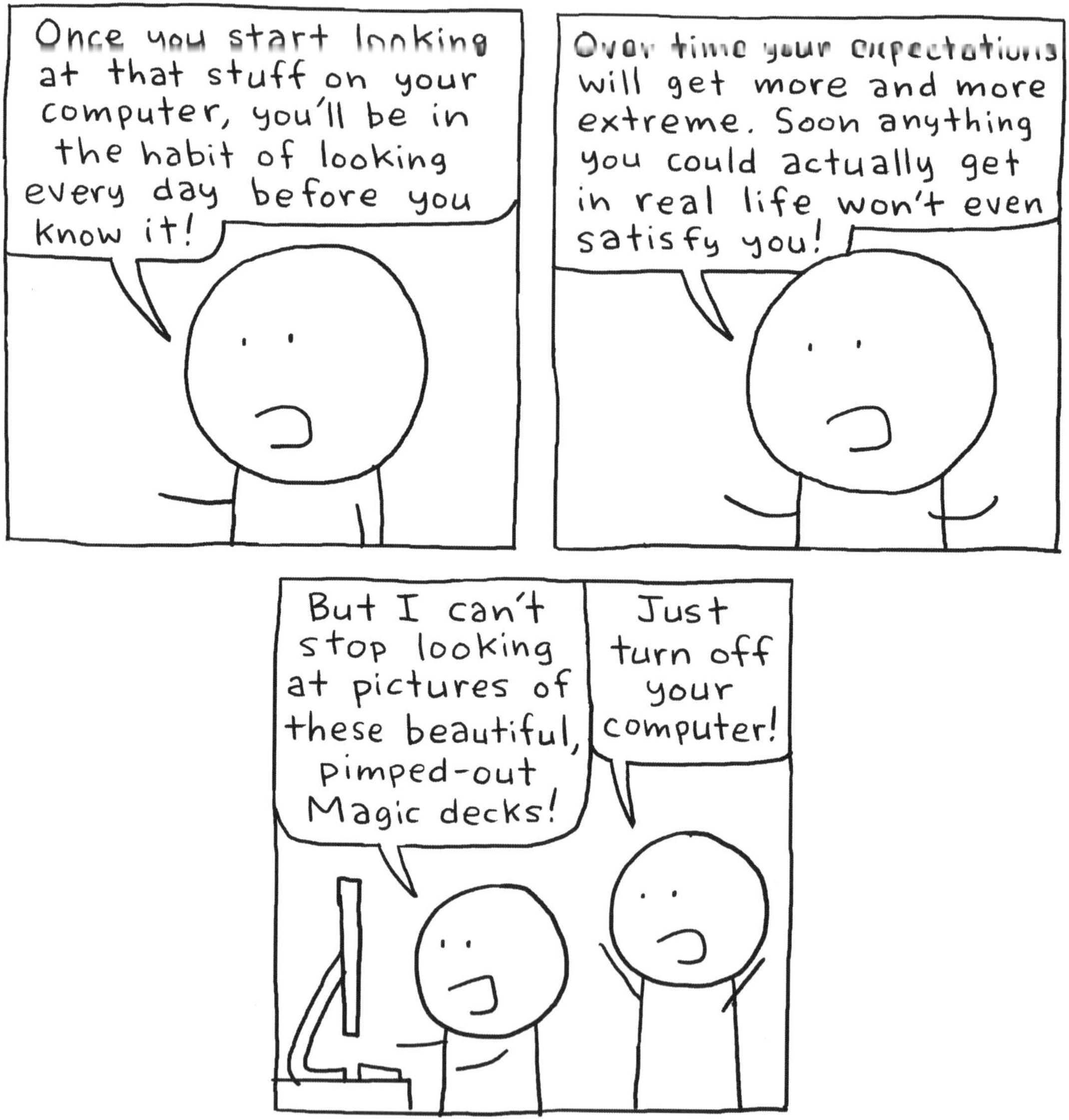
Once you start looking at that stuff on your computer, you'll be in the habit of looking every day before you know it!
Over time your expectations will get more and more extreme. Soon anything you could actually get in real life won't even satisfy you!
But I can't stop looking at pictures of these beautiful, pimped-out Magic decks!
Just turn off your computer!

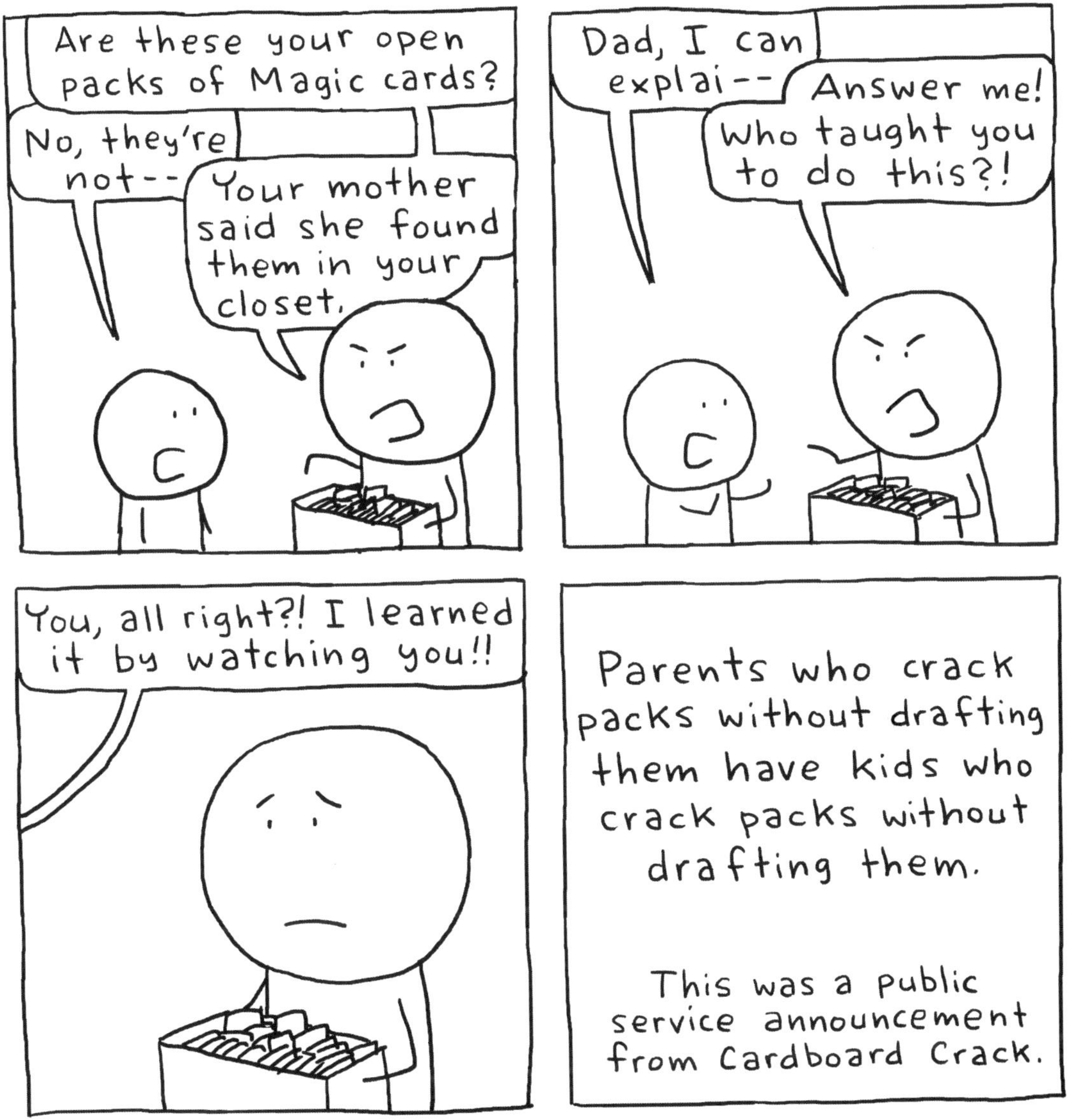
Are these your open packs of Magic cards?
No, they're not--
Your mother said she found them in your closet.
Dad, I can explai--
Answer me! Who taught you to do this?!
You, all right?! I learned it by watching you!!
Parents who crack packs without drafting them have kids who crack packs without drafting them.
This was a public service announcement from Cardboard Crack.

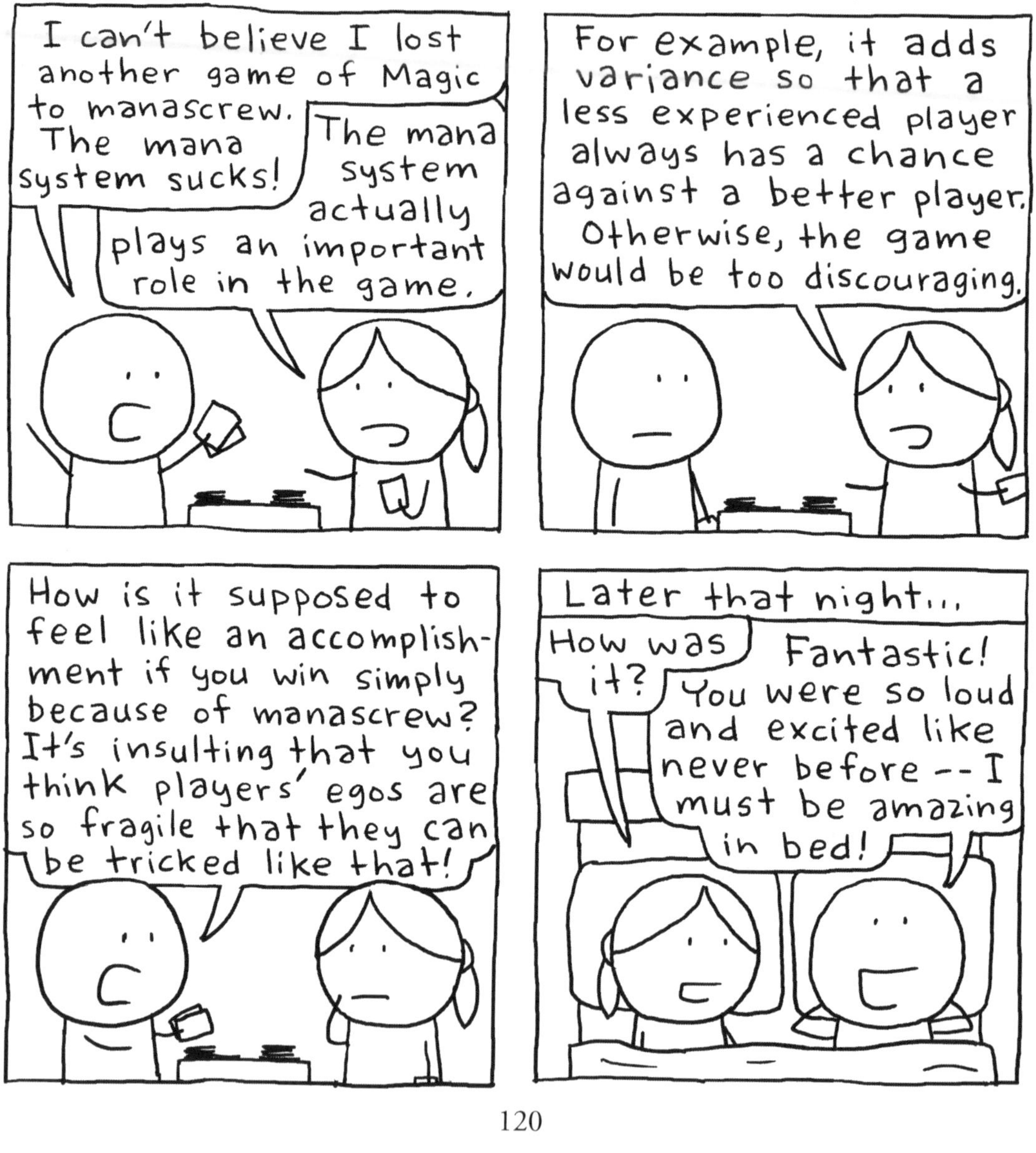
I can't believe I lost another game of Magic to manascrew. The mana system sucks!
The mana system actually plays an important role in the game.
For example, it adds variance so that a less experienced player always has a chance against a better player. Otherwise, the game would be too discouraging.
How is it supposed to feel like an accomplish-ment if you win simply because of manascrew? It's insulting that you think players' egos are so fragile that they can be tricked like that!
Later that night...
How was it?
Fantastic! You were so loud and excited like never before -- I must be amazing in bed!

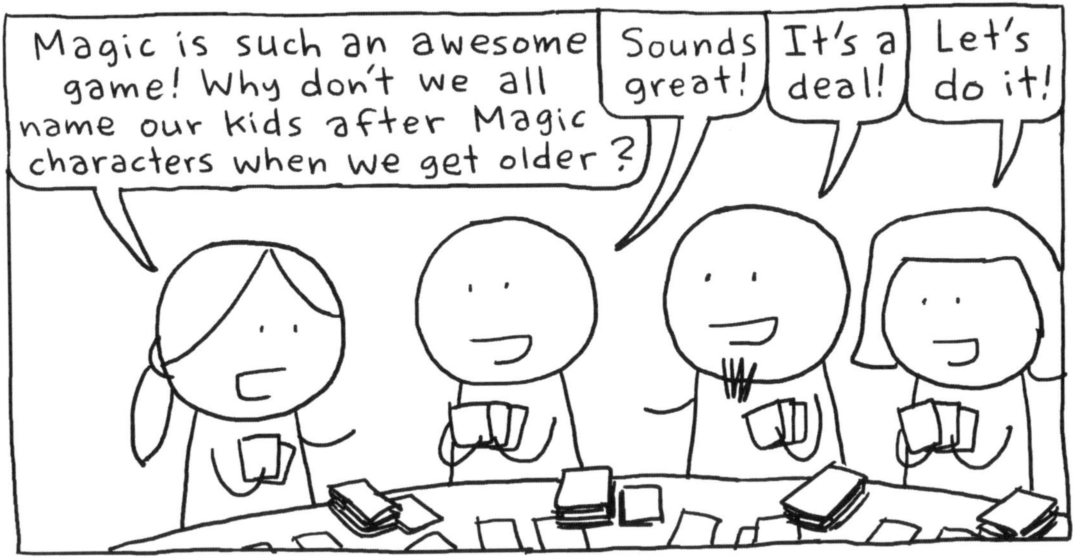
Magic is such an awesome game! Why don't we all name our kids after Magic characters when we get older?
Sounds great!
It's a deal!
Let's do it!

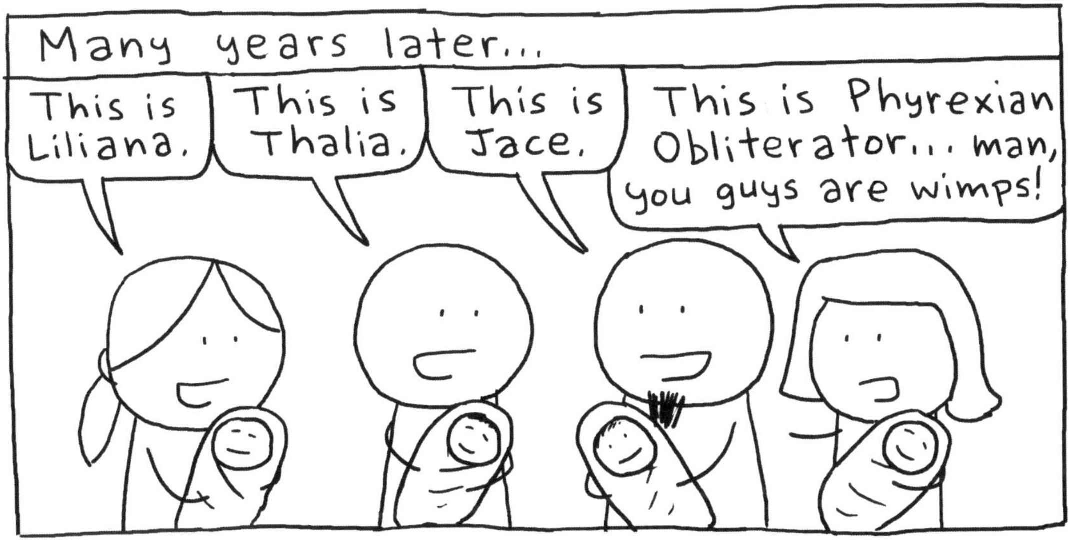
Many years later...
This is Liliana.
This is Thalia.
This is Jace.
This is Phyrexian Obliterator... man, you guys are wimps!

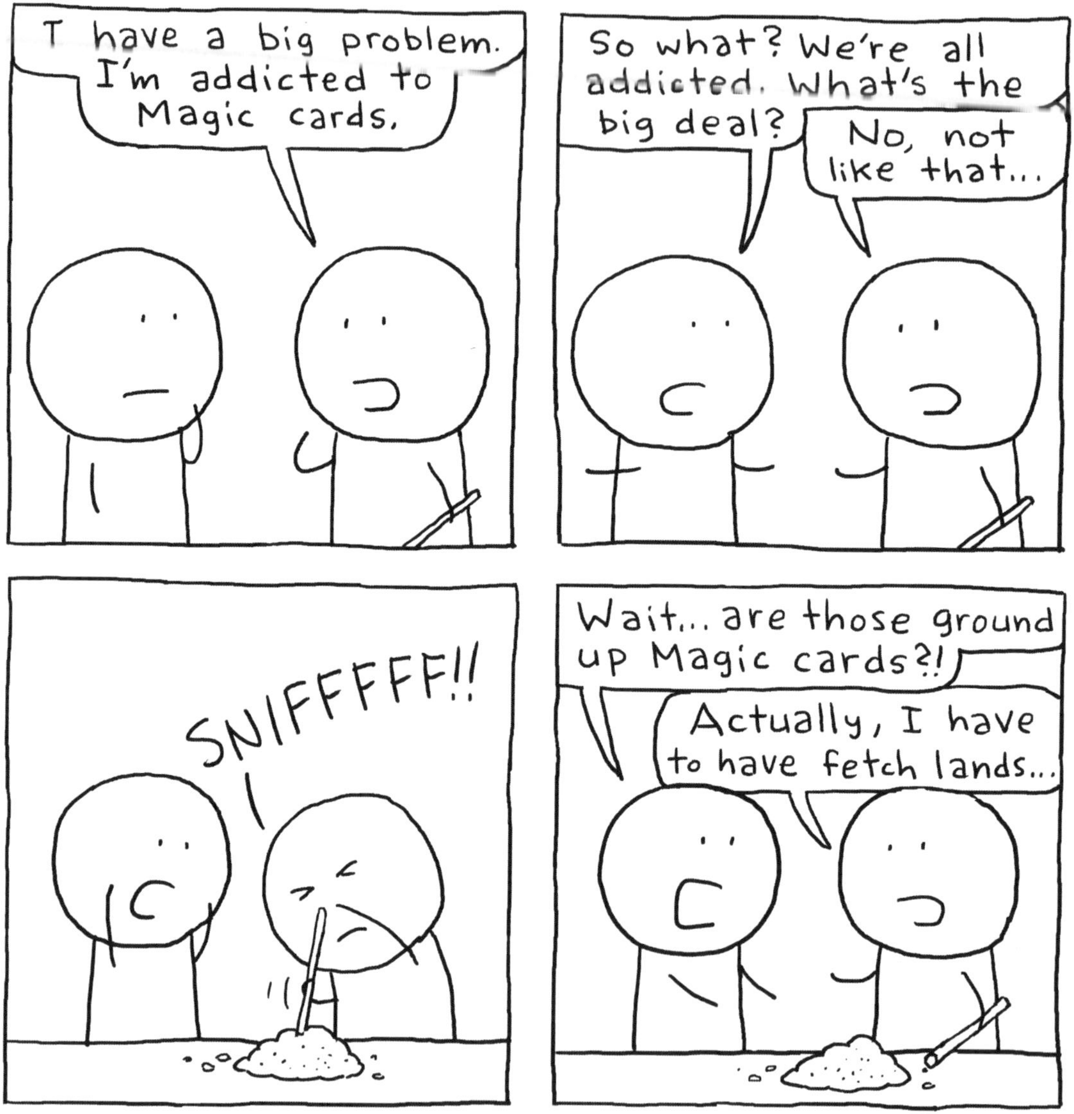
I have a big problem. I'm addicted to Magic cards.
So what? We're all addicted. What's the big deal?
No, not like that...
SNIFFFFFF!!
Wait... are those ground up Magic cards?!
Actually, I have to have fetch lands...

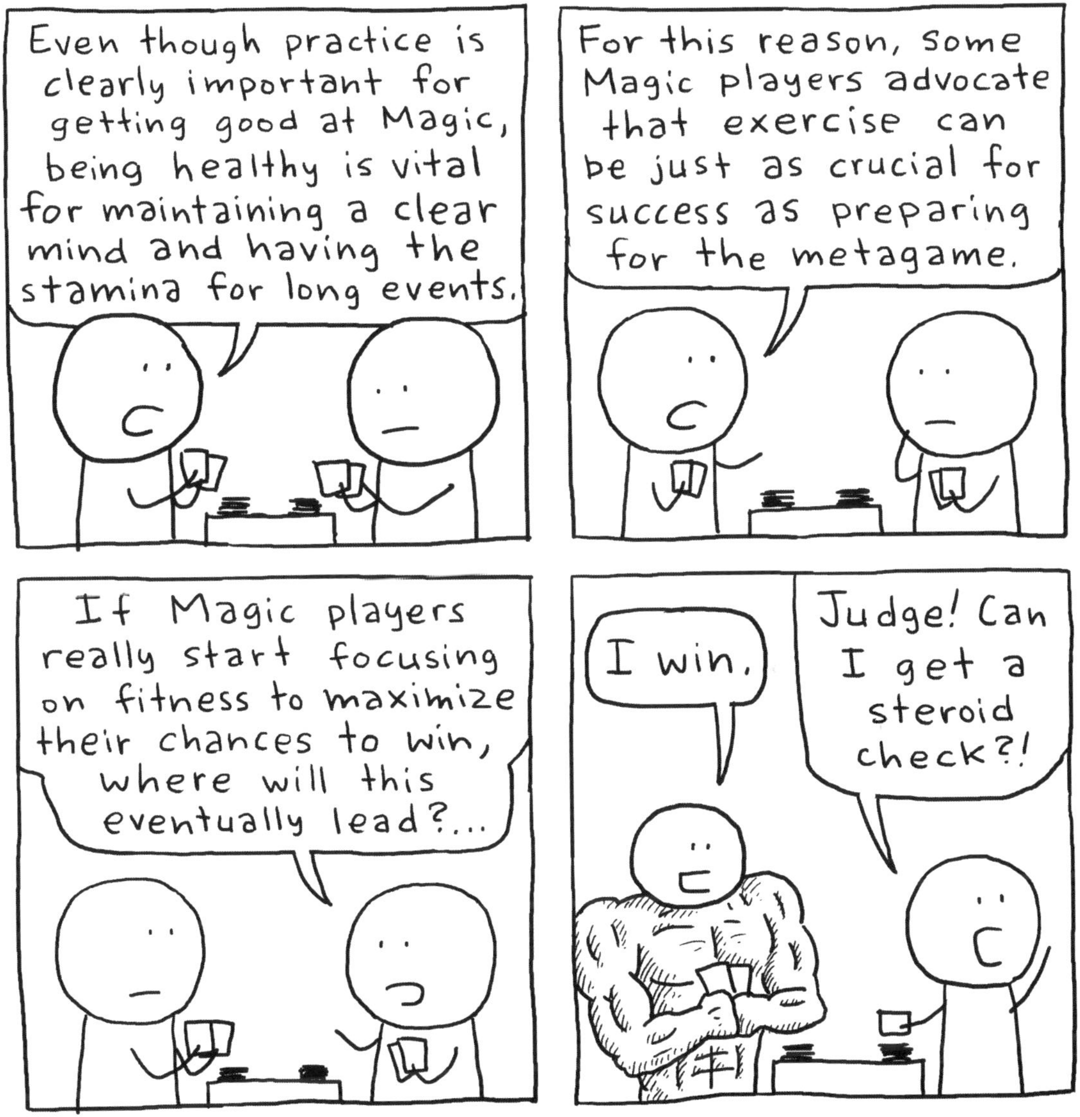
Even though practice is clearly important for getting good at Magic, being healthy is vital for maintaining a clear mind and having the stamina for long events.
For this reason, some Magic players advocate that exercise can be just as crucial for success as preparing for the metagame.
If Magic players really start focusing on fitness to maximize their chances to win, where will this eventually lead?...
I win.
Judge! Can I get a steroid check?!

The hardest part of transitioning from being a beginning Magic player...

I finished my first tournament level deck. What do you think?

Looks good! Now just spend between $100 and $400 on your mana base and you'll be good to go!

You're screwing with me, right?

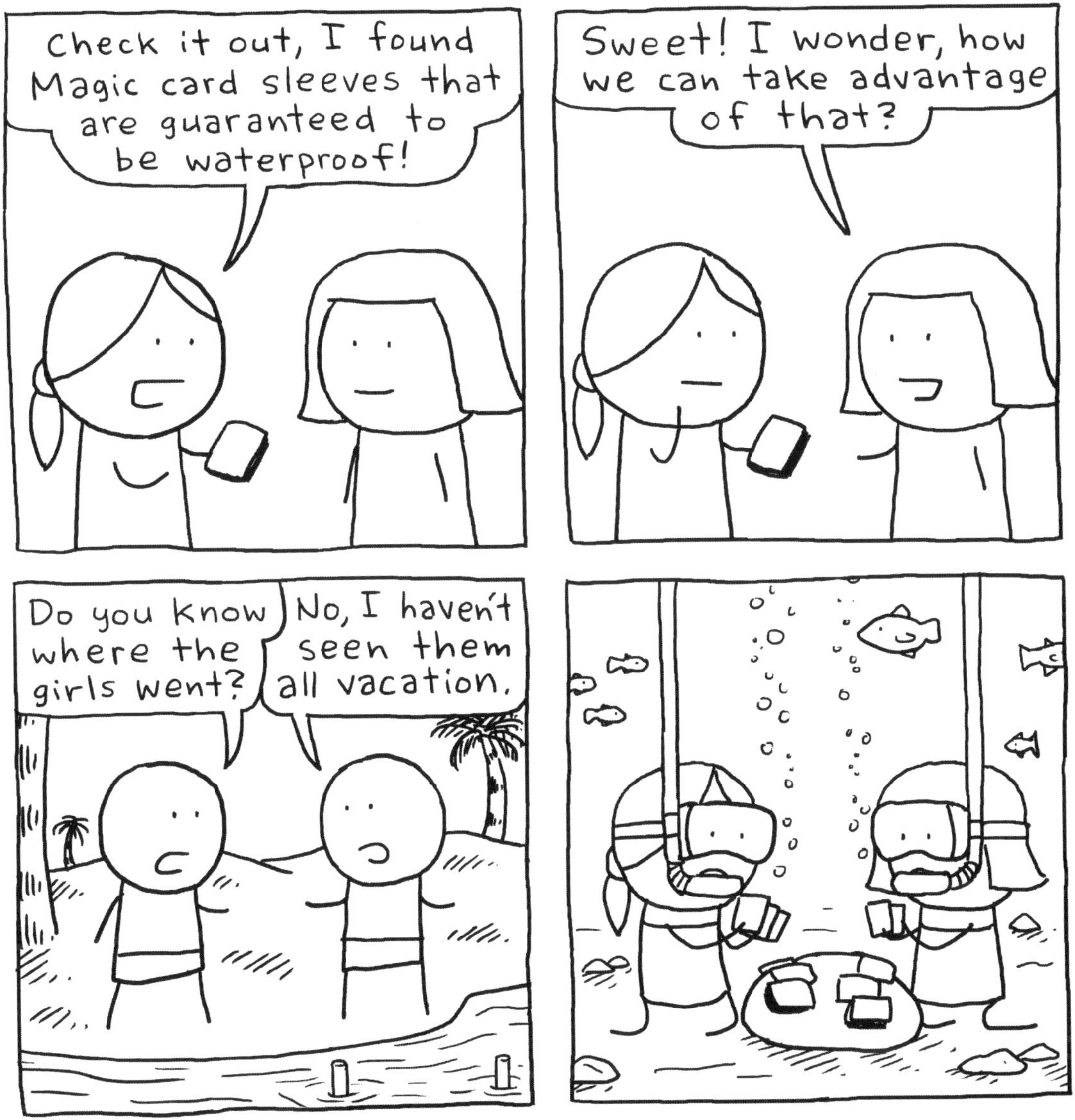
Check it out, I found Magic card sleeves that are guaranteed to be waterproof!
Sweet! I wonder, how we can take advantage of that?
Do you know where the girls went?
No, I haven't seen them all vacation.

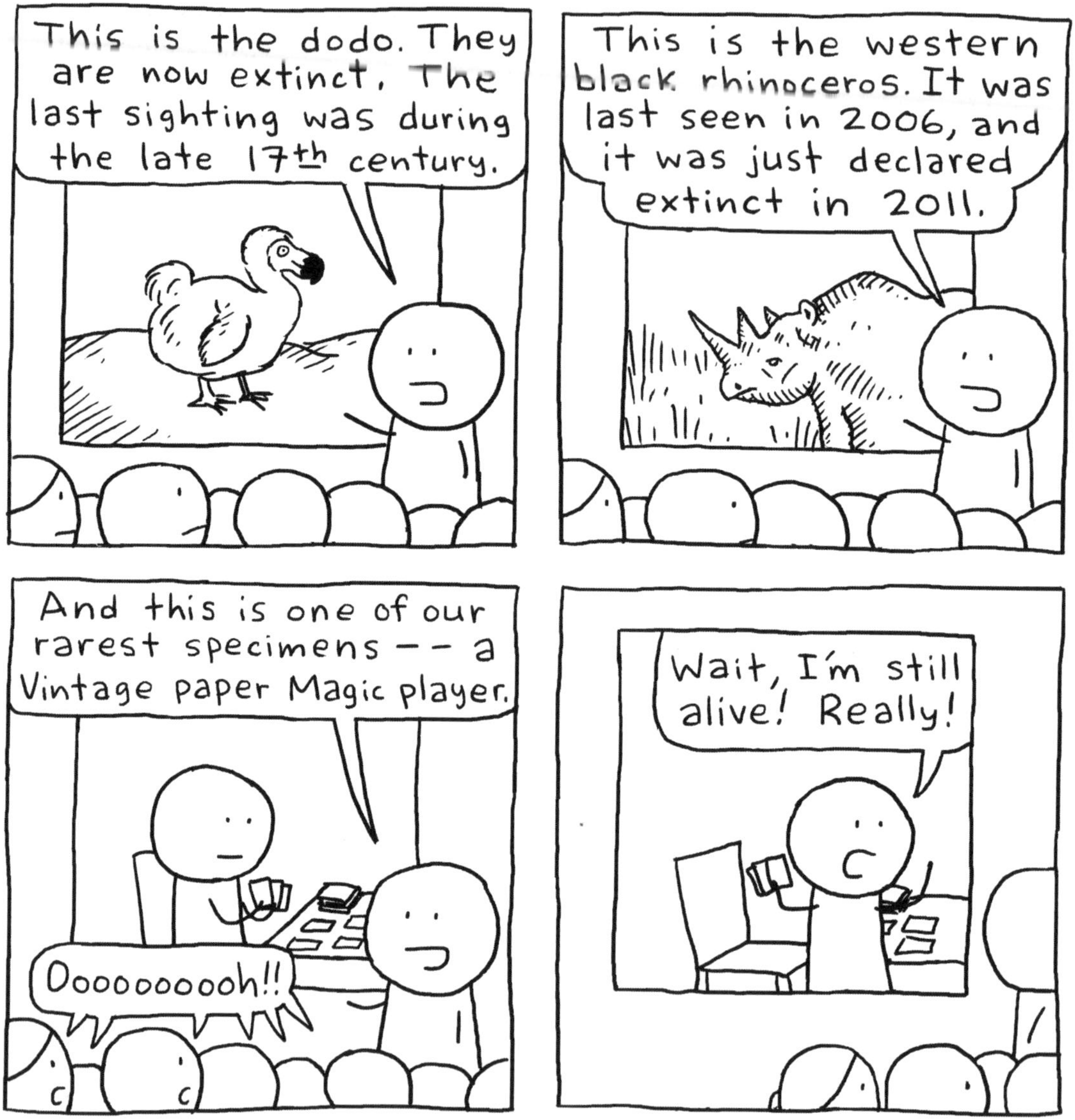
This is the dodo. They are now extinct. The last sighting was during the late 17th century.
This is the western black rhinoceros. It was last seen in 2006, and it was just declared extinct in 2011.
And this is one of our rarest specimens -- a Vintage paper Magic player.
Ooooooooooh!!
Wait, I'm still alive! Really!

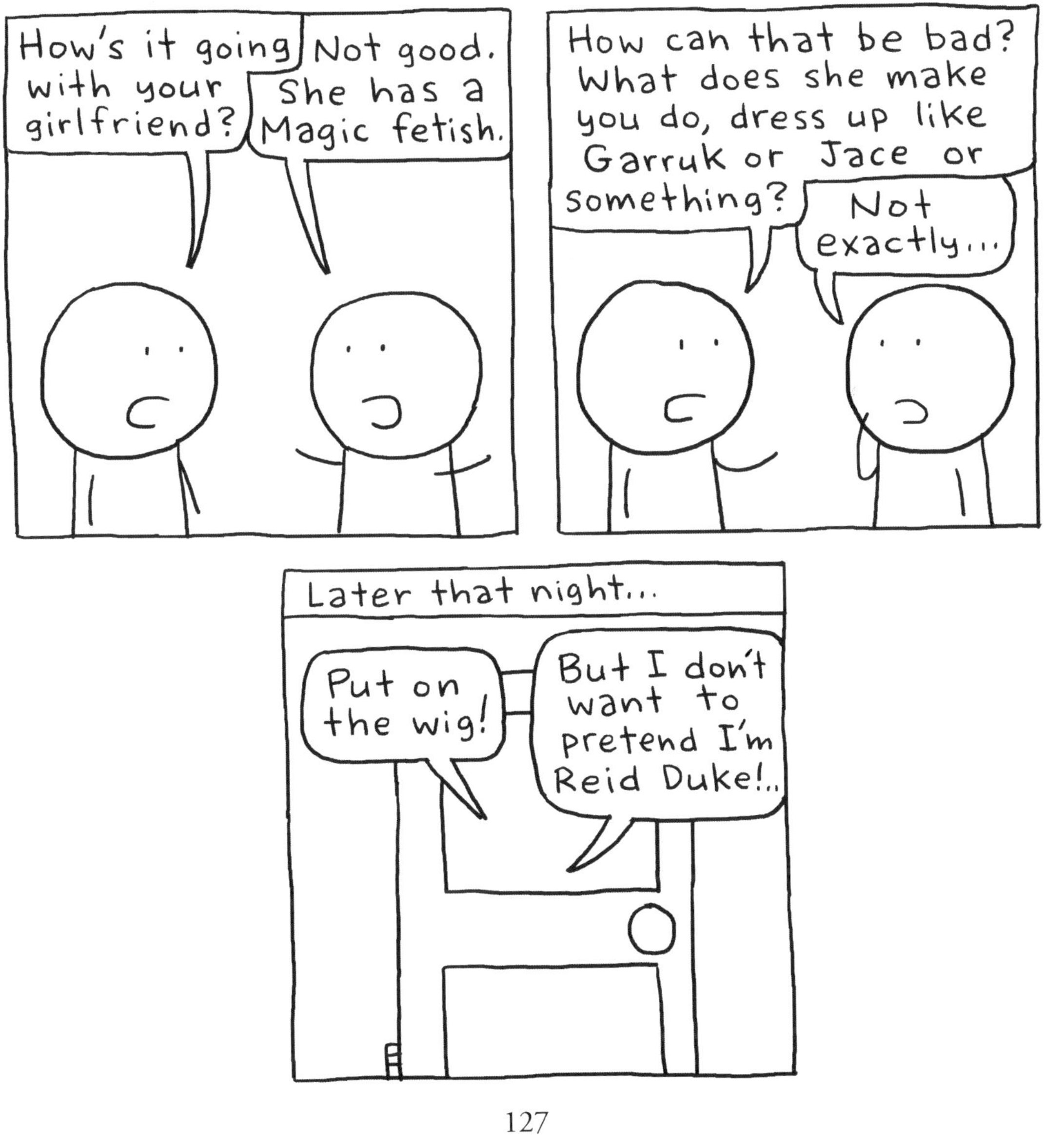
How's it going with your girlfriend?
Not good. She has a Magic fetish.
How can that be bad? What does she make you do, dress up like Garruk or Jace or something?
Not exactly...
Later that night...
Put on the wig!
But I don't want to pretend I'm Reid Duke!..

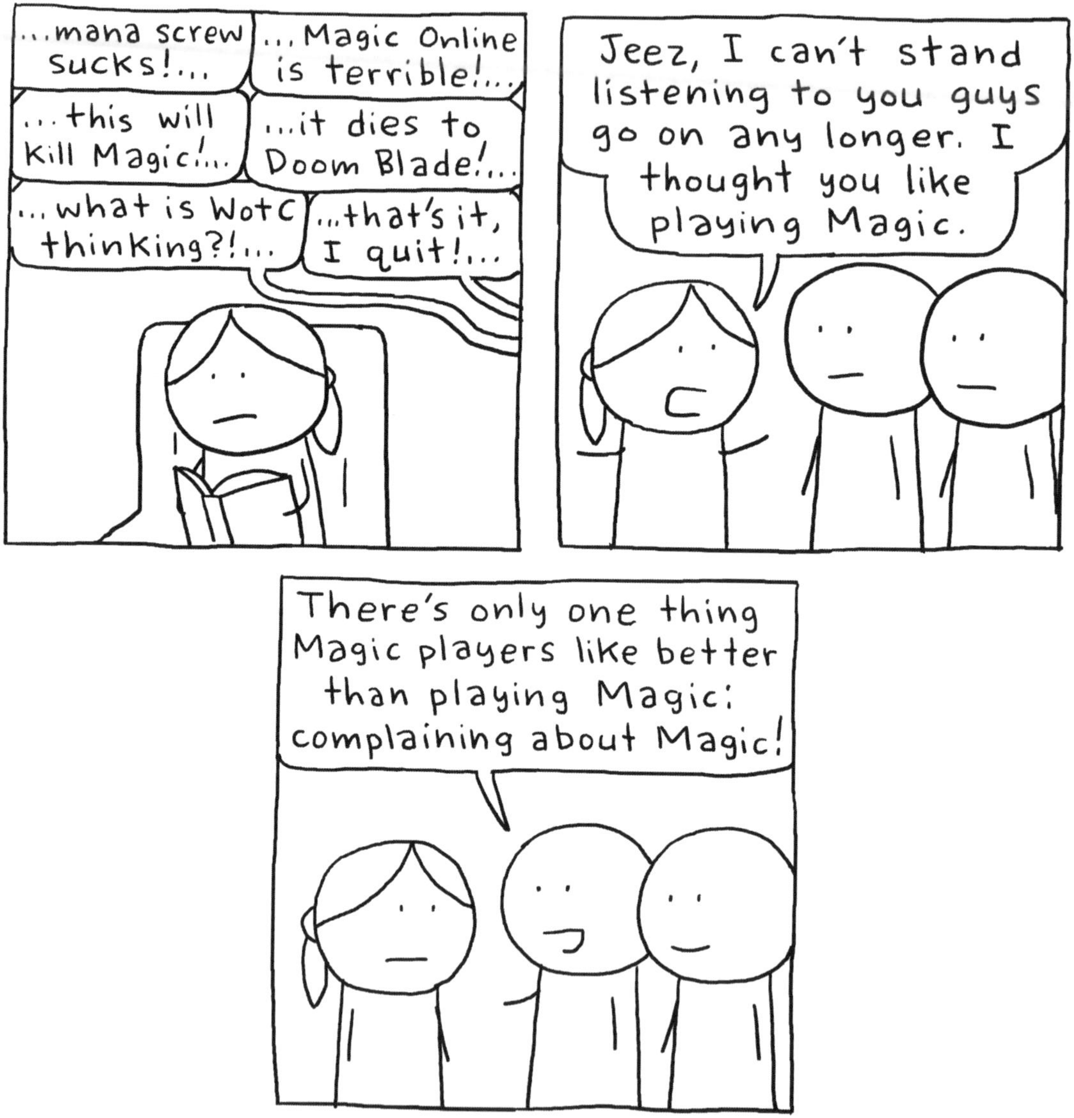
...mana screw sucks!...
...Magic Online is terrible!...
...this will kill Magic!...
...it dies to Doom Blade!...
...what is WotC thinking?!...
...that's it, I quit!...
Jeez, I can't stand listening to you guys go on any longer. I thought you like playing Magic.
There's only one thing Magic players like better than playing Magic: complaining about Magic!

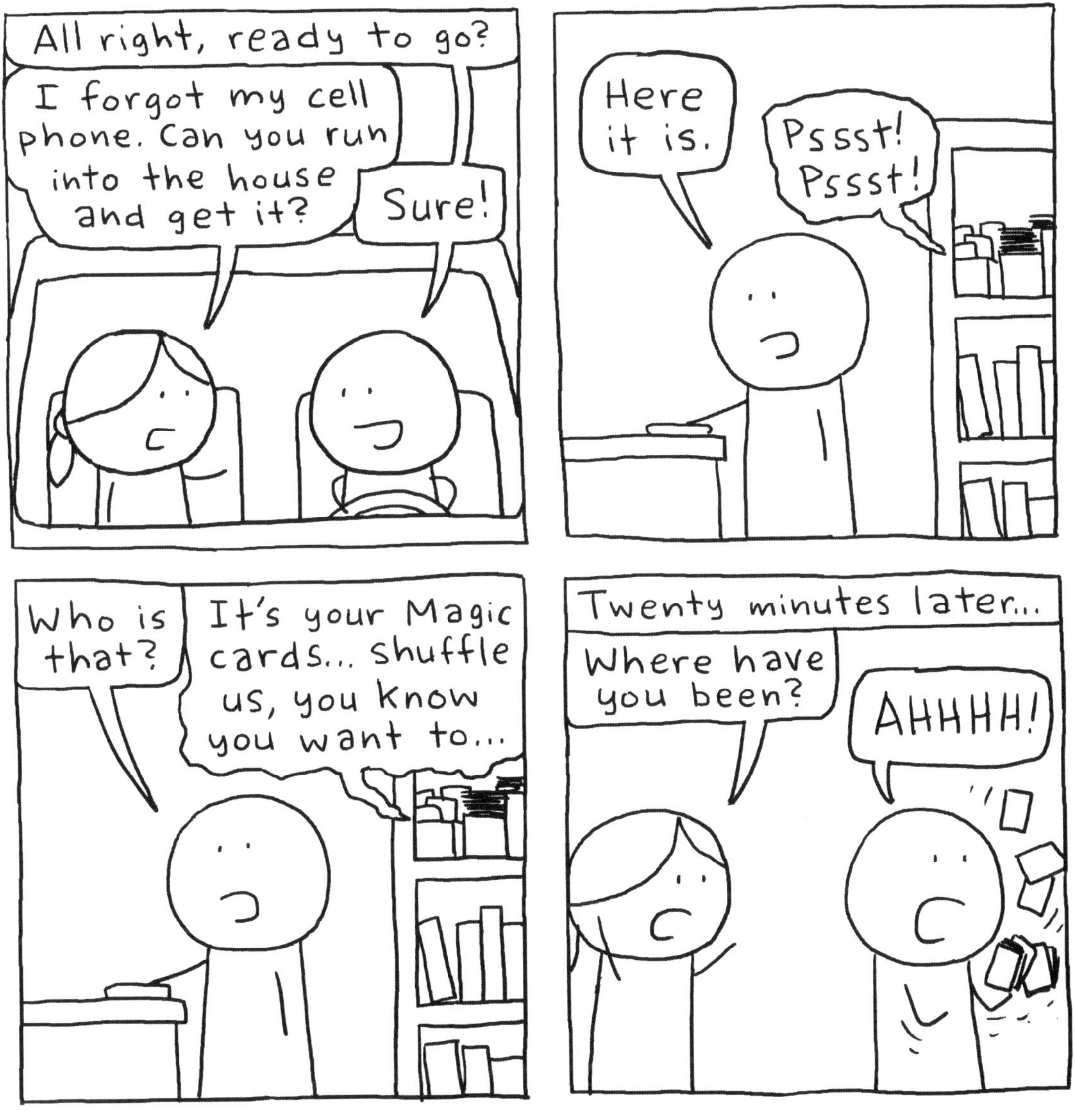
All right, ready to go?
I forgot my cell phone. Can you run into the house and get it?
Sure!
Here it is.
Pssst! Pssst!
Who is that?
It's your Magic cards... shuffle us, you know you want to...
Twenty minutes later...
Where have you been?
AHHHH!

Bonus Comics

The following pages feature comics that are exclusive to this book and have never appeared on the Cardboard Crack website. I hope you enjoy the chance to see them here for the first time!

Have you ever heard of a phantom limb? It's the sensation that a missing limb is still attached to the body, even though it's not.
It's amazing how the human body reacts to being separated from something it's used to. I can't imagine what that must be like!
By the way, you're not holding any Magic cards right now.
Oh, I'm not?

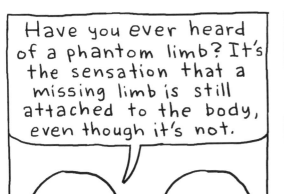

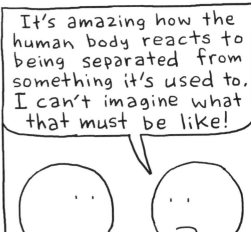

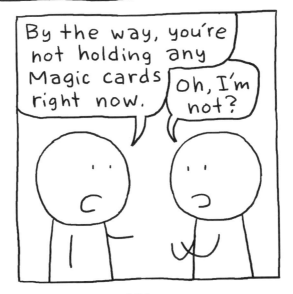

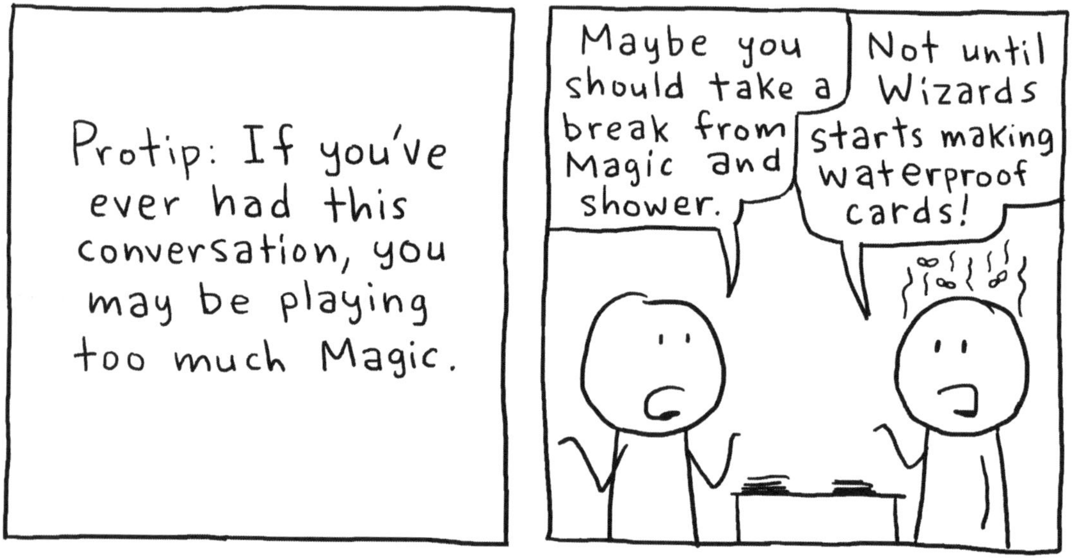
Protip: If you've ever had this conversation, you may be playing too much Magic.
Maybe you should take a break from Magic and shower.
Not until Wizards starts making waterproof cards!

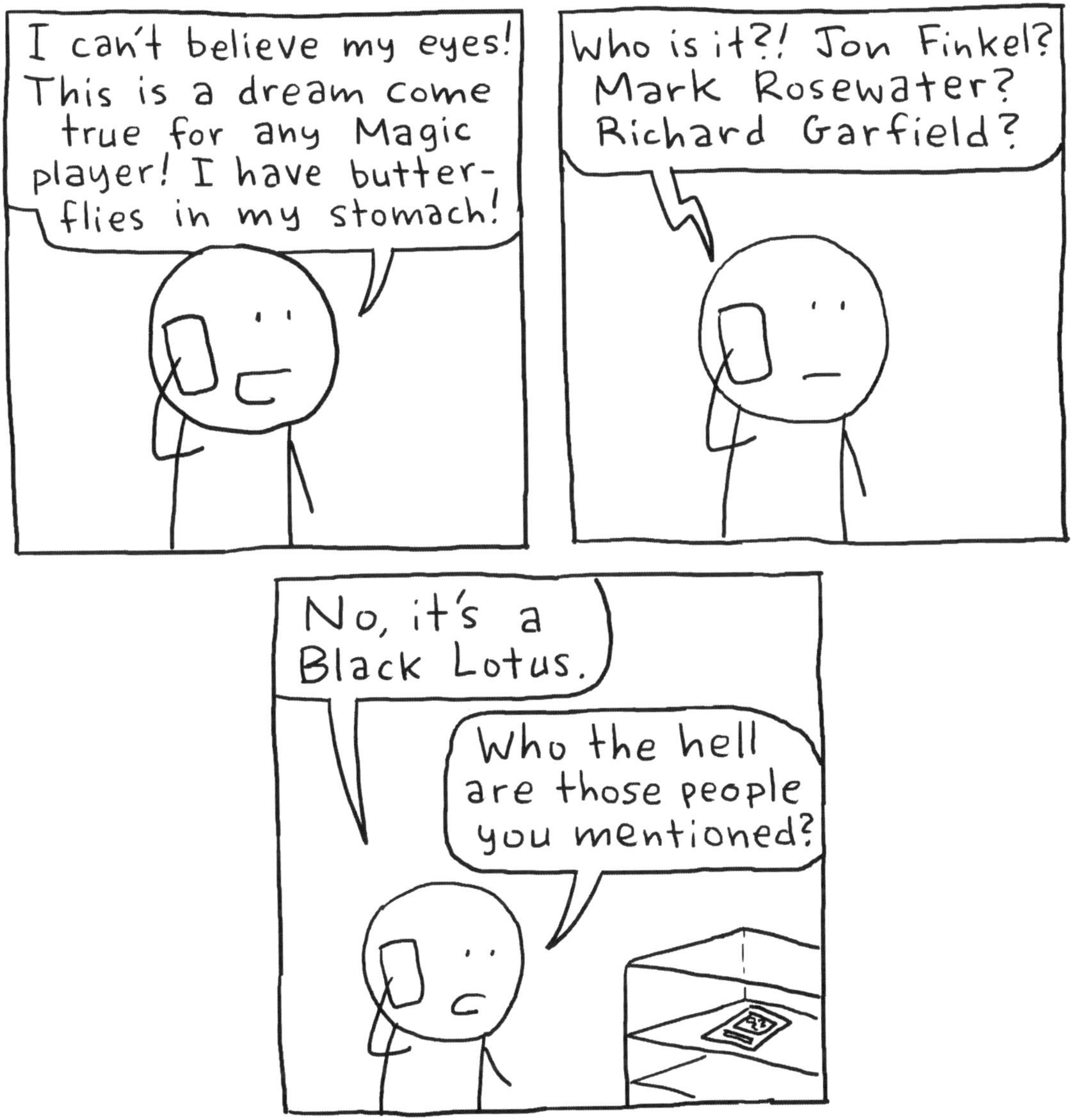
I can't believe my eyes! This is a dream come true for any Magic player! I have butter-flies in my stomach!
Who is it?! Jon Finkel? Mark Rosewater? Richard Garfield?
No, it's a Black Lotus.
Who the hell are those people you mentioned?

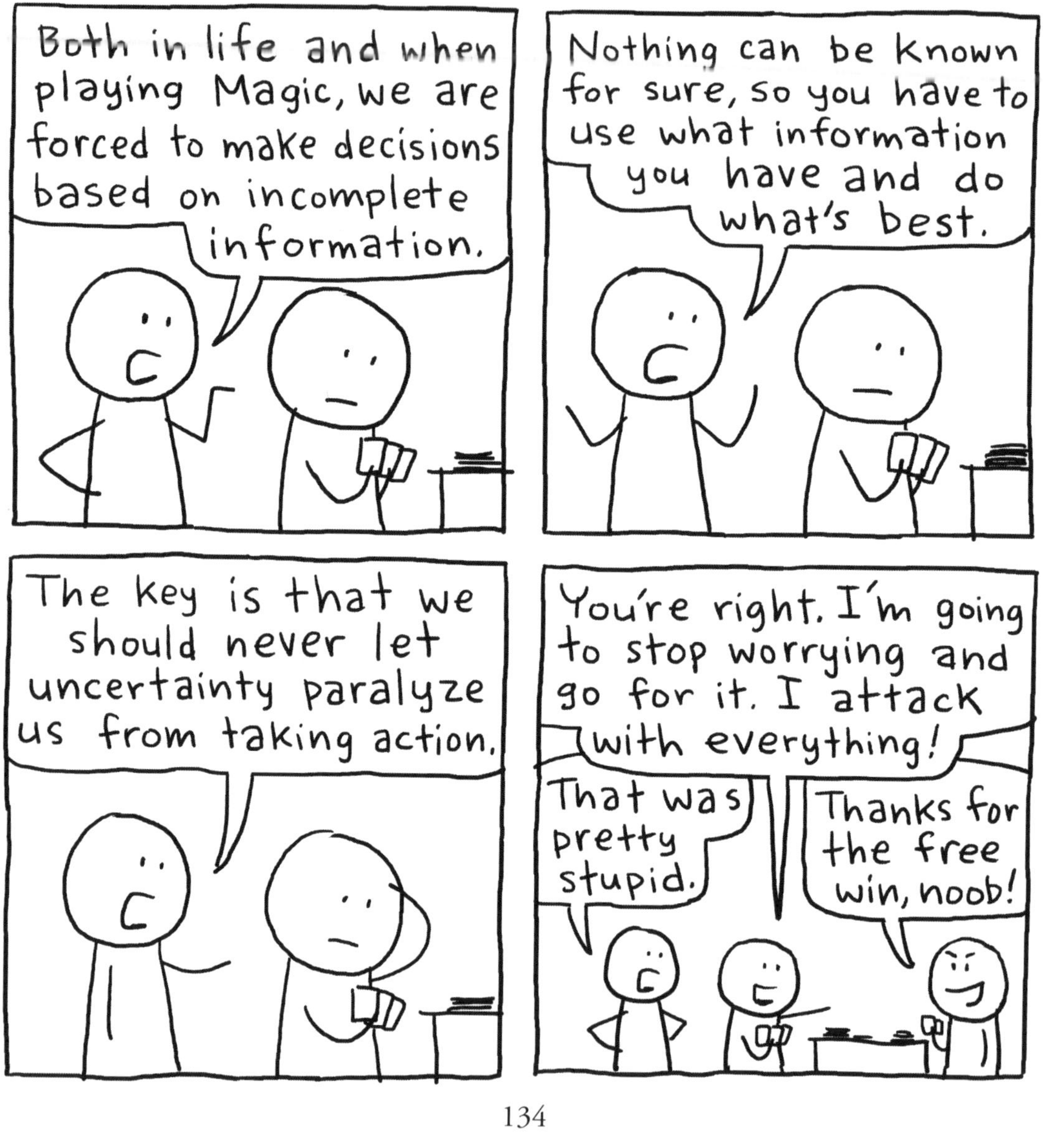
Both in life and when playing Magic, we are forced to make decisions based on incomplete information.
Nothing can be known for sure, so you have to use what information you have and do what's best.
The key is that we should never let uncertainty paralyze us from taking action.
You're right. I'm going to stop worrying and go for it. I attack with everything!
That was pretty stupid.
Thanks for the free win, noob!

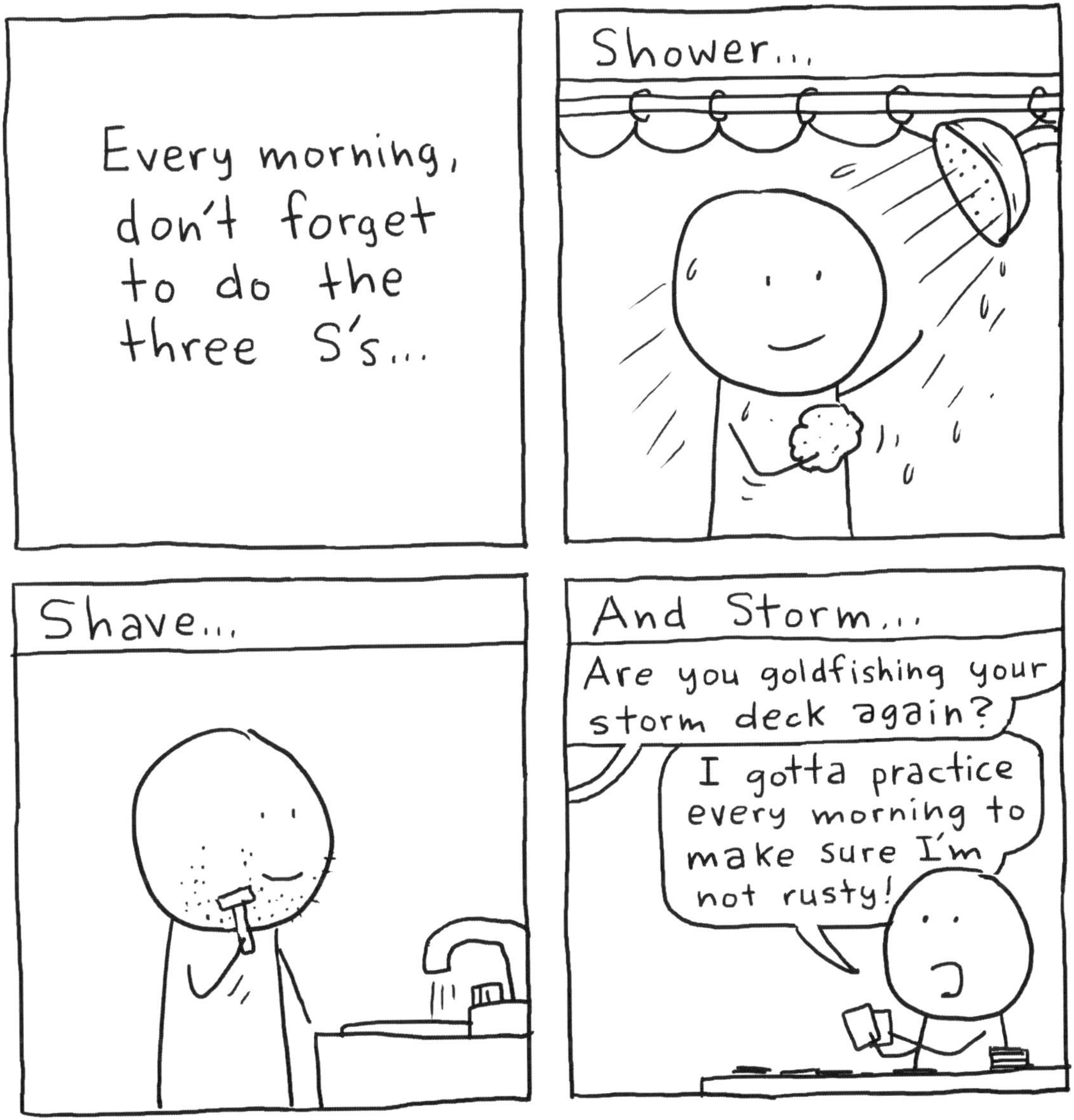

Every morning, don't forget to do the three S's...
Shower...
Shave...
And Storm...
Are you goldfishing your storm deck again?
I gotta practice every morning to make sure I'm not rusty!

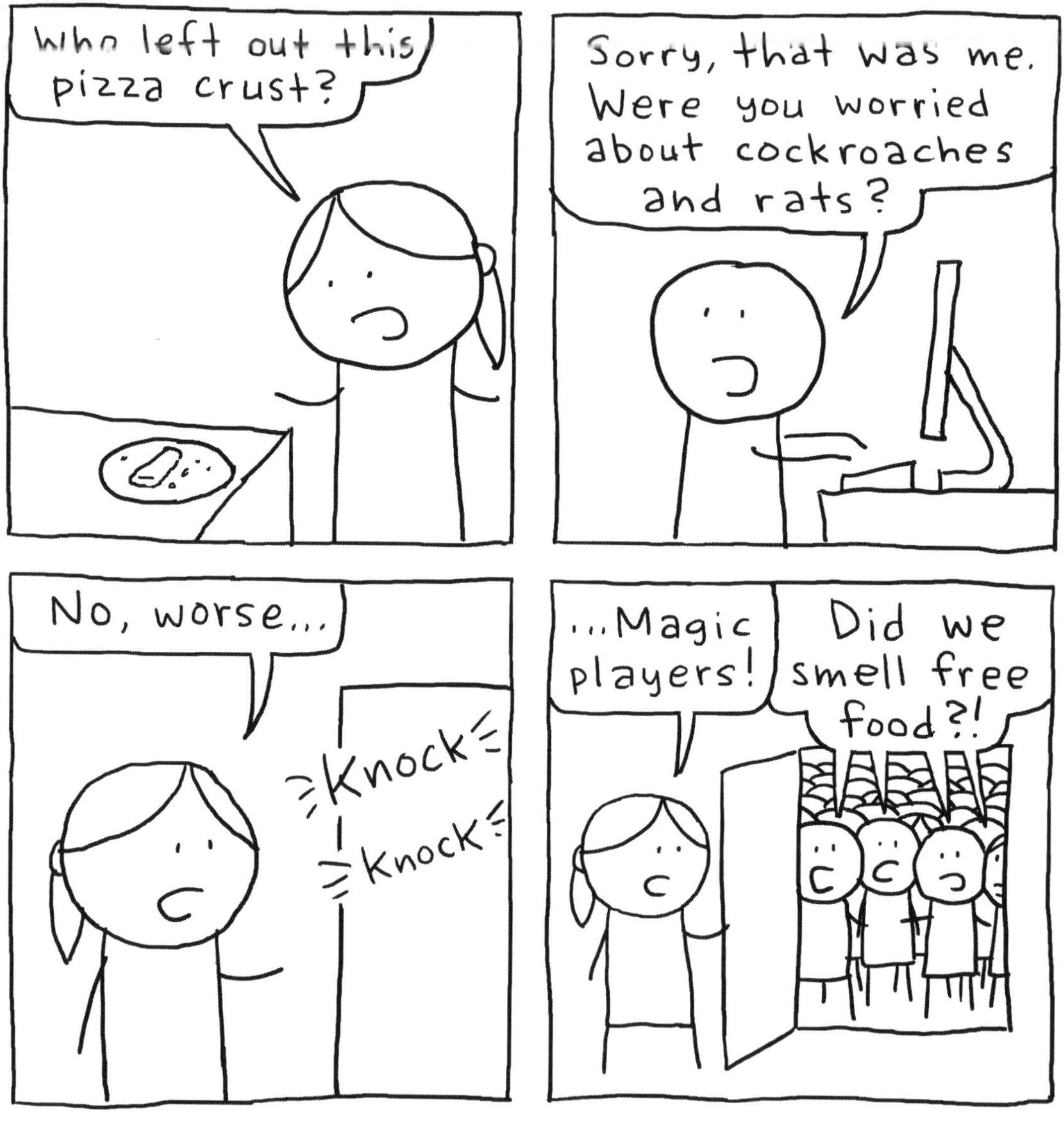
Who left out this pizza crust?
Sorry, that was me. Were you worried about cockroaches and rats?
No, worse...
Knock
Knock
...Magic players!
Did we smell free food?!

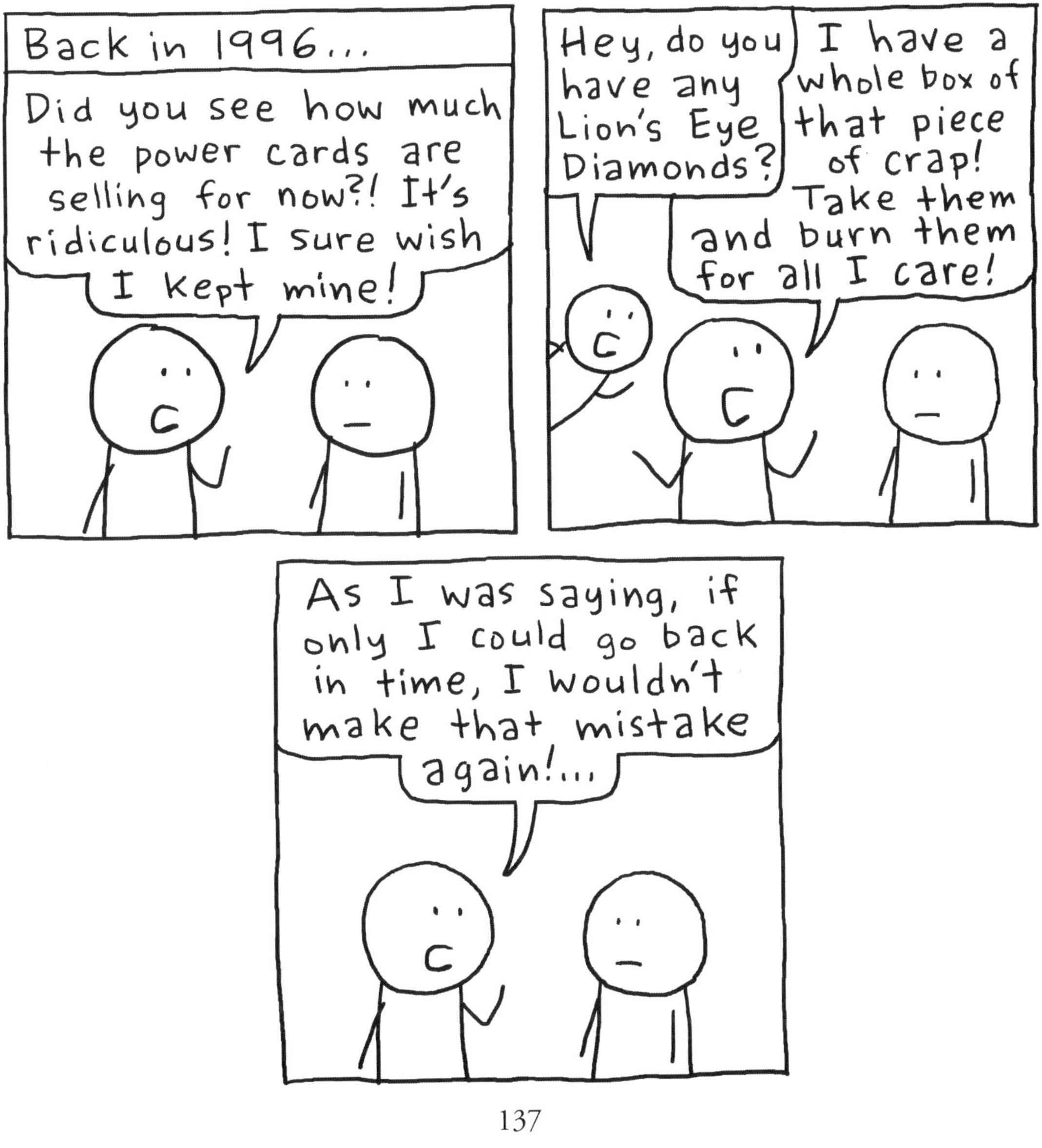
Back in 1996...
Did you see how much the power cards are selling for now?! It's ridiculous! I sure wish I kept mine!
Hey, do you have any Lion's Eye Diamonds?
I have a whole box of that piece of crap! Take them and burn them for all I care!
As I was saying, if only I could go back in time, I wouldn't make that mistake again!...

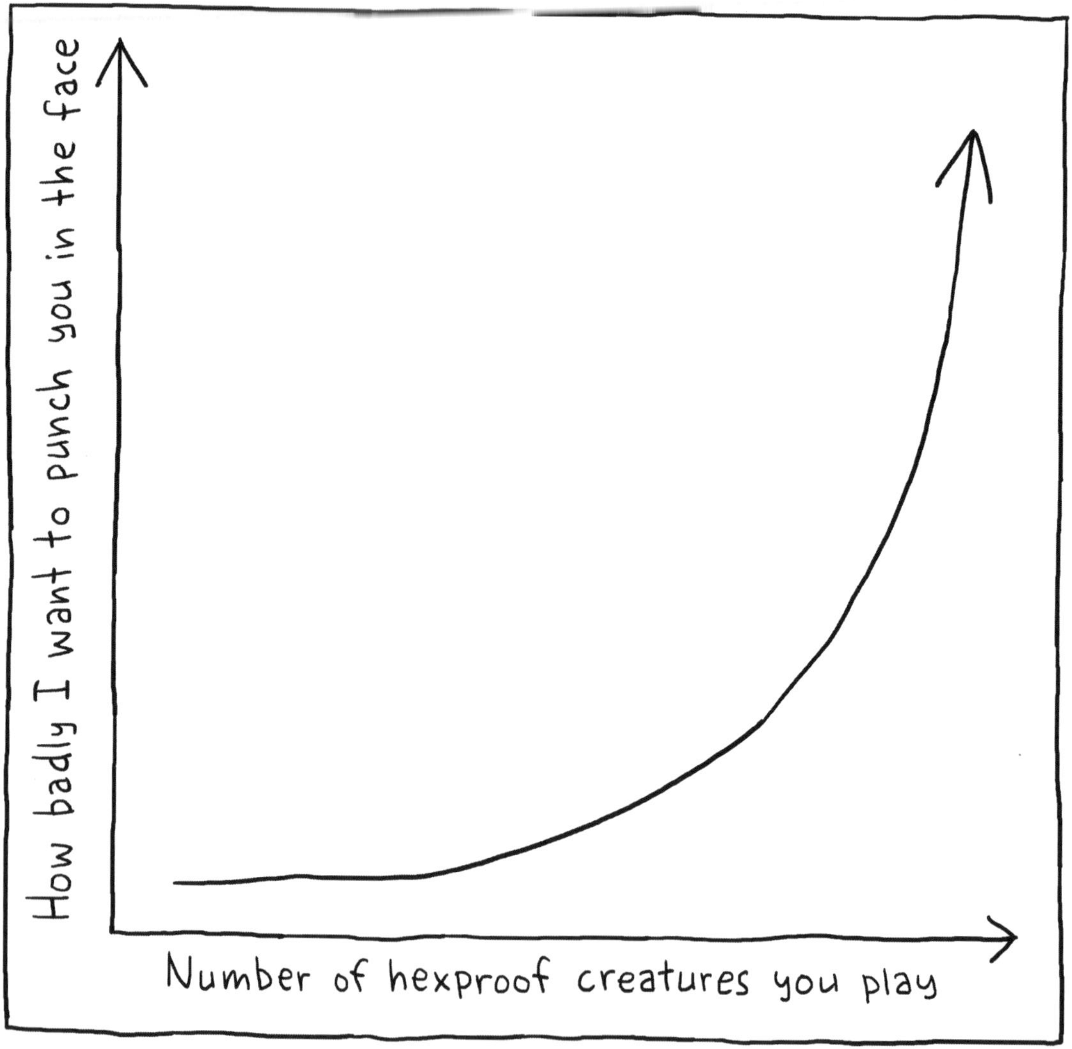
How badly I want to punch you in the face
Number of hexproof creatures you play

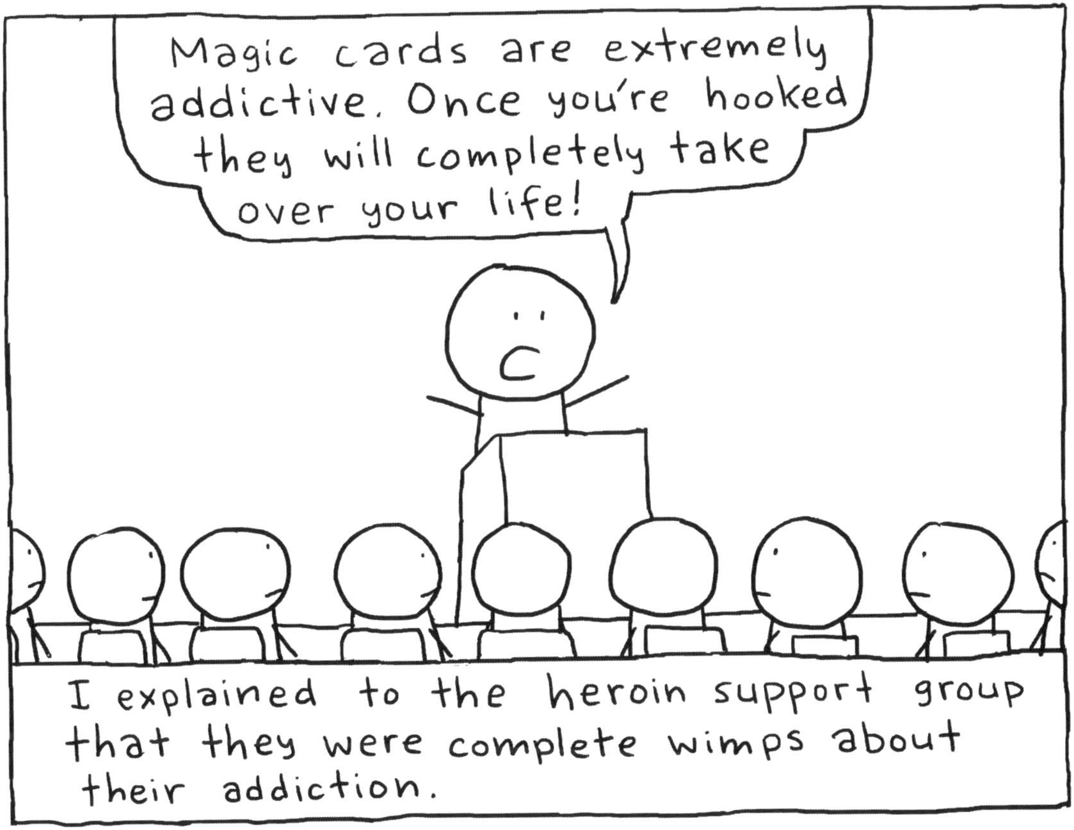
Magic cards are extremely addictive. Once you're hooked they will completely take over your life!
I explained to the heroin support group that they were complete wimps about their addiction.

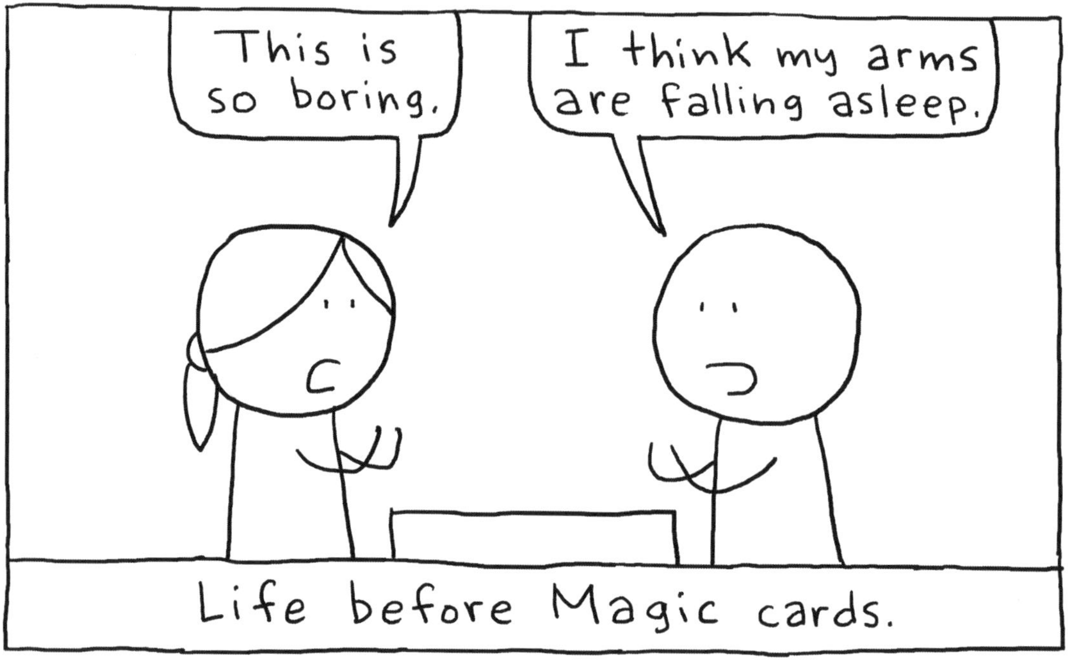
This is so boring.
I think my arms are falling asleep.
Life before Magic cards.

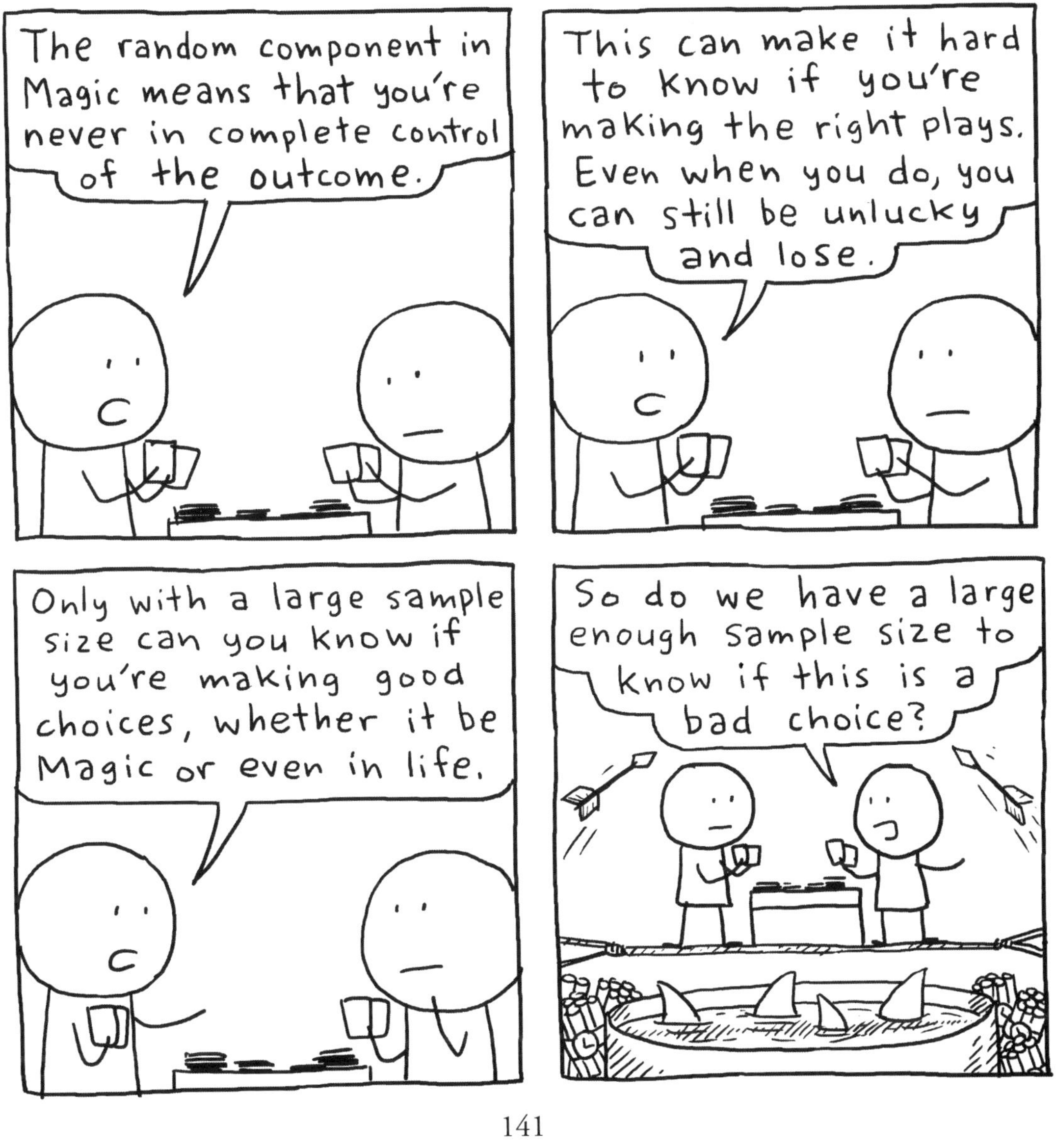
The random component in Magic means that you're never in complete control of the outcome.
This can make it hard to know if you're making the right plays. Even when you do, you can still be unlucky and lose.
Only with a large sample size can you know if you're making good choices, whether it be Magic or even in life.
So do we have a large enough sample size to know if this is a bad choice?

Cardboard Crack has been online since March 25, 2013, exclusively featuring comics about the world's most addictive game, Magic: The Gathering. Since that time, the Cardboard Crack website has gained many thousands of followers and many millions of page views. It has received links from a wide variety of prominent personalities in the Magic community, from Aaron Forsythe (current director of Magic: The Gathering R&D) to Jon Finkel (widely regarded as one of the greatest Magic players of all-time). Cardboard Crack is also featured in the weekly newsletter of StarCityGames.com (the world's largest Magic store).

New comics can be found regularly at:
cardboard-crack.com
facebook.com/CardboardCrack

Check out these other Cardboard Crack books:
Cardboard Crack
I will never quit Cardboad Crack

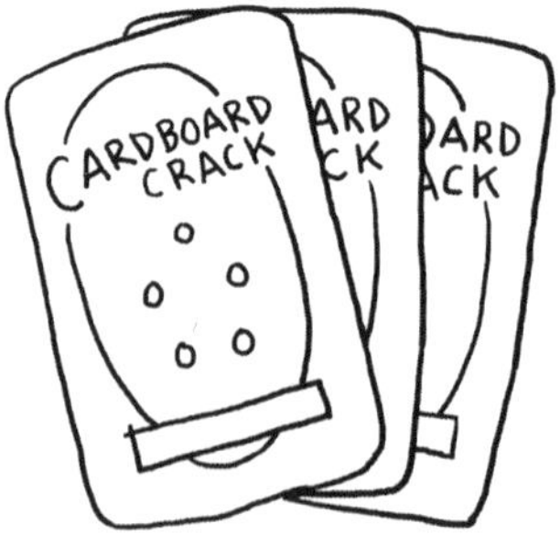
CARDBOARD CRACK

Printed in Great Britain
by Amazon.co.uk, Ltd.,
Marston Gate.